The economic theory of
social institutions

The economic theory of social institutions

ANDREW SCHOTTER

New York University

CAMBRIDGE UNIVERSITY PRESS

Cambridge
London   New York   New Rochelle
Melbourne   Sydney

Published by the Press Syndicate of the University of Cambridge
The Pitt Building, Trumpington Street, Cambridge CB2 1RP
32 East 57th Street, New York, NY 10022, USA
296 Beaconsfield Parade, Middle Park, Melbourne 3206, Australia

First published 1981

Printed in the United States of America
Typeset by University Graphics, Inc., Atlantic Highlands, New Jersey
Printed and bound by Vail-Ballou Press, Inc., Binghamton, New York

Library of Congress Cataloging in Publication Data

Schotter, A

The economic theory of social institutions.

Bibliography: p.

Includes index.

1. Economics. 2. Social institutions – Economic aspects.
3. Institutional economics. 4. Game theory.
I. Title.
HB171.S3815   306′.3   80-20731
ISBN 0 521 23044 6

To my parents

Contents

Contents

Preface

Ideas, once conceived, often undergo long gestation periods and are brought forth with great pain. When in the process they grow into monographs or books, one must realize that despite their mature appearance they are still only infants. This book presents a theory of social institutions that is still in its infancy and in no way purports to be fully mature. However, it does, I think, capture the essence of the phenomenon under investigation and present a formal way of dealing with it.

In judging the pages that follow, we must first ask what it is that a theoretical social scientist can attempt when he tries to make sense out of a particular aspect of the real world. It is my feeling that the first step he must take is to strip the phenomenon under study of its misleading worldly trappings and to lay bare its true nature. What may often be discovered is that the exotic phenomenon under investigation is isomorphic to a phenomenon with which we are quite familiar and comfortable. It is in the identification of these structural similarities that the essential qualities of the phenomenon are discovered and it is this process that any social scientific theory must attempt before going on to deal with more complicated questions. This is exactly what I have attempted to do in this book. I have tried to lay bare the essence of social institutions and the structure of the evolutionary problems they are called upon to solve. In doing this I have relied heavily upon the theory of n-person, noncooperative games, in both their extensive and normal forms, and upon the entire corpus of modern microeconomic theory. Game theory is used because it is the most natural tool available to study the phenomenon we are interested in. It is still only a tool, however, and I hope that its use will not deflect you from the essential objective of the book.

It is never easy to know when one should stop thinking and reading and start writing. I have decided to write this book now, not because I have either exhausted all my thoughts on the topic or totally come to grips with what a social institution is, but rather because I am at the stage in my thinking where abstraction has ceased and the task of concrete application has just begun. Consequently, instead of waiting to produce an exhaustive work, which might never see the light of day, I decided to present my ideas now on a more abstract and theoretical level and let myself and future investigators (if any are interested) apply these ideas to specific real-world situations. The drawback of this decision, however, is that much of what is contained here is quite abstract and, some might find, detached from reality. I cannot apologize for this, however, because such abstraction is a necessary first step in the construction of a social-scientific theory–and this book is just that, a first step. I hope that when the reader is finished he will have a better understanding of what social institutions are and how they evolve. Those, quite simply, are my only objectives.

In writing this book, I have benefited greatly from the advice and encouragement of a large number of friends and colleagues. My greatest debt, however, is to my wife, Dr. Anne Howland Schotter, who willingly or not discussed all my ideas with me and continuously pointed out flaws in my logic as well as several outright absurdities. In addition, her editorial eye greatly improved the style and clarity. I could not have written the book without her.

This book also reflects the influence of my teacher, the late Oskar Morgenstern, who inspired me to study economics. Despite being ill, Oskar read the first discussion papers from which this book grew. My phone rang constantly bringing his advice and encouragement, which I will never forget.

It is an extremely flattering experience when colleagues take the time to read and criticize one's rough ideas in typescript form. In this connection, I must thank William Baumol, Geoffrey Brennan, Lewis Kornhauser, Bill Sharkey, and Martin Shubik, all of whom read the entire manuscript and forced me to clarify both my thinking and my exposition. In addition, I must thank Albert Alexander, Juan Eugenio de la Rama, and Bob McGovern, who met weekly with me to discuss my book as it was being typed. They gave me a good sense of how sophisticated graduate students would react to the material presented.

The work in Chapter 3 is the product of a collaborative effort, for which I express my profound gratitude to Simeon Berman of the Courant Institute of Mathematical Sciences. Simeon's expertise, patience, and knack for simplification led to the creation of a mathematically tractable model. These few sentences cannot adequately reflect his contribution.

Probably the greatest inspiration for one's work comes from informal discussions and correspondence with friends and colleagues. I thank Bernard Wasow, who allowed me to consume many an afternoon coffee break on the thirteenth-floor lounge of the Courant Institute with my talk of norms and institutions. In addition, I thank Janusz Ordover, who devoted a pleasant summer afternoon we shared in Warren, Vermont, to reading Chapter 2 and discussing it with me. In our countless other discussions I have always come away with greater insight into economic theory.

I would also like to thank Gerhard Schwödiauer, with whom I have discussed my ideas at length many times. It is Gerhard to whom I owe a delightful month in Vienna, where I wrote Chapter 2 at the Institute for Advanced Studies. I was also fortunate to have had the opportunity to discuss this book with Ned Phelps. I again thank Lewis Kornhauser, who because he is well versed in mathematics, economics, philosophy, and law, enabled me to economize my efforts to discuss my ideas. Finally, Steven Brams both discussed my ideas with me in person and wrote to me about the material in Chapters 1 and 2.

One can never really know whether one's ideas are well formed until one verbalizes them and receives a reaction. Here I was lucky in being able to present my ideas in the spring of 1979 at the Austrian Economics Seminar at New York University, which is run by Israel Kirzner. Israel had read an earlier version of Chapter 1 and greatly helped me put my ideas in perspective.

Anyone who has done research knows that it is a time-intensive activity and that, unless one is able to block out large, uninterrupted periods to think and write, one will never be able to complete very much. I have been extremely fortunate in having had the support of the Office of Naval Research (contract number N00014-78-C-0598) and the association of Randy Simpson and Tom Varley. Their support has allowed me to devote a large portion of my time to active research.

Finally, I must thank Colin Day, Senior Economics Editor at Cambridge University Press, for all that he has done in making this book a reality. Colin's faith in the project never seemed to fade and was one of the things that encouraged me to continue my work.

ANDREW SCHOTTER

New York
October 1980

1 The nature and function of social institutions

This book considers the nature, function, and evolution of economic and social institutions. Most simply, it is a first step in an attempt to liberate economics from its fixation on competitive markets as an all-encompassing institutional framework. It views economic problems as evolutionary ones in which economic agents have finite lives and pass on to their successors a wide variety of social rules of thumb, institutions, norms, and conventions that facilitate the coordination of economic and social activities. In time, the institutional structure of the economy becomes more and more complex as more and more social and economic institutions are created and passed on from generation to generation. In some instances these institutions supplement competitive markets, and in some instances they totally replace them. Some of the institutions are explicitly agreed to and codified into law; others are only tacitly agreed to and evolve spontaneously from the attempts of the individual agents to maximize their own utility. Some lead to optimal social states; others are dysfunctional. In any case, each arises for a specific reason. It is the purpose of this book to investigate these reasons and analyze the types of institutions that evolve.

But what are social institutions, and what functions do they serve? These questions can be answered only by viewing economic problems in an evolutionary light. Doing this, as Veblen (1898) points out, takes the emphasis away from equilibrium analysis and places it on the disequilibrium aspects of the economic process.[1] The proper analogy to make is between the evolution of an economy and the evolution of a species. Biologists know that a particular animal reveals a variety of features that it has developed to solve specific evolutionary problems. If these problems cease to exist, the animal is left with vestigial features whose function is a mystery to us. But if the problems remain, the function of the feature may be obvious for all to see. The problem for the scientist is one of inferring from observed appearances the evolutionary problem that must have existed to produce what we observe today.

In the social world the problem is similar. Economic and social systems evolve the way species do. To ensure their survival and growth, they must solve

1

a whole set of problems that arise as the system evolves. Each problem creates the need for some adaptive feature, that is, a social institution. Analogously, then, the problem facing social scientists is to infer the evolutionary problem that must have existed for the institution as we see it to have developed. Every evolutionary economic problem requires a social institution to solve it. For instance, the problem of multilateral exchange in neoclassical economies (economies satisfying all of the "proper" neoclassical assumptions) is solved by the creation of competitive markets, and the evolutionary source of this institutional feature is evident today. However, this is just one of many institutions that "successful" economies must develop. Those societies that create the proper set of social institutions survive and flourish; those that do not, falter and die. The distressing fact is that what is functional to meet today's problem may be totally inadequate in meeting the tests our society faces tomorrow. Social institutions are our adaptive tools; we cannot survive without them.

This point was made by Alfred Marshall in his *Principles of Economics*. Greatly influenced by the emerging biological sciences,[2] he perceived that those aspects of economic institutions that are most prominent today are those most likely to have developed recently and consequently will give no hint of the original purpose of the institution. He writes:

> In this matter economists have much to learn from the recent experiences of biology: and Darwin's profound discussion of the question throws a strong light on the difficulties before us. He points out that those parts of the structure which determine the habits of life and the general place of each being in the economy of nature, are as a rule not those which throw most light on its origin, but those that throw least.
>
> The qualities which a breeder or a gardener notices as eminently adapted to enable an animal or a plant to thrive in its environment, are for that very reason likely to have been developed in comparatively recent times. And in like manner, those properties of an economic institution which play the most important part in fitting it for the work which it has to do now, are for that very reason likely to be in a great measure of recent growth. [Marshall 1920, p. 50]

More recently, James Buchanan (1975) contends, in a book that is heavily institutional and evolutionary in its approach, that if one is to study institutions, one must study them in a historical–evolutionary context: "Once it is recognized that observed institutions of legal-political order exist in a historical setting, the attraction of trying to analyze conceptual origins independently of historical process is severely weakened" (Buchanan 1975, p. 53).

The following example should be illuminating. Consider the existence of a commodity money in an exchange economy. Clearly, the social convention that specifies a certain commodity as a means of exchange did not always exist. Furthermore, the particular commodity chosen is arbitrary except that we would expect it to be light in weight, durable, and relatively abundant. Consequently, if the proverbial creatures from outer space were to arrive and

observe this phenomenon, they would have to explain why all trade is monetized, and why, in addition, this one commodity out of the whole set of possible
commodities was the one chosen. The answer to the first part of the question
is simple. Money evolves because at some point in the history of an economy
the problem of efficient multilateral trade arises. Its solution requires a method
of exchange that uses as few social resources as possible to achieve a Pareto-
optimal set of trades. The obvious evolutionary solution, in addition to markets,
was to monetize trade by using one good as a means of exchange. Thus money
was a social convention that satisfied the important economic need for an efficient exchange of goods and services. Once this problem was solved, its solution
was passed on from generation to generation: money was institutionalized. This
explanation would, of course, not be obvious to our visiting creatures. They
would have no clue to the evolutionary problem for which money was the
solution. It is, therefore, the object of science to provide one for them.

If we attempted to answer the question of why one particular commodity
was chosen as money, we would find greater difficulties. Although, as we said,
the commodity must be durable, lightweight, and abundant, many commodities
have these qualities. Consequently, our explanation would have to involve a
certain amount of indeterminacy. This is not grounds for despair, however.
The nature of the analysis in this book is such that we can never expect to
isolate a unique institutional form as stable; rather, we must content ourselves
with a set of forms that, when taken together, are stable. This is all we can, or
should, expect from a theory.

*see Nelson
+ Winter.*

1.1 Toward a new view of economics

The approach to economics outlined so far has dramatic consequences for the
way in which we look at the scope and method of economics. Before we discuss
this in detail, however, let us briefly look at some previous attempts at integrating institutions into economics.

There have been, historically, two distinct interpretations of the rise of social
institutions in economics. One explanation, put forth in John Commons's
Institutional Economics, may be called the "collectivist" explanation. The other
explanation, given in Karl Menger's *Untersuchungen über die Methode der
Sozialwissenschaften und der politischen Ökonomie insbesondere* (1883; translated by Francis J. Nock in 1963 as *Problems in Economics and Sociology*),
may be called the "organic" theory.

The difference between these two approaches is simple. Commons saw social
institutions as the expression of the conscious collective action of rational economic agents. For him, economics was to be freed from the "psychological" or
individualistic economics of Adam Smith and the neoclassical economists and

put on a new foundation in which collective action and a "negotiational psychology" were to replace atomistic maximization. As Commons puts it:

> Collective action, as well as individual action, has always been there, but from Smith to the Twentieth Century it has been excluded or ignored, except as attacks on trade unions or postscripts on ethics or public policy. The problem now is not to create a different kind of economics–"institutional economics"–divorced from preceding schools, but how to give collective action, in all its varieties, its due place throughout economic theory. [Commons 1934, p. 5]

For Commons, then, the universal principle behind institutional behavior is the collective and purposeful action enforcing it: "If we endeavor to find a universal principle, common to all behavior known as institutional, we may define an institution as Collective Action in control of Individual Action" (Commons 1934, p. 69).

Menger's explanation of the rise of institutions is quite different. He saw them as arising out of the selfish interaction of a myriad of individual economic agents, each pursuing his own self-interest. They evolve "organically," not by collective design or will. Therefore, Menger believed that what Commons called "psychological economics" need not be thrown away in order to construct a theory of social institutions. Rather, this forms its theoretical superstructure. Just as Adam Smith's invisible hand can, in a decentralized fashion, lead economic agents to reach a Pareto-optimal competitive equilibrium, it can also lead them to create social institutions that will facilitate their interaction when competitive outcomes are not optimal.[3] Another way to phrase the same problem is to say that "competitive" economics deals with only one institution–the market–which arises organically out of the maximizing behavior of individual agents. However, a host of other institutions, norms, and rules are also created that help to allocate resources in an optimal fashion. It is the organic development of these other institutions with which Menger was concerned. He considered the "most noteworthy problem of the social sciences" to be the question of "how . . . institutions which serve the common welfare and are extremely significant for its development came into being without a *common will* directed toward establishing them" (Menger 1883, p. 147). Menger went on to say: "The solution of the most important problems of the theoretical social sciences in general and of theoretical economics in particular is thus closely connected with the question of theoretically understanding the origin and change of 'organically' created social institutions" (Menger 1883, p. 147).

Interestingly, both Menger [in his *Principles of Economics* (1950) and in *Untersuchungen*] and Commons study the rise of the institutions of money and law as examples for their arguments. More recently, Robert Nozick (1975) has given an explanation of the rise of the state as a social institution in *Anarchy, State, and Utopia*, which is very close to Menger's conception of social institutions arising organically.[4] James Buchanan (1975) has explained the rise of property and societal law in an analogous manner in *The Limits of Liberty*.

Our conception of the role of economics in social science is very close to Menger's, and it is on this conception that we will base our definition of *economics* as *the study of how individual economic agents pursuing their own selfish ends evolve institutions as a means to satisfy them*. This definition is quite distinct from the one offered by Lord Robbins in 1935, which is still the standard one in textbooks:

> The economist studies the disposal of scarce means. He is interested in the way different degrees of scarcity of different goods give rise to different ratios of valuation between them, and he is interested in the way in which changes in ends or changes in means–from the demand side or the supply side–affect these ratios. *Economics* is the science which studies human behavior as a relationship between ends and scarce means which have alternative uses. [Robbins 1935, p. 16]

Robbins's definition differs from ours in two distinct ways. First, it concentrates totally on the individual, whereas ours sees the individual as a selfish, maximizing agent who is capable of coordinated social action (i.e., institution building). Second, Robbins's definition, in his reference to the forces of supply and demand, clearly implies that he sees only one social mechanism through which human economic behavior can manifest itself–that of competitive markets; ours explicitly recognizes a variety of mechanisms or institutions. As a result, our definition is broader than his and our analysis sees competitive economics as an extreme case.

Using our definition of positive economics, welfare economics can be defined as the study of the welfare aspects of comparative social institutions. This definition then simply says that if our positive economic theory is going to study the effect of social institutions on resource allocation, the associated prescriptive theory should study comparative social institutions. This, however, includes within it neoclassical welfare economics, because if neoclassical theory deals only with perfectly competitive economies, the only institutions they deal with are markets, and welfare economics becomes the study of comparative market organizations.

1.2 Welfare economics and comparative social institutions: the optimal rules of the game

If, for a second, we let ourselves be all-powerful social planners who have the power to create any society or economic structure we want, what will that society or economy look like? In trying to answer this question, we would probably lay out some general rules or principles for the members of that society to follow. These rules could be codified into law and would prescribe the type of behavior that is acceptable in specific situations. In economics, such rules would include antitrust laws, safety requirements, and minimum-wage legislation.

John Rawls, in *A Theory of Justice* (1971), attacks just this problem. He seeks a set of rules to be the basis of a contract among selfish, maximizing social agents, which they would agree to under a "veil of ignorance." His view of social justice concentrates not so much on the comparison of social states as on the comparison of social systems and institutions. He states:

> For us the primary subject of justice is the basic structure of society or more exactly, the way in which the major social institutions distribute fundamental rights and duties and determine the division of advantages from social cooperation. By major institutions I understand the political constitution and the principal economic and social arrangements. Thus the legal protection of freedom of thought and liberty, competitive markets, private property and the means of production, and the monogamous family are examples of major social institutions. Taken together as one scheme, the major institutions define men's rights and duties and influence their life prospects, what they can expect to be and how well they can hope to do. [Rawls 1971, p. 7]

When discussing institutions and formal justice, Rawls permits himself to be a social planner and shows that social planning involves not allocation by fiat but the development and administration of rules, laws, and institutions that lead to socially optimal states:

> In designing and reforming social arrangements one must, of course, examine the schemes and tactics it allows and the forms of behavior which it tends to encourage. Ideally, the rules should be set up so that men are led by their predominant interests to act in ways which further socially desirable ends. The conduct of individuals guided by their rational plans should be coordinated as far as possible to achieve results which although not intended or perhaps even foreseen by them are nevertheless the best ones from the standpoint of social justice. [Rawls 1971, p. 57]

Our view of the role of theoretical welfare economics has much in common with Rawls's view of the study of justice. (Notice how close Rawls is here to Menger.) We view welfare economics not as a study that ranks social states or prescribes optimal resource allocations, but as one that ranks the system of rules which dictate social behavior. We view government in competitive and mixed economies as an agent whose role it is to prescribe a set of taxes, laws, and rules of behavior that limit the strategy sets of social agents in an optimal way. In essence, *welfare economics is the study of the optimal rules of the game for economic and social situations*. Its purpose is, like Rawls's rules and institutions, to structure competitive social and economic situations that further societal welfare while preserving individual sovereignty.[5]

The main point made here, then, is that welfare economics must study the comparative optimality of rules, laws, and institutions that form the rules of the game of social conduct, together with the outcomes that these rules help determine. The philosophical justification for such a view can be found in quite disparate works. John Rawls (1971) views justice through a "contractarian" point of view. He sees a just society as one whose rules, laws, and institutions are exactly those that would be chosen by its agents if they were placed under a "veil of ignorance" as to who they would be in that society. These rules are the rules that would form a contract by which the members of the society would agree to conduct themselves.

From the other side of the political spectrum comes additional support for our view. Robert Nozick (1975), in discussing fair income distributions, states that one cannot rank two income distributions–social states–by themselves in terms of social desirability, for the process by which the income distributions were achieved–the rules of the game determining them–is equally important. He argues that an extremely skewed income distribution can be fair as long as it is arrived at in a fair way and without coercion. In addition, a totally egalitarian income distribution could be undesirable if it were arrived at by immoral acts such as murder: "The entitlement theory of justice in distribution is historical; whether a distribution is just depends upon how it came about. In contrast, *current-time-slice* principles of justice hold that the justice of a distribution is determined by how things are distributed (who has what) as judged by some structural principle(s) of just distribution" (Nozick 1975, p. 153).

Still another philosophical view, "rule utilitarianism" (in contrast to the more typical "act utilitarianism" used widely by economists), can be called upon to support our institutional emphasis. This view ranks social actions not on the basis of the social states they alone determine, but on the basis of the eventual social state that would result if those types of actions became rules of conduct or conventions of behavior for the agents in the society. The rule-utilitarian view is, then, a type of Kantian approach, which views all human conduct in terms of the payoffs that would result if that conduct became a convention of behavior for all agents in society.[6]

Thus we have seen that welfare economics must be the study of the comparative "rules of the game" of social and economic behavior. Its role is not only to rank social states and prescribe which is best, but also to compare the rules of conduct by which those outcomes are determined.

1.3 Who should study social institutions?

Why should an economist be interested in social institutions? Why not leave the problem to the anthropologists and sociologists? The reason, as we will see more clearly in Chapter 2, is that economics as it exists today is hampered by an institutional short-sightedness that greatly inhibits its analysis of social problems. The short-sightedness results from our fixation on market institutions and our failure to introduce a more varied set of institutions into our analysis. This short-sightedness may lead to the advocacy of market solutions where other institutional arrangements might be more efficient.

To be a little more precise, economics focuses on the price relationships of commodities conditional on one particular institutional structure–competitive markets. When the phenomena in question fit appropriately into this framework–when there are no externalities or nonconvexities–its limited institutional assumptions are no hindrance. However, many institutions are created that allocate goods and services when competitive markets are not a realistic assumption to make, and a truly comprehensive theory must explain their creation together with the resulting value relationships, which may no longer be equivalent to equilibrium price ratios. As an illustration, consider the following rather fanciful game.

Game 1.1: The traffic game

Two cars, C and D, are driving toward each other on a street and are approaching an intersection, A. They are driving at the same speed and will approach the intersection at the same time. Both drivers are in a hurry and want to get to their destinations, which are marked g and f, respectively, in Figure 1.1. Therefore, C wants to make a left-hand turn and D wants to go straight ahead. The game that is determined by this scenario is a variant of the "battle of the sexes" game, pictured in Matrix 1.1. Clearly, the Pareto-optimal

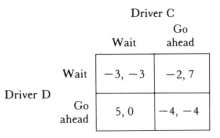

Matrix 1.1

states occur on the off-diagonal elements of the matrix, and some mechanism is needed for the agents in the economy to coordinate their activities. What mechanism should society use? To a theoretical economist, the obvious answer would be that a market should be set up that would sell the right to use the intersection. This right should be sold at auction. The argument here would be that the only reason a problem exists in the first place is because of a market failure in the right of way. Consequently, we may picture an auctioneer, who stands in the middle of the intersection and instantaneously accepts bids from both drivers, selling the right to use the intersection first to the higher bidder.

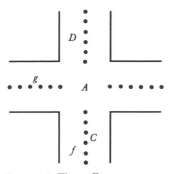

Figure 1.1. The traffic game.

Clearly, the price would be set between 5 and 7 and the car turning left would get the right to use the intersection first. This is, of course, a highly unlikely mechanism. However, even if it were feasible and the auctioning process were extremely efficient, this scheme would be cumbersome and costly.

Another scheme, however, would be to initiate traffic rules and force each person to learn them before he is allowed to drive on the streets. If this scheme were utilized, a rule of thumb would be established in which drivers wishing to make turns at intersections must wait for oncoming cars before proceeding. The person making the turn would wait, and the decisions would be costlessly coordinated.

The point of this example is that price mechanisms, except for the textbook variety, are not costless and are in many circumstances rather clumsy systems to run. Therefore, we might find situations in which decentralized informational schemes, such as rules and norms, are more efficient allocating mechanisms. However, if economic analysis is so fixated on the market that it ignores other institutional arrangements, it is destined to be analytically myopic.

1.4 Institutions defined

It is not an easy task to define social institutions, because they are amorphous and require a definition general enough to encompass all of them without being meaningless. Consequently, I have chosen a definition that is similar to David Lewis's definition of social conventions (1969): regularities in behavior which are agreed to by all members of a society and which specify behavior in specific recurrent situations. However, social institutions are different from social conventions in terms of the mechanisms necessary to enforce them. Social conventions, such as language, table manners, driving on the right side of the street, and allowing only one person to speak at a time in a conversation, are fundamentally self-policing. According to Lewis, they evolve as the noncooperative solution to social coordination games. For instance, consider the telephone game described by Lewis (1969, p. 42).

Game 1.2: The telephone game

In Oberlin, Ohio, the phone company used to cut all phone conversations off at the end of 3 minutes. Consequently, if party 1 called party 2 and was cut off, he faced the following problem: If I call him back, and he tries to call me, we will get a busy signal and will not be able to speak. If I do not call him back and he does not call me, we cannot speak either. We can speak only if I call him back and he does not call me, or if I do not call him back and he does call me. Party 2 has the same problem. Assuming that all calls are free, what will happen?

According to Lewis, the game can be represented as a coordination problem[7] (Matrix 1.2). The game, although simple, is by no means trivial. It can be

		Callee	
		Call back	Do not call back
Caller	Call back	0, 0	8, 8
	Do not call back	8, 8	0, 0

Matrix 1.2

solved only if both parties can find a way to coordinate their activities. This coordination can be achieved by establishing a social convention or regularity in behavior to govern these situations, which specifies whether the caller or the person called is to call back. Which specific convention will evolve is indeterminate, yet both are in equilibrium, because not only does neither party have an incentive to deviate from the convention, both desire that the other not deviate either. The convention determines equilibrium behavior. More formally, Lewis defines a social convention as follows.

Definition 1.1: A social convention. A regularity R in the behavior of members of a population P when they are agents in a recurrent situation S is a *convention* if and only if it is true that and is common knowledge in P that (1) everyone conforms to R; (2) everyone expects everyone else to conform to R; and (3) everyone prefers to conform to R on the condition that the others do, since S is a coordination problem and uniform conformity to R is a coordination equilibrium in S (Lewis 1969, p. 58).

Although social institutions are predominantly concerned with solving social coordination problems, they are not necessarily self-policing and may require some external authority, such as the state, to enforce them. For instance, a system of property rights is a social institution in which the behavior of individual agents is circumscribed to conform. It defines a regularity in behavior that is socially agreed to. Yet this institution is not in equilibrium because each person has an incentive to steal from others. As a result, some external authority must be instituted to enforce these rights–the state.[8] Consequently, we will have to modify Lewis's definition to read as follows: *A social institution is a regularity in social behavior that is agreed to by all members of society, specifies behavior in specific recurrent situations, and is either self-policed or policed by some external authority.* In these situations, the regularity may be the use of a particular commodity, such as money, in the exchange of goods and services or the regularity in prices charged by public utilities that specifies the behavior of regulated firms. In other situations, it might be a code that exists which dictates the contribution individuals make in paying for public or club goods, or it may be the percentage gratuity left as a tip for waiters in restaurants. Whatever it is, once it is incorporated in the study of economics, the institutional framework of our science is immediately expanded and we can proceed to rigorously analyze a great many problems in a fresh way without forcing the analysis into one particular institutional framework: competitive markets.

A social institution can then be more formally defined as follows.

See R. Roberts.

Definition 1.2: A social institution. A regularity R in the behavior of members of a population P when they are agents in a recurrent situation Γ is an *institution* if and only if it is true that and is common knowledge in P that (1) everyone conforms to R; (2) everyone expects everyone else to conform to R; and (3) either everyone prefers to conform to R on the condition that the others do, if Γ is a coordination problem, in which case uniform conformity to R is a coordination equilibrium; or (4) if anyone ever deviates from R it is known that some or all of the others will also deviate and the payoffs associated with the recurrent play of Γ using these deviating strategies are worse for all agents than the payoff associated with R.[9]

Clearly, the class of social institutions is broader than the class of social conventions. For instance, it is common knowledge that the famous prisoners' dilemma game can be solved through the use of a binding contract that is enforceable by an external authority. Consequently, in an oligopolistic industry a particular pricing behavior may be instituted that specifies behavior for the firms in their recurrent play of prisoners' dilemma. This regularity, if violated, would be punished by some jointly randomized strategy on the part of the double-crossed firms. Consequently, although this pricing institution is not a convention in Lewis's sense because it is not self-policing, it is an institution under our definition.

1.5 Methodology

The chapters that follow present an approach to economic issues that is not typical. Although it is fundamentally game-theoretical, it differs from classical game-theoretical formulations in being evolutionary rather than static or dynamic. In classical game theory, players are treated as abstract entities totally described by their information and the strategy sets and by their preferences. They act strategically, given total information about the extensive form of a static or dynamic game. Consequently, in choosing strategies, the only information they are allowed to use is that which is formally contained in the description of the game before it is played.

We, however, start with the hypothesis that the most interesting games are not one-shot games or games that are played once and only once between a fixed set of players, but are, rather, recurrent supergames or games that are iterated over and over. In addition, the players in these recurrent situations are constantly changing as the agents who fill certain abstract roles in the game leave. Consequently, games, or the social situations they describe, are not viewed as static phenomena but as evolutionary situations with constantly changing players. The result of this approach is that, as the games we analyze are repeatedly played, the players develop certain societally agreed to rules of thumb, norms, conventions, and institutions which are passed on to succeeding generations of players. Consequently, our players have more information than classic players of n-person games, because they know not only the game in its extensive form but also a whole set of institutions that classic game theory ignores as being extra-game-theoretical. The rigorous inclusion of this information into a game-theoretical analysis is one of the contributions of this book.

In our analysis, players are real, not abstract beings. They are capable of developing trust, creating rules of thumb and social institutions, and following their dictates. In Chapter 3 we see the full impact of this approach.

1.6 Institutions and indeterminacy

As we saw earlier regarding the evolution of money, a theory of institutions may not yield unique results. In other words, although it can be expected to delimit a stable set of institutions that may evolve in an economy, there is no reason to expect the institutions that could theoretically evolve to be unique. Such determinacy should not be expected of any theory in the social sciences. This indeterminacy is not a weakness of the theory, however. As von Neumann and Morgenstern (1947) have said, the role of social science is not to find a solution to a problem but rather to define the set of all solutions. They state:

Since solutions do not seem to be necessarily unique, the complete answer to any specific problem consists not in finding a solution, but in determining the set of all solutions. Thus the entity for which we look in any particular problem is really a set of imputations. This may seem to be unnaturally complicated in itself. . . . Concerning these doubts it suffices to say: First, the mathematical structure of the theory of games of strategy provides a formal justification of our procedure. Second, the previously discussed connections with "standards of behavior" (corresponding to sets of imputations) and the multiplicity of "standards of behavior" on the same physical background . . . makes just this amount of complicatedness desirable. [von Neumann and Morgenstern 1947, p. 44]

In this book we investigate the evolution of stable social institutions. Consequently, we will see that although there might be great indeterminacy in the predicted value of price relationships in some of our models, the range of institutional indeterminacy will be rather small. As an example, consider the following three-person constant-sum game.

Game 1.3: Buddies

Three players exist, eeny, meeny, and miny, and one external millionaire, moe. Moe offers the three players the following deal. If any two of them can agree on how they will split it, moe will give them $1 million. Or if they can all agree on how to split the million dollars, he will give it to all three of them.

The game can be depicted by the following characteristic function, which describes the payoff that any coalition, if it forms, can guarantee itself:

$$V(\text{eeny}) = V(\text{meeny}) = V(\text{miny}) = 0$$
$$V(\text{eeny, meeny}) = V(\text{eeny, miny}) = V(\text{meeny, miny}) = \$1,000,000$$
$$V(\text{eeny, meeny, miny}) = \$1,000,000$$

What should be the solution to this game or social situation? The answer can be found in the first chapter of von Neumann and Morgenstern's *The Theory of Games and Economic Behavior* (1947). It should consist of a set of payoffs–possibly infinite–together with a set of social institutions (called "standards of behavior" by von Neumann and Morgenstern) which are stable in the sense that no payoff/institution pair in the set dominates the other, and any payoff/institution pair not in the set is dominated by at least one pair in the set.

To be more precise, in our example there are two obvious institutional arrangements that might evolve. First, two players might join and split the reward in half, excluding the third player. The set of symmetric payoffs associated with this institutional arrangement is

$$V = \begin{cases} \overset{\text{eeny}}{500{,}000} & \overset{\text{meeny}}{500{,}000} & \overset{\text{miny}}{0} \\ 500{,}000 & 0 & 500{,}000 \\ 0 & 500{,}000 & 500{,}000 \end{cases}$$

In addition, we might envision a discriminatory institutional arrangement in which all three players join together; one is offered a fixed payment, possibly zero, and the other two split the remainder equally. This institution has the following set of symmetric payoffs associated with it:

$$V' = \begin{cases} \alpha_1 = \alpha_2, 0 < \alpha_3 < \$500{,}000 \\ \alpha_1 + \alpha_2 + \alpha_3 = \$1{,}000{,}000 \end{cases}$$

where α_1, α_2, and α_3 are the payoffs to any of the players eeny, meeny, miny, respectively.

The result of the analysis is then indeterminate. However, although the set of imputations may be infinite, the analysis has greatly delimited the range of possible institutional arrangements. In fact, only two stable institutional arrangements exist.

The point that von Neumann and Morgenstern (1947) were making is that many distinct standards of behavior or institutions may evolve from the same physical background (i.e., from the same social situation or game as described by its rules) and that social science should be responsible for predicting that set of institutions that is in some sense stable.

Let us now assume that, as all mortals, eeny, meeny, and miny must someday die, but that moe is immortal. Assume that when they do, their offspring will take their place in the game "Buddies," which is run by moe, and another division game will be played. If they are allowed to transfer the knowledge they have accumulated to their children, they will inform them of the particular payoff/institution pair chosen in their generation and it is likely, although not certain, that this will affect the solution to the next period's game. In other words, particular, arbitrary institutional arrangements may become fossilized in the economy, and these arrangements become parameters or permanent features of the society as it continues to evolve. Consequently, many generations later, a payoff/institution pair may exist that governs this game or situation, without it being obvious why that particular pair is chosen.

In oligopolistic markets, firms establish working relationships or industry ethics as they repeat the play of the same price, quality, or quantity game. Their working relationships are then institutionalized and passed on to their successors. Observing these industries, it is often hard to explain the origin of these institutions. Institutions are often bastard children whose true parents are hard to trace.

1.7 Some game-theoretical terminology

Before describing how we will proceed with our analysis of social institutions in succeeding chapters, I think it appropriate to define some simple game-theoretical terms that will be used throughout. This is done because I hope the book will be accessible to all modern social scientists, not merely to the technically trained high theorist. Those who are already familiar with basic game-theoretical terms are urged to go directly to Section 1.8. I hope also that the game-theoretical purist will forgive my lack of rigor in this section.

To begin, a *game* is defined as a set of rules for a particular situation that delimits the actions available to the *players* (the agents engaged in the situation) and awards payoffs to them on the basis of the actions chosen. Each player has a set of actions or *strategies* from which to choose, which we will call his *strategy set.* The payoff he receives is determined not only by the strategy he chooses, but also by the strategies the other players have chosen. If the payoff to each player were independent of the actions or strategies of all the other players, the situation being investigated would not be called a game but, rather, would consist of a set of independent maximization problems–a situation of considerably less interest.

Now the rules of the game typically specify whether the players are allowed to communicate with each other and whether they are allowed to arrange binding contracts that will allow them to jointly correlate their strategies. If both communication and binding contracts are possible, the game is called a *cooperative game;* if no communication is possible, the game is called *noncooperative.* Cooperative and noncooperative games differ from each other not because the players in one cooperate whereas in the other they do not, but because the communication and contracting possibilities within them are different.

Consider the set of strategies available to player i. Call it S_i, player i's strategy set. If there are n players in the game and if we choose one strategy from each S_i, the resulting n choices will be called a *strategy n-tuple* and be denoted $s = (s_1, s_2, \ldots, s_n)$, $s_i \in S_i$, $i = 1, 2, \ldots, n$. The set of all such n-tuples is called the *strategy space* for the game.

To finish our description of a game we must define the payoffs that result when any given n-tuple is chosen. To do this we merely specify a *payoff function,* which is a function that assigns each player a payoff based on the strategy n-tuple chosen by the players. Hence a payoff function assigns a payoff vector $(\Pi_1(s), \ldots, \Pi_n(s))$ to each n-tuple $s = (s_1, \ldots, s_i, \ldots, s_n)$, where $\Pi_i(s)$ represents the payoff to player i resulting when the n-tuple s is chosen by the players.

With this background we can depict an abstract game by the triple $(N; S; \Pi)$, where N is the set of players in the game, S the strategy space, and Π the payoff function. Describing the game in this way is called describing its *normal form*. In Chapters 2 and 3 we will be concerned almost exclusively with games in normal form. In Chapter 4 we turn our attention to games in what is called *extensive form,* and discuss them in detail.

From our discussion of the telephone game and our definitions of a social convention and a social institution, it should be clear that we will be engaged with problems or games that are recurrent or are played repeatedly by a fixed set of players. Consequently, we will be forced to analyze games that are created by the infinite iteration of static games described in normal form. The game that is defined by this infinite iteration is called a *supergame* and will be the focus of our attention in Chapter 3.

To finish our discussion of games in normal form, we must discuss two common equilibrium concepts–because games are usually studied for the specific purpose of discovering their equilibria. Let $\Pi_i(s_1, \ldots, s_i, \ldots, s_n)$ be the payoff function for player i. If this player has a strategy that yields a higher payoff than any other strategy, no matter what the other $n - 1$ players in the game do, this strategy is called a *dominant strategy* for player i. If in a game $(N; S; \Pi)$ all players have dominant strategies, a *dominant strategy equilibrium* exists. Typically, however, games do not have dominant strategy equilibria. For those situations in which dominant strategy equilibria do not exist, we are forced to fall back on a more general equilibrium notion called the *noncooperative, or Nash equilibrium*. This concept is quite easy to understand. We say that a game is in noncooperative or Nash equilibrium if, given the strategy n-tuple chosen by the players, no player has any incentive to deviate and choose another strategy. In other words, a strategy n-tuple $s^* = (s_1^*, \ldots, s_n^*)$ is in noncooperative or Nash equilibrium if no player, given the strategy choice of the other $n - 1$, could increase his payoff by changing his own strategy choice. As we will see, Nash equilibrium can be defined for games that are played once and only once as well as for iterated or supergames.

To complete this quick game-theoretical review, it is necessary to describe the notion of a cooperative game in *characteristic function form* and one solution concept for such a game, *the core*. In doing this, remember that in cooperative games the players are able to communicate with each other and make binding contracts. Let us assume that there is a set of N players in the cooperative game we are investigating and that a subset of them, $S \subseteq N$, decides to form a *coalition* and coordinate their strategy choices. If we denote $V(S)$ as the most this coalition can guarantee its members no matter what the other players in the game do against them, $V(S)$ is called the *value of the characteristic function for coalition S*. The *characteristic function* is a set-valued function that describes the best that any coalition $S \subseteq N$ can do for itself if it were to form. If there exists some good in the world for which all players have linear utilities, transferring this good becomes equivalent to transferring utility and the game is said to have *transferable utilities*. Let $x = (x_1, \ldots, x_n)$ be a payoff distribution awarding a payoff to each player in the game. If $\Sigma_i \, x_i = V(N)$ and $x_i \geq V(i)$, where $V(i)$ is the value of the characteristic function for player i, then $x = (x_1, \ldots, x_n)$ is called an *imputation*. The analysis of n-person cooperative games is nothing more than the search for imputations that are stable in some sense.

Suppose that we found an imputation $x = (x_1, \ldots, x_n)$ and that this imputation were proposed to the players with a request that they accept it. Clearly, if any coalition of players, S, could get together and do better for themselves [by distributing $V(S)$] than by accepting $x = (x_1, \ldots, x_n)$, they would *block* this imputation proposal. If an imputation exists that cannot be blocked by any coalition, that imputation is in the core of the game. The core can be defined as the set of imputations that cannot be blocked by any coalition.

With these concepts behind us, we can now discuss how we will proceed in succeeding chapters.

1.8 A preview of things to come

It is usual at this point in any economics monograph for the author to tell the reader that only a smattering of high school algebra is necessary for a total understanding of the material in the book. Rather than make such a statement, I will try to specify the exact strategy that any reader should follow, realizing that some parts are more difficult than others.

The aim of Chapter 2 is to bring into focus the major point of this book: that economic and social institutions emerge in society in response to a set of recurrent societal problems. The commonly adhered to solution to these problems becomes the set of social institutions that help to structure social interaction and order our social lives. In Chapter 2 four basic recurrent problems (coordination problems, problems of the prisoners' dilemma type, inequality-preserving problems, and problems of the cooperative game type) are delineated and presented as the major categories of problems for which economic and social institutions are the solution. A wide variety of examples discuss the evolution of such institutions as conventions of war, property rights, money, the week, and the state. In addition, a basic methodological point is made–that if economists are going to study the function and evolution of social institutions, they should start their analyses in an institutional "state of nature" and study which institutions emerge from this initial state. Such an analysis is presented in Chapter 2.

Chapter 2 should be clear to practically all modern social scientists, regardless of their mathematical training or field. Although some elementary game theory is used, it is essentially self-explanatory (except for the treatment of the evolution of the state in Section 2.2).

In Chapter 3 I present a mathematical theory of social institutions, which is a model that will allow us to predict which equilibrium social institution will emerge from a given recurrent situation if many such institutions are possible. Actually, the model provides us with a distribution defining the probability that any particular equilibrium institution will emerge. More formally, the model depicts the process of institution creation as a stochastic diffusion process in which a set of social norms are created upon which a social institution is built. The institutional problem is phrased as a supergame.

Because the material in Chapter 3 is more difficult, I present it in two parts. The first part presents the model in a two-person prisoners' dilemma world and tries to give an intuitive version of it. Although this discussion is somewhat formal, no mathematical prerequisites exist except a tolerance for notation. I urge all readers to try the first part. The second part of Chapter 3 formalizes and generalizes the discussion of the first part and will probably be followed only by those readers who have the stomach for some mathematics, although the level is not too high. Finally, at the end of the chapter, I present an example that illustrates the salient characteristics of the model and demonstrates how it could be implemented to solve the institutional problem posed: Which equilibrium institution will emerge from the recurrent societal problem as its solution?

In Chapter 4 I spell out the exact function that social and economic institutions serve. I demonstrate that social and economic institutions are informational devices created to supplement the informational content of competitive prices when these prices are insufficient to coordinate economic activity. Using simple Edgeworth box diagrams, I demonstrate the informational function of these institutions. In order to measure their informational content, I present an entropy measure first developed by C. E. Shannon and demonstrate that social institutions are entropy-minimizing devices which help create order out of the chaos that would exist without them.

The prerequisites for this chapter are few and it can be read by any trained economist. Some game-theoretical background concerning games in extensive form is presented and, using this material, all readers should find the going relatively easy.

In Chapter 5 I briefly survey some recent work on the theory of teams, hierarchies, and bounded rationality that relate to the analysis presented in Chapters 1 to 4. In addition, I try to point out the consequences that our neo-institutional approach has for the study of economics. Finally, I end this chapter with the disturbing thought that we may not be the total ruler of our institutional fate, and that the institutional forms that we see being created may represent the manifestation of some biogenetic bias preprogrammed in all of us. In other words, if social institutions are the institutionalized solution to a series of recurrent societal problems, then if we are innately predisposed or biased toward certain of these solutions, the types of institutions we build are to some extent beyond our control. In short, this chapter asks whether we can escape the sociobiological challenge of E. O. Wilson (1975) in our analysis of social institutions. Are we really conducting our own institutional symphony or are we merely improvising on a score written before we get on the podium?

Robert Nozik, in the introduction to *Anarchy, State and Utopia* (1975), states that he hopes there is room in the world for authors whose words are not the last words on a subject. My hope is that there is room in the world for books such as this one, which, far from being the last word, is in essence a first word. The ideas presented are not meant as much to replace existing economic theory as to rephrase and reemphasize it. If there is value in looking at old ideas in a new light, this book should be of value.

2 State-of-nature theory and the rise of social institutions

If, as we have indicated in Chapter 1, economics is going to study the rise and evolution of social institutions, a very simple methodological approach is suggested. We should start our analyses in a Lockean state of nature in which there are no social institutions at all, only agents, their preferences, and the technology they have at their disposal to transform inputs into outputs. The next step would be to study when, during the evolution of this economy, such institutions as money, banks, property rights, competitive markets, insurance contracts, and the state would evolve. Looking at economics this way has distinct pedagogical advantages, because it allows us to connect a highly abstract economic theory with the world as we view it through the institutions we observe in everyday life.

The type of method suggested in this chapter is not new. In political science, theorists have tried to deal with the evolution of the state as a "social contract" among free individuals and, as a result, have depicted the institution of the state as emerging from a state of nature. Recently, Robert Nozick (1975) has used such a state-of-nature approach to study how the state can arise in a noncoercive way or at least in a manner that is consistent with individual liberties. He is, as a matter of fact, convinced that we can learn a great deal about such social institutions as the state by understanding how the institutions could have evolved that way. He states:

A theory of state-of-nature that begins with fundamental general descriptions of morally permissible and impermissible actions, and of deeply based reasons why some persons in any society would violate these moral constraints, and goes on to describe how a state would arise from that state-of-nature will serve our explanatory purposes, *even if no actual state ever arose that way.* . . . State-of-nature explanations of the political realm are fundamental potential explanations of this realm and pack explanatory punch and illumination, even if incorrect. We learn much by seeing how the state could have arisen, even if it didn't arise that way. If it didn't arise that way, we also would learn much by determining why it didn't; by trying to explain why the particular bit of the real world that diverges from the state-of-nature model is as it is. [Nozick 1975, pp. 8–9]

20

In economics, a fascinating article by Radford (1945) described the evolution of a wide variety of social institutions in a prisoner-of-war camp during the Second World War. He demonstrated convincingly that if all social and economic institutions were destroyed tomorrow and their memory erased from everybody's mind, the people surviving would proceed to create a new set of institutions which, although possibly different in form from the earlier ones, would serve the same function. Social institutions are human-made, and the only way to destroy them is to destroy human beings themselves. Short of that, we cannot be prevented from creating social mechanisms that make our lives more efficient.

If we are to study how institutions evolve from an institutional state of nature, the institutional form emerging will be an endogenous variable in the model. It emerges without any agent or group of agents consciously designing it–through human actions but not human design. This emphasis on the endogenous unplanned aspect of social institutions is counter to the usual social-scientific view of institutions as planned or designed mechanisms given exogenously to the theorist. The role of the social scientists in that analysis is one of studying the properties of these preordained institutions and not of studying their "organic" evolution. One of the few social scientists to have attacked this conventional point of view is F. A. Hayek, who states:

It is a mistake to which careless expressions by social scientists often give countenance, to believe that their aim is to explain conscious action. This, if it can be done at all, is a different task, the task of psychology. For the social sciences the types of conscious actions are data. . . . The problems which they try to answer arise only in so far as regularities are observed which are not the result of anybody's design. If social phenomena showed no order except in so far as they were consciously designed, there would be, as is often argued, only problems of psychology. It is only in so far as some sort of order arises as a result of individual action but without being designed by any individual that a problem is raised which demands theoretical exploration. [Hayek 1955, p. 39]

Basically, what Hayek is saying is that if one feels that the task of social science is to explain planned behavior or consciously planned social institutions, then all that remains to be studied are the preferences of the planner. But the study of the origin of preferences is the study of psychology; hence, if that were true, all social science would reduce to just that. That may be a fortunate or an unfortunate state of affairs, but, as Hayek rightly points out, a possibly more interesting field of endeavor might be to study the unplanned or unconscious interaction of social agents in order to investigate the spontaneous or unintended social institutions they create. I believe that the types of problems that Hayek feels demand a theoretical explanation can be answered through the use of what we are calling a "state-of-nature method."

In this chapter I present a wide variety of admittedly extreme models that employ this state-of-nature methodology to analyze the evolution of various social institutions. Some of the institutions studied and their analyses will be familiar, others will probably be new; some will discuss the creation of empirically significant institutions, other more frivolous ones. The point will always be the same, however: to demonstrate the type of problem from which social institutions emerge as a solution. Consequently, it is important to make clear that this chapter presents neither a formal theory of social institutions nor a realistic model of the emergence of any particular one–that will be attempted in Chapter 3. Rather, in this chapter we merely attempt to offer some examples of phenomena for which the method just described would be of value and to classify those situations for which social institutions are created. The examples presented are meant only to be illustrative and are in no way complete models of the phenomena described.

2.1 Situations likely to lead to the creation of social institutions

Social institutions, as we have stated, are created to help the agents in an economy solve certain recurrent problems that they face. From each problem there emerges a different social institution whose function is to solve the problem with a minimum of social resources. Consequently, it seems that a simple classification of social institutions is implied by the types of problems they are created to solve, together with the actual way they are created: organically, as Menger thought, or explicitly, as Commons suggested. In a recent book entitled *The Emergence of Norms* (1978), Edna Ullman-Margalit offers three types of situations or problems from which social institutions (which she calls norms)[1] will emerge. Although these three categories are not exhaustive, Ullman-Margalit feels that they cover the most empirically relevant cases.

In a nutshell, the three categories of problems are:
1. Problems of coordination.
2. Problems of the prisoners' dilemma type.
3. Problems of inequality preservation.

In addition, I will treat a fourth category not covered by Ullman-Margalit, which I call problems of the cooperative-game type. Before we turn to our examples, let us look more closely at these four categories.

Problems of coordination

A problem is a *coordination problem* if the payoff space of the game it defines is such that at any equilibrium point, not only does no player have any incentive to change his behavior, given the behavior of the other players, but no player wishes that any other player would change either. To understand

Matrix 2.1. (a) Prisoners' dilemma problem (b) Coordination problem

how such problems are different from other noncooperative game problems–especially prisoners' dilemma problems–consider Matrix 2.1. Looking at Matrix 2.1a, we notice that at the equilibrium (2, 2) no player has any incentive to deviate given the other players' strategy choice. The point (2, 2) is therefore a Nash equilibrium point. This is also true for the two equilibrium points circled in Matrix 2.1b, because if both players happened to choose strategy 1 [leading to payoff (6, 4)] or both chose strategy 2 [leading to payoff (3, 7)], neither would have any incentive to change his strategy given the other's choice. The difference between these equilibria and the one in Matrix 2.1a, however, is that at the equilibrium in Matrix 2.1a, although neither player has any incentive to deviate, each would certainly like the other player to have chosen differently, because this would increase his payoff from 2 to 8; whereas in Matrix 2.1b, not only does each player not want to deviate from his chosen strategy, he does not want the other to deviate either. Their preferences are *locally* parallel, although globally divergent.

The strategic problem for each player in this type of game, then, is that he wants to "coordinate" his choice of strategy with his opponents, because for any given choice by his opponent, it is always beneficial to coordinate, yet he is not indifferent as to the exact strategy n-tuple they coordinate on.[2] If a coordination game were a recurrent feature of a given economy or society, rather than trying to solve the game each time it reappears, it would be reasonable to expect the agents in the economy to establish some equilibrium mode of behavior or convention and adhere to it each time the problem arises. Such a convention of behavior, if adhered to, is a social institution and would allow the agents to avoid the occurrence of inefficient nonequilibrium payoffs.

The problem, then, for each agent in a recurrent coordination game is to avoid recurrent nonequilibrium payoffs by always coordinating his activities with those of the others, yet to try to have the n-tuple of coordinated strategies be one that is best for him. In other words, in the game depicted by Matrix 2.1b, both players clearly prefer the diagonal equilibria to any off-diagonal nonequilibrium payoffs, yet player 1 would prefer the payoff pair (6, 4) and player 2 would prefer (3, 7). [The game is what Thomas Schelling (1960) calls a mixed-motive game.]

Prisoners' dilemma games

Prisoners' dilemma games are games in which for any noncooperative equilibrium, there exists at least one payoff vector associated with some *nonequilibrium* pure strategy *n*-tuple that is Pareto-superior to it. Consequently, if societies faced prisoners' dilemma games recurrently, it would be efficient for them to evolve some regularity of behavior that would avoid the repeated use of equilibrium, but inefficient, strategies. Again, such a regularity would be a social convention that would prescribe behavior for the agents in this recurrent situation and would be adhered to. The institutional rule would specify the use of some nonequilibrium *n*-tuple to be played recurrently as the game reappears. However, since the game is of the prisoners' dilemma type, at each iteration there is an incentive to deviate from the institutional rule. The consequences of such a deviation must be spelled out in the definition of the institution itself.

As we will see later, it is important that the situations under investigation be recurrent ones because social institutions can best be described as noncooperative equilibria of supergames that involve the repeated play of some particular constituent game, not as features of one-shot games. The institutions that evolve, then, are in equilibrium only with respect to the supergame and its payoff, not with respect to the constituent game making it up. This distinction will concern us later. At present, the relevant point to make is that prisoners' dilemma situations are clearly situations for which we might expect social institutions to emerge.

To illustrate the need for social institutions in the solution to prisoners' dilemma problems, Michael Taylor (1976) has discussed the possibility that stable social institutions (in the form of stable supergame equilibria) may be established to solve public-goods problems modeled as prisoners' dilemma games in order to avoid nonoptimal outcomes. Consider Matrix 2.2. In this

| | | II | |
		Give true information	Lie
I	Given true information	8, 10	1, 12
	Lie	12, 1	3, 3

Matrix 2.2. Public-goods game

game two agents are being asked to contribute to the construction of a public good. The amount of the good constructed will depend upon the marginal rates of substitution between this good and an all-purpose private good that the agents report to the economy's central planner. The public good is assumed to last only one period, after which it vanishes and the game will have to be played again. The strategies of the two agents in any period are either to lie or to tell the truth to the planner when he asks their marginal rates of substitution. Based on these reports, the planner will determine the amount of public good to provide.

This recurrent problem is clearly a prisoners' dilemma game, and, as is customarily thought, if no binding contracts can be enforced between the agents, a nonoptimal equilibrium will result in which the public good would be underprovided. However, if the game were recurrent and the players realized this, both of them might realize that the repeated use of a lying strategy would be self-destructive, and as the situation is iterated, we might expect a norm of truthful revelation of preferences to be developed upon which the convention of telling the truth would be built. Consequently, we could expect social institutions to evolve to solve recurrent prisoners' dilemma games.[3]

The two types of problems, coordination and prisoners' dilemma, are not necessarily mutually exclusive. Prisoners' dilemma games may have coordination elements associated with them (although the reverse is not true). Consider Matrix 2.3. Here we have a 6 × 6 game that is composed of three subgames,

| | II | | | | | |
	1	2	3	4	5	6
1	4, 4	1, 8	0, 0	0, 0	0, 0	0, 0
2	8, 1	2, 2	0, 0	0, 0	0, 0	0, 0
3	0, 0	0, 0	5, 5	3, 6	0, 0	0, 0
4	0, 0	0, 0	6, 3	4, 4	0, 0	0, 0
5	0, 0	0, 0	0, 0	0, 0	6, 6	4, 10
6	0, 0	0, 0	0, 0	0, 0	10, 4	5, 5

I (rows 1–6)

Matrix 2.3. A coordination–prisoners' dilemma game

each of which is a 2 × 2 prisoners' dilemma game. Although each subgame is of the prisoners' dilemma variety, even if no binding contracts could be made that would stabilize the game at the *nonequilibrium* payoff (6, 6), the players still have an incentive to coordinate their actions and choose strategy 6, which determines that *equilibrium* payoff (5, 5) which is Pareto-superior to any other *equilibrium* payoff. The game then includes elements of both the prisoners' dilemma and the coordination variety.

Inequality-preserving social institutions

The third type of social institution that Ullman-Margalit considered is what she calls "norms of partiality" and what I call *inequality-preserving institutions*. Actually, these institutions are really not a separate category because they are a subclass of coordination institutions, as we will soon see. For reasons of taxonomy, however, it does make sense to classify them separately. These are institutions created to preserve a status quo position of inequality among various economic agents. The type of institution envisioned here would be something like a property right or an inheritance law that establishes a convention in which property of certain types, or the right to use such property, is agreed to be safe from theft or violation by others. The important point about the type of situation leading to the creation of such inequality-preserving institutions is that one equilibrium payoff vector in the situation is given special importance by being designated as the status quo, and all of the analysis takes this as a starting point. This sanctification of the status quo is what makes the situation different from a coordination problem or a prisoners' dilemma problem.

To understand this type of problem more thoroughly, consider Matrix 2.4 (Ullman-Margalit's Matrix 4.16). Assume that this game is a recurrent game

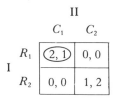

Matrix 2.4. Inequality preservation games: coordination game with a status quo

in which the same 2 × 2 matrix game is played over and over again by the same two players. As such, it appears to be a simple coordination game in which there are two noncooperative equilibria (R_1, C_1) and (R_2, C_2), each favoring a different player. From what we said about coordination games and institutions, we can expect that, if this game were iterated, the players would create some convention of behavior for themselves that would specify which one of these equilibria they would adhere to in every iteration of the game.

In situations leading to the formation of inequality-preserving institutions, the problem is identical to the one described above except that one equilibrium outcome, the one circled, is specified "historically" as the status quo. Consequently, the question under investigation is *not* which equilibrium will emerge as the societally agreed upon social convention, but rather whether the historically predetermined convention prescribing an unequal distribution of utility will be adhered to or whether the unfavored party will try to deviate from it. To understand why an incentive for deviation exists, consider Matrix 2.4 and the game at the iteration in which the equilibrium (R_1, C_1) has been played for $t - 1$ periods and is by now an institutional fact of life or established convention of behavior (in the sense of Lewis). At the time it may be rational for the column player to try to change the equilibrium (or status quo) from (R_1, C_1) to (R_2, C_2), because as far as he can see, the game is symmetric and there is no reason why the historically fossilized convention (which is unfavorable to him) is any more justifiable than (R_2, C_2), in which case he would be doing better. Consequently, we can expect (as Ullman-Margalit argues) the column player to try to break this noncooperative equilibrium and move it from (R_1, C_1) to (R_2, C_2). He will do this by (as Schelling describes it) trying to commit himself totally to choosing C_2, in which case the row chooser is forced into choosing between the payoff associated with (R_1, C_2) and the payoff assciated with (R_2, C_2). Here the row chooser would prefer (R_2, C_2), which is better for the column chooser than (R_1, C_1), the status quo. The column chooser's hope is that if he can inflict a low payoff on the row chooser often enough in the iteration of the game, he can convince him that he is totally committed to C_2 and can thereby break the previously established convention. If the convention is well defined, however, such an attempt would be impossible because, by definition, the institutional rule supporting (R_1, C_1) not only specifies (R_1, C_1) as the accepted mode of behavior, but also specifies punishing behavior for the column chooser if he tries to deviate. This punishing behavior involves having the row chooser continue to choose R_1 no matter what. Consequently, social institutions emerge and perpetuate historically determined but possibly unequal distributions of utility, and to that extent they are inherently conservative.

Although we have classified these situations as distinct and separate circumstances leading to the creation of social conventions, we will not treat them separately, because the distinction between inequality-preserving institutions and institutions created to solve coordination problems is artificial. This is true because by separately classifying each of these situations, we are merely drawing a distinction between the analysis of a coordination problem before and after a social institution has been created. In other words, if we started with a coordination problem and a convention evolved establishing (R_1, C_1) as the socially agreed upon and stable social institution, then, once established, the situation immediately becomes one requiring an inequality-preserving institution. However, such an inequality-preserving institution has already been established, because it is included in the institution created to solve the coordination problem. Consequently, if stable institutions are created that, as is often the case, determine unequal distributions of income, the policing strategies defined by the institution are, in and of themselves, inequality-preserving institutions. There is no need to create a separate category here, and consequently we will not formally treat such situations in this book.

Explicitly and organically determined social institutions in cooperative game contexts

One common characteristic of the type of situation leading to the creation of social institutions in the cases described above is that all of the games specified are played noncooperatively or without communication among the agents. They emerge organically by human action but not by human design and are the result of individual but not collective human behavior. Now, of course, many social institutions are created in one stroke by a social planner or by the agents of society meeting in a face-to-face manner and bargaining about the type of institution they would like to see created. Here the exact form of the institution that emerges is the result of explicit human design (in the case of a planner) or multilateral bargaining (in the case of a legislature). Probably the best example of such institutions is presented by James Buchanan and Gordon Tullock (1962) in their classic book, *The Calculus of Consent,* where they discuss how various characteristics of state constitutions are determined. Here such social conventions or institutional rules as the majority needed to pass bills are explicitly set and bargained for, and the constitution creation game is played cooperatively, with communication.

We will not discuss these types of institutions in this book, for two reasons. First, if the social institutions we are investigating are created by a social planner, their design can be explained by maximizing the value of some objective function existing in the planner's mind. Such an exercise, as Hayek (1955) has pointed out, is of less theoretical interest and need not warrant our consideration here, unless the problem of preference revelation exists, which we will discuss later. On the other hand, if the form of the social institution created is the outcome of a multilateral bargaining process, a bargaining theory would be required. Such an analysis, however, is probably best left to others. What remains is the study of social institutions created to help solve those societal problems that exist and are created organically or spontaneously. It is to these that we devote our attention.

This does not mean that the study of explicitly or consciously defined social institutions is not an interesting topic. Quite the contrary is true, as Leonid Hurwicz (1973a) has demonstrated. In fact, the design of desirable social institutions can be considered one of the major contributions of game theory to economics, as has been argued by Schotter and Schwödiauer (1980). The point made by Hurwicz and others is that each social institution can be considered as a set of rules that specify or constrict the behavior of agents in various social and economic situations. If these situations can be specified as games of strategy whose equilibria can be calculated, then, if the planner can indicate the type of outcomes he desires to see emerge from the game, the proper institutional structure (rules of the game) can be determined that yields these outcomes as equilibria. Such a study becomes the study of the creation of optimal rules of games.

This view of social institutions, as embodied in the rules of the game, is different from the view presented in this book because here we view social institutions not as various sets of rules but as various and alternative standards of behavior (strategy n-tuples) that are elements of the equilibrium of the game. In other words, our social institutions are not part of the rules of the game but part of the solutions to iterated games of strategy. It is for this reason that we do not consider what we have called explicitly created social institutions.

There are, however, social institutions that emerge organically from a social situation equivalent to cooperative n-person games which are not the product of human design but appear as properties of the equilibrium solution to the game under investigation. Here the institutions are created through the interaction of individual and group maximizing behavior, none of which has as its purpose the creation of a social institution. One of the best examples of such an institution is given by Robert Nozick (1975) in his explanation of how the state can emerge from a Lockean state of nature without an agent actually planning it and without the players being coerced to accept it. As we will see, the state in Nozick's analysis is a property of the core of what we will call the *state-of-nature theft game*. The important point to keep in mind, however, is that although the agents who create the state are able to speak with each other and bargain in a face-to-face manner, the type of institutional arrangements that emerge from these negotiations may be totally unintended and qualify completely as what Menger called organically created social institutions.

Since we are interested in all organically created social institutions, we will pay some attention to these types of cooperative game institutions as well. However, the attention will be limited to the one example we offer in Section 2.2.

As a result of our discussion, we can construct a 4 × 2 classification of social institutions (see Table 2.1) according to the way they are created (organically or explicitly) and the type of problem they solve (coordination, prisoners' dilemma, inequality-preserving, or cooperative).

From this description it is clear why we will limit ourselves to the analysis of institutions that are created to solve either noncooperative coordination problems or problems of the prisoners' dilemma type and take the form of noncooperative equilibria to infinitely repeated supergames or cooperative game problems in which the social institution created is a feature of the solution con-

Table 2.1. *Classification of social institutions*

| | Method of creation | |
Type of problem	Organically	Deliberately
Coordination problem	Studied here	Bargaining problem—not studied here
Prisoners' dilemma problem	Studied here	The creation of binding and explicit contracts—not studied here
Inequality-preserving problem	Not studied here (part of the coordination institution)	Unequal distribution of income enforced by the state or some coercive force—not studied here
Cooperative game problem	Studied here, but limited to one example in Section 2.2	Problems of planning—not studied here

cept used. Although this admittedly leaves out a wide variety of social institutions, it does include many that are of extreme empirical significance and, in addition, treats those cases that are of the most interest theoretically.

To give a better picture of the type of analysis envisioned in this book, let us turn to a series of examples presented to illustrate the type of real-world situation that requires the creation of a social institution, together with a demonstration of what we have called a state-of-nature method. It must again be pointed out that these examples are not meant to be realistic models of social phenomena as much as motivating examples illustrating an institution-generating problem. As Nozick states, we can learn a great deal about social institutions by studying how they could have evolved from a state of nature even if, in fact, they did not evolve that way. Consequently, although we do not claim that the social institutions used to illustrate our approach actually did evolve to solve the exact problem described, we can learn a great deal about social institutions by studying the type of situation that cries out for the creation of one. This is what I hope to do in the remainder of this chapter. I apologize if at times the presentation of the examples seems too formal for the purposes of illustration. I have tried, whenever possible, to make the examples as intuitive as possible while remaining precise. It has not always been an easy task.

2.2 Some examples

Now that we know the type of situation for which social institutions are created, let us investigate a series of real-world problems that have been settled by the development of some social institutions. We will classify the examples into the four categories discussed above.

Coordination problems and coordination institutions

The evolution of the week. It is interesting to contemplate why time is divided into weeks.[4] Clearly, this is an arbitrary division, because there is no natural event, such as the rotation of the moon, which corresponds to the week. Yet in almost all parts of the world, time is divided into weeks, usually consisting of 5 or 6 working days and 2 or 1 day of leisure, respectively.[5] The division of time into weeks is clearly a man-made social convention or institution; it is an artifact of human existence.

What facts explain the existence of the week? What function does it serve? To answer these questions, we shall assume that we are observing an agrarian society in which time is totally undifferentiated except for its division into days–a society that has not yet evolved the concept of the week as a social institution.

To offer a possible explanation of how the week evolved, let us assume that the society described above is composed of a set of n farmers and that the farms they inhabit are arranged in a circle around a central city (Figure 2.1). To help our analysis, let us make some fanciful assumptions that will serve to highlight the coordination problem of interest to us in this chapter. First, assume that each farmer grows only one crop on his soil, so that farmer i grows only crop x_i, and that all farmers have a utility function of the following type:

$$U_i = A x_1^{\alpha_1} x_2^{\alpha_2} \cdots x_{i-1}^{\alpha_{i-1}} x_{i+1}^{\alpha_{i+1}} \cdots x_n^{\alpha_n}$$

Notice that each farmer gains no utility from the consumption of his own crop but most consume every other crop in positive amounts to obtain any utility at all. Next, assume that there is no disutility or utility to be derived from work and that the amount of crop available to be harvested by farmer i at time t is

$$x_i^t = \psi^i(\tilde{t}_i)$$

where $\tilde{t}_i$ is the amount of time that has elapsed since the last harvest of i's crop and ψ^i is a concave, twice-differentiable function of $\tilde{t}_1$. Finally, assume that all trade must take place in the city; that there are transportation costs c_i involved for farmer i each time he brings a crop to the city; and that, after harvesting, crops cannot be stored but must be consumed during that market day or they will spoil. Each farmer must bring his produce to the city to be sold (because he gains no utility from the consumption of the crop that he alone produces), but each trip to the market is costly.

When a farmer brings his goods to the city, he takes them to a marketing

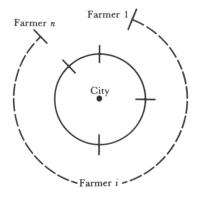

Figure 2.1. Coordination of distribution in an agrarian society.

institution that we assume evolved at an earlier time, whose function it is to allocate the goods brought to it each day. Consequently, at the end of any given day, each farmer must decide if he wants to travel to the city with his crop. We assume that if he goes, he takes all of his harvestable crop with him; therefore, the game we will describe will not include quantity as a strategic variable. The only strategic variable for each farmer is when to go to the city. When all the farmers who have decided to go on a given day arrive, they hand over all their produce to the central marketing agent, whose existence is assumed and not explained, and who is fully informed about the utility functions of all farmers. This central marketing agent then defines a set of equilibrium prices based on the supplies that have been brought to the market and upon the known utility functions of the farmers, from which he derives his demand functions. At these prices he calculates the utility-maximizing bundle for each farmer and allocates the bundles accordingly. All farmers then consume the bundles allocated to them.

Some things are now obvious. First, unless all farmers arrive in the city on the same day, all prices must be zero. This is true because unless a farmer can consume positive amounts of each good, he will be unwilling to demand any good at a positive price. However, because a farmer's income can be positive only if the good he produces receives a positive price, his income will be zero on any day in which not all farmers come to the city. On those days the farmer's utility from consumption must be zero and his final payoff from traveling to the city on that day will be $-c_i$, because it cost him c_i to travel to the city and yet he gained no utility when he got there.

More generally, it is possible to express the payoff to player i when he arrives at the market simultaneously with all other farmers as being strictly a function of $\tilde{t} = (\tilde{t}_1, \ldots, \tilde{t}_n)$ or $P_i = \xi^i(\tilde{t})$, because any vector $\tilde{t}$ determines the supply of goods available on a given day, which, when juxtaposed to the demand curves derived, determines the equilibrium prices and allocations. The problem that results is a simple coordination problem in which all agents must tacitly agree to arrive in the city on the same day if any agent is to receive a positive payoff. Consequently, a recurrence pattern must be specified that indicates the number of days between market days. Such regularity in behavior or recurrence pattern, if unanimously adhered to, is exactly what Lewis has called a social convention and what we are calling a social institution. The length of time between market occurrences is the week, and the institution of the week is a coordination equilibrium, because no agent would choose to deviate from it or have anyone else deviate.[6]

In describing the normal form of the game, we can think of the game being played as follows. Starting on day 1, each farmer will choose some number in the interval $[0, \infty]$, which we will call his recurrence time in the city. This time will specify the number of days that he will allow to elapse between visits to the city. Consequently, the strategy space for our game will be the product set $T = \Pi_{i=1}^{n} [0, \infty]$, and an n-tuple $t = (t_1, \ldots, t_n)$ will represent a vector of choices, one for each farmer. The payoffs to any farmer when a given vector $t = (t_1, \ldots, t_n)$ is chosen, that is, when he chooses the recurrence pattern t_i and all other players choose the recurrent pattern $\bar{t}_i = (t_1, \ldots, t_{i-1}, t_{i+1}, \ldots, t_n)$, is

$$\Pi_i = \sum_{t \in T_i^*} \alpha_i^{t-1}[\xi_i^i(\tilde{t}) - c_i] - \sum_{t \in \bar{T}_i} \alpha_i^{t-1}[c_i]$$

where α_i is the discount rate for farmer i; T_i^* is the set of time periods in which, given the vector of recurrence times $t = (t_1, \ldots, t_i, \ldots, t_n)$, farmer i arrives in the city and all other farmers are there; and $\bar{T}_i$ is the set of time periods during which farmer i travels to the city and not all farmers are there.

What this payoff function tells us is that on those days in which farmer i goes to the city and all other farmers are there (those $t \in T_i^*$), he will receive a payoff of $\xi_i^i(\tilde{t}) - c_i$, whose discounted value is $\alpha_i^{t-1}[\xi_i^i(\tilde{t}) - c_i]$; whereas in those periods in which farmer i travels to the city and not all other farmers are there (those $t \in \bar{T}_i$), his payoff is $-c_i$, whose present discounted value is $\alpha_i^{t-1}[-c_i]$.

As a result, we can define the payoffs to the farmers in the recurrence game in normal form, strictly in terms of the n-tuple of recurrence times chosen by the farmers, as $\Pi_i = \Pi_i(t)$. In addition, we can specify utility functions, production functions, and discount rates such that for all i, any vector for which $t_1 = t_2 = \cdots t_n = t^*$ determines a greater payoff for him than does a vector for which he or anyone else deviates and sets $t_i \neq t^*$.

The problem, then, is a pure recurrent coordination problem that is best looked upon as a supergame in which each player must decide upon an infinite sequence of 0s and 1s, in which each 1 would indicate a choice to go to the city on a given day and each 0 would indicate a choice to stay at home. The week would be institutionalized when all the sequences of the players are identical. In addition, assumptions can be made in the simple model presented, such that it is in every farmer's interest to establish the week and every t^* days to stop work and go to the city. The possibility that the week might have actually evolved for the purpose of solving a marketing coordination problem is perhaps suggested by the fact that in Brazil the days of the week are called "first market day," "second market day," and so on.

Although every agent in the economy has some interest in establishing the week, the preferences of the players over the actual length of the week are certainly not identical. Depending on the parameters that characterize the farmer, the optimal length of the week may differ very greatly. More precisely, if each farmer could control the length of the week, he would determine a length that would maximize the following expression:

$$\max_{t_1,\ldots,t_n} \Pi_i(t_1, \ldots, t_n; c_i, \alpha_i)$$

In other words, each farmer, if he were allowed to choose the length of the week, might actually choose a different optimal length. The preferences of the players are then identical in establishing the existence of the week, but their preferences are conflicting in determining its length.

The relevant questions at this point in our analysis are: How long will the week that is established actually be, and how many periods can be expected to pass until it is established? A successful theory of social institutions would have to answer these questions in a rigorous manner. Although we must wait until Chapter 3 for an attempt to answer this type of question, it is clear that any analysis that gives a determinate answer to such a question cannot be valid. The exact form of any social institution can be specified only probabilistically. The development of the week will be greatly influenced by the coincidence with which people start to converge on the city and see each other. What develops is a snowballing effect in which people come to the city in a particular pattern, see that other people are also following this pattern, and continue to return or not, according to whether their pattern is popular. Eventually, a universal pattern is established and institutionalized, but the exact pattern that is institutionalized is actually randomly determined.

As we will see in our formal model, the history or path of the game will have a dramatic influence upon the type of institution that is created, and to the extent that different coincidental paths occur, different institutions are possible. The problem is clearly a dynamic one, however, and can only be modeled in extensive form or as a supergame with dynamic properties.

Finally, it is clear that the size of the week that finally evolves from a given society may not be Pareto-optimal.[7] For instance, consider the two-person

		Farmer 2		
		Every day	Every 2 days	Every 3 days
Farmer 1	Every day	6, 5	3, 4	2, 3
	Every 2 days	5, 5	8, 10	0, 0
	Every 3 days	3, 2	0, 0	9, 6

Matrix 2.5. The week game

society shown by Matrix 2.5, in which the players have to play the recurrence game explained above but the number of days from which they can choose is limited to three. Here we see that although each farmer would rather have a week established no matter what its length, farmer 1 would prefer its length to be 3 days, then 2 days, and then 1 day, whereas farmer 2 would prefer it to be 2 days, then 3 days, then 1 day. Notice, however, that there exists a length of week–the 1-day week–that is Pareto-inferior to the 2- and 3-day weeks but may still evolve as an equilibrium pattern. Consequently, the efficiency of the institutions that evolve from a given situation may be rather low.

The evolution of money. Money, like the invention of the week, is a man-made artifact. There is nothing in nature that says that corn or gold or silver shall function universally as money or that money should exist at all. To the extent that these commodities do function as a means of exchange, they do so because of a tacit (or explicit, in the case of fiat money) agreement among the agents in the economy to accept these goods as payments for other goods and services. Menger states

that every economic unit in a nation would be ready to exchange his goods for little metal disks apparently useless as such, or for documents representing the latter is a procedure so opposed to the ordinary course of things. . . . The problem, which science has here to solve consists in giving an explanation of a general homogeneous course of action pursued by human beings when engaged in traffic which taken concretely makes unquestionably for the common interest and which seems to conflict with the nearest and immediate interest of contracting individuals. [Menger 1892, pp. 239–40]

In a recent article in the *Journal of Political Economy,* Robert Jones (1976) presents a probabilistic model of the evolution of a medium of exchange in which he derives stable solutions for an economy in which full monetization, full barter, and intermediate amounts of monetization or trade evolve. As such, it is a prime example of a model that employs the type of methodology being called for here. However, since Jones's model is non-game-theoretical, we attempt our own simple game-theoretical model here, which, I hope, will highlight the salient aspects of the problem, whose solution lies in the creation of money.

To begin, consider the agrarian economy studied above, which, at present, has two institutions–a week of duration t^* and a marketing institution. Assume that a technological breakthrough has occurred and it is now possible for the marketing agent to pick up each farmer's goods on market day and deliver them to a central warehouse at zero cost. Consequently, any farmer i no longer need incur a cost of c_i when he wants to deliver his goods to the market, but need only incur a cost of g_i to transport himself there, with $g_i < c_i$ for all farmers in the economy. Further assume that every week, the marketing agent arrives, picks up the supplies of goods, deposits them in his warehouse, and, given the known and fixed utility functions of the agents, calculates what would be the competitive equilibrium price vector for the economy if competitive markets existed.

Because the week is always the same length, all crops grow in a stationary manner according to $x_i^t = \psi^i(t_i^*)$, all utility functions are unchanging, and there is no capital investment, the economy is in a stationary state in which the set of equilibrium prices determined each week is identical, as are the resulting incomes of the farmers and their weekly bundles. Hence each week each farmer would receive the same utility from transacting in the market. There is one problem, however, which we will assume is that the marketing agent is not actually capable of executing trades and consequently must rely on an external mechanism to do this. To discover how the evolution of money might solve this problem, let us assume that in addition to the crops existing in the economy, there are also m different plastic chips, each of a different color, in which all trade must take place but which yield no utility. Consequently, once the equilibrium prices are announced each week, each trader takes a number of chips equal to his equilibrium income with him to the city and attempts to buy his equilibrium bundle at those prices. (Each chip of any color is given an exogenously determined price of 1 so that they can all function as the *numéraire* in the economy.) Consequently, at the recurrent set of equilibrium prices, each farmer i will take with him to the city a number K_i of possible m different colored chips (indexed $m = 1, 2, \ldots, M$) equal to $K_i = p_i^* \psi^i(t_i^*)$, where p_i^* is the equilibrium price for the good he produces and $\psi^i(t_i^*)$ is the amount that he recurrently brings to the market. Each period, the distribution of income is given by $K = (K_1, \ldots, K_n)$ and each farmer chooses a distribution of chips to take to the market, $d^i = (d_1^i, \ldots, d_j^i, \ldots, d_m^i)$, $d_j^i \geq 0$ and $\Sigma_j d_j^i = K_i$.

At any given week, then, there exists a set of n farmers each with income K_i and each with a portfolio of chips represented by d^i. When in the city, the farmers conduct trade as follows. There are n trading booths at which the n goods are traded. The prices of the goods are known by all farmers and they calculate their optimal bundles on these prices, so that the only strategic problem involved is one of actually executing the set of equilibrium trades. To do this, each farmer must make two decisions. One concerns how he wants to be paid for the goods he sells (i.e., in what chip or what combination of chips he will accept payment) and the other concerns how he will decide to pay for the goods he wants to buy. In other words, each farmer must decide upon a pair of distributions $s_i = (f^i, r^i)$ in which $f^i = (f^i_{11}, \ldots, f^i_{Mn-1})$ is an $n - 1 \times M$ dimensional vector in which f^i_{mj} indicates the amount of chips m brought to the city by farmer i that he wants to allocate in purchasing good j. Feasibility requires that $d^i_m \geq \Sigma_j f^i_{mj}$ for all m. In other words, a farmer cannot decide to pay for goods in a way that requires him to use more of any color plastic chip than he has brought to the city, and $\Sigma_m \Sigma_j f^i_{mj} \leq K_i$. In addition, the farmer must decide upon an M-dimensional vector $r^i = (r^i_1, \ldots, r^i_M)$ that defines the way he wants to be paid for the goods he supplies. By feasibility, $\Sigma^M_{m=1} r^i_m \leq K_i$–a farmer cannot ask to be paid in such a way that the sum of payments to him are greater than his income.

Clearly, we have defined a recurrent game that the set of farmers play with each other each week when they arrive in the city and try to execute trades. The game can be described as follows. Time starts at the market day defined in week 1. At that time all supplies of crops are collected and brought to the city and all prices and incomes are determined. At these prices all farmers calculate the equilibrium bundles and then attempt to purchase them. To do this each farmer makes a choice of a pair of vectors $s_i = (f^i, r^i)$ such that $\Sigma_m \Sigma_j f^i_{mj} \leq K_i$ and $\Sigma_m r^i_m \leq K_i$. Letting S_i be the set of all such feasible strategy choices for player i (a closed compact convex set), the strategy space for the game is $S = \Pi^n_{i=1} S_i$. To determine the payoffs of the game, let us look at player j. Assume that he supplies good j. Then he will agree to sell all of his good only if he is paid in the way he specifies [i.e., according to $r^j = (r^j_1, \ldots, r^j_M)$]. This will be true if $r^j_m = \Sigma_{i \neq j} f^i_{mj}$ for all m. Consequently if $r^j_m = \Sigma_{i \neq j} f^i_{mj}$ holds for all j and m, it will be true that the manner in which all farmers have specified that they want to be paid exactly balances the paying plans of each of the others. In this case all goods brought to the market will actually be sold, and a Pareto-optimal equilibrium payoff will be determined. If, however, for farmer j, $r^j_m > \Sigma_{i \neq j} f^i_{mj}$, for any chip m, in which case the farmers fall short by $e^j_m = r^j_m - \Sigma_{i \neq j} f^i_{mj}$ of paying farmer j the r^j_m chips m he specified, farmer j will refuse to sell $b^j = E^j/p^*_j$ units in the market, where $E^j = \Sigma^m_{m=1} e^j_m$. In other words, if E^j is the sum of farmer j's shortfalls on the m types of chips, then at price p^*_j for his goods he will hold E^j/p^*_j units from sale. As a result, because there is a shortage of the right kind of chips being offered for good j at trading booth j, a limited supply of the good will be allocated by giving each of the $n - 1$ farmers demanding the product a fraction of the available supply $J = \psi_j(t_j^*) - b^j$ equal to

$$Z_i = \frac{\sum\limits_{m=1}^{M} f_{mj}^i}{\sum\limits_{m}\sum\limits_{i} f_{mj}^i} \, (J)$$

This means that if the manner in which the farmers want to pay for good j does not coincide with the manner in which farmer j wants to be paid (i.e., not in the chip or chips he will accept for payment), the resulting shortfall in supply is allocated in such a way that farmer i receives a fraction of the available supply equal to his fraction of the demand for that good at the equilibrium.[8]

From this description we can clearly see that we have defined a recurrent coordination game in normal form in which the strategy space for each player is a pair of vectors $s_i = (f_j^i, r^i)$ such that $\Sigma_j \, \Sigma_m f_{mj}^i \leq K_i$ and $\Sigma_m r_m^i \leq K_i$ and the payoff function is a mapping $\gamma\colon \Pi_{i=1}^n\colon S_i \to R^N$ describing the vector of utility payoffs determined for each n-tuple of pairs $s = (s_1, \ldots, s_n)$. It is the solution to this problem for which the convention of money emerges, because if each farmer agreed to receive his income in one and only one type of chip and to pay all other farmers in exactly the same type of chip, and all other farmers chose to do the same, then the equilibrium conditions specified above would be trivially satisfied in each period, and in each period the farmers would receive the payoffs associated with the competitive equilibrium of the economy. If this occurred, the economy would be fully monetized and there would emerge a chip that would function as *the* medium of exchange. However, it may be that the farmers recurrently decide to bring a mix of colored chips to the market and ask to be paid with a mix of chips and yet our equilibrium conditions are still satisfied. (There may exist mixed-strategy equilibria.) In this case, although the economy would execute all equilibrium trades in each period, we could not say that *a* money exists for the economy, and trade would not be considered fully monetized. The question of which chip will evolve as *the* chip of exchange in this economy and what the probability is that one actually will emerge is typical of the types of questions that we hope to answer in this book.

In conclusion, although our model is admittedly abstract and highly stylized, I feel that it presents the type of problem that has historically led to the evolution of money. Most succinctly, the problem is one of executing trade in the least costly manner, and this can be done only if the agents in the economy will accept one particular good in exchange when they trade. The problem is, of course, that they have to agree implicitly on the same good (or chip), and it is in tracing how this one good gets established as money that our problem takes on its intellectual interest.

Prisoners' dilemma problems and social institutions

Many social situations can be represented as prisoners' dilemma games. The metaphor has become so commonplace, in fact, that it is a standard phrase in the vocabulary of social scientists. But prisoners' dilemma games as described in textbooks rarely exist in the real world. This is so because the classic prisoners' dilemma situation is a static one-shot situation in which the players face each other one and only one time and must choose strategies for that one play only. Most real-world situations of any interest, however are *repeated situations* in which a set of players *repeatedly* face each other in the same situation. This is clearly true in international relations, where countries repeatedly test each other in situations of conflict in various parts of the world. It is also true in military conflicts, because each side in a conventional war knows that this will not be the only such war they will fight in the course of their history and therefore will realize that their behavior now will affect the type of behavior they can expect in future wars. Consequently, their behavior is likely to be different from what it would be in a one-shot war game.

The distinctive characteristic of all these situations is that in all of them there is a learning process going on in which the players learn the type of behavior they can expect from each other and build up a set of commonly held norms of behavior. It is upon these commonly established norms that a social convention of behavior or institution is established that prescribes behavior for each participant in the conflict. Consequently, countries that fight conventional wars in the world today do not use certain types of strategies (germ warfare, infanticide, nuclear weapons, the bombing of civilian population centers, etc.), because they know that if they introduce such tactics, and future wars occur, the present value of the payoffs associated with the fighting of the future wars would be so low that they would be better off to fight the present war without them than to introduce such tactics. Similarly, oligopolists must concern themselves with the effects their present actions will have on the set of industry norms and realize that although a low-price strategy now may be beneficial in the short run, in the long run it could lead to a protracted price war that would be mutually damaging to all members of the industry. Consequently, in these recurrent prisoners' dilemma games, we can expect some type of social convention to be established by the players in the game that will allow them to avoid the payoffs predicted by the one-shot analysis. Let us look at some examples.

The rules of war and rule utilization. The cliché that all is fair in love and war notwithstanding, it is commonly agreed that all is not fair in war and that a strict code of conduct exists that prescribes the type of conduct "allowable" in military confrontations. Rules of war exist and are enforced by the knowledge of the state of affairs that would exist if they were abandoned. The introduction of a new weapons system or technique has severe consequences for the way future wars are fought.

To try to visualize how such rules of war evolve, consider a two-country world with country A and country B. Assume that these countries will, over a period of years, continually fight wars with each other, and assume that each country has access to three types of weapons: x, y, and z. If this is so and we define a weapons system as a combination of one or more of these weapons, each country could employ a total of $2^3 - 1 = 7$ weapons systems against the other if they were to fight a war.

To formalize this, let $X_A = \{x, y, z\}$ and $X_B = \{x, y, z\}$ be the set of weapons for countries A and B, respectively, and let χ_A and χ_B be the power sets of X_A and X_B or the set of all subsets (weapons systems) that can be formed using elements of X_A and X_B, respectively. Let $\Pi_A(s_A, s_B)$ and $\Pi_B(s_A, s_B)$ be the payoff functions for countries A and B defined when country A chooses a weapons system $s_A \in \chi_A$ and country B chooses a weapons system $s_B \in \chi_B$. The strategy space for the game is $\chi = \chi_A \times \chi_B$.

If the weapons system chosen by one country contains all the weapons chosen by the other country and more (i.e., the set of weapons in its weapons system includes the set of weapons in the other country's weapons system as a proper subset) or if it includes a larger number of weapons absolutely (no matter which ones they are), the payoff to that country will be larger than the other country's payoff (i.e., it has a higher expectation of winning any battle they may fight). If this were so, the game we have just described would be a prisoners' dilemma game in which it is a dominant strategy to use all three weapons but for which the payoff associated with the pair of strategy choices is not optimal. Because we are assuming that this type of war will be fought repeatedly over time, the real payoffs to the players will be the discounted values of these conflicts as the participants contemplate them. Consequently, if α_A and α_B are the discount parameters of country A and B, respectively, the payoffs to the countries will be

$$P_A = \sum_{t=1}^{\infty} \alpha_A^{t-1} \Pi_A(s_A^t, s_B^t) \quad \text{and} \quad P_B = \sum_{t=1}^{\infty} \alpha_B^{t-1} \Pi_B(s_A^t, s_B^t)$$

where s_A^t and s_B^t are the weapons systems used by countries A and B, respectively, in period t, $\alpha_A = 1/1 + r_A$, $\alpha_B = 1/1 + r_B$, and r_A and r_B are the discount rates for players A and B, respectively.

The relevant question for us in this book is: How will wars be fought between these countries? Will the countries fight them in a "no-holds-barred" manner, employing all weapons at each conflict and thereby continually inflict a destructive outcome upon each other, or will they restrict their strategy sets in a way that is optimal for them in the long run, although possibly irrational in the short run? If they restrict their strategy sets, which subset will emerge as the sanctioned subset with which to fight wars? Will these rules of war emerge organically, or will they have to be agreed to formally in a set of articles of war? The answer that we reach in this book is that as countries continually fight each other and recognize their interdependence in fighting future wars, they will evolve rules of war some of which will be codified into signed agreements but many of which will be tacitly agreed to and administered. The set of rules that emerges will have various optimality properties, and it is the utilitarian comparison of these various rules of war upon which we can make value judgments. Consequently, the conventions that countries create to fight wars can be compared on a rule-utilitarian basis and judged accordingly.[9]

The important quality of prisoners' dilemma games that distinguishes them from coordination games is that the social conventions or institutions established for repeated prisoners' dilemma games must involve a sanctioning rule that specifies what reaction the other $n-1$ players will have when any given player deviates from the behavior specified by the institution. This is needed because at any time during the game, owing to its prisoners' dilemma quality, there is always an incentive for a player to deviate and play his dominant ($|s_A|$, $|s_B| = 3$) strategy, and this is indeed what he will do if the sanctions placed against him are not great enough. In coordination games, however, no additional punishing strategy need be spelled out, because once the institution is established at a coordination equilibrium, no one has an incentive to deviate or wishes anyone else to deviate.

In the final analysis, when countries fight wars, they have more information at their disposal upon which to make strategic choices than merely the strategic capabilities of the conflicting parties and their preferences. They have, in addition, knowledge of a whole set of tacitly agreed to rules of conduct or conventions of war to which they adhere. To analyze military situations without paying attention to these conventions and the norms of behavior upon which they are based is to miss a large mass of potentially important information. All is not fair in war, and what is considered fair is unambiguously spelled out in the existing set of social conventions.[10] Adherence to these conventions is beneficial to all parties. [For a discussion of rule utilitarianism and rules of war, see Brandt (1974) and Haire (1974).]

Oligopolistic markets. One of the most problematical areas of economic research is the theory of oligopoly. Even optimistic judgments of the field conclude that a thorough theory of oligopoly does not yet exist, and pessimistic judgments would have us believe that a real theory is not even possible. Wherever the truth lies, it is clear that many modern theories of oligopoly are inadequate because they view the phenomenon as a static one-shot game, when, in essence, it is a dynamic iterated game in which a set of firms repeatedly play either the same or a similar price quantity or quality prisoners' dilemma game over and over through time.

To illustrate this point, let us consider an industry with a homogeneous product x and a product demand curve $p = f(x)$. Let $dp/dx < 0$ and $d^2p/dx^2 > 0$. Assume that there are n firms indexed $i = 1, 2, \ldots, n$, and denote the output of firm i by x_i. Each firm's cost function is given by $c_i(x_i)$, where

$$\frac{dc_i(x_i)}{dx_i} > 0 \quad \text{and} \quad \frac{d^2c_i(x_i)}{dx_i^2} > 0$$

With this information we can specify the profit function for each firm as

$$\pi_i = f(x)x_i - c_i(x_i)$$

where

$$x = \sum_{i=1}^{n} x_i$$

This industry can be depicted as a game in which the strategy set for each firm is the interval $0 \leq x < \infty$ and the payoff to the firm is a function π_i: $\prod_{i=1}^{n} [0, \infty) \rightarrow R^1$, which is strictly concave in x_i, bounded from above, differentiable, and continuous. As such, the industry has a unique noncooperative Nash equilibrium in which the equilibrium n-tuple $x^* = (x_1^*, \ldots, x_n^*)$ is suboptimal for the firms in terms of their profits or in which there exists another n-tuple, $x' \in \pi_{i=1}^{n} [0, \infty)$, for which $\pi_i(x') > \pi_i(x^*)$ for all i [see Friedman (1977, theor. 2.2)].

In the typical textbook analysis of this problem, this is all the information that the analyst is given except for some information concerning the "conjectural variations" assumed in the model or information concerning the type of model being considered (i.e., Cournot, Bertrand, von Strackelberg, etc.). However, if this is going to be a true theory of oligopoly or industry behavior, it would seem that we would need more information than cost and demand functions in order to describe or predict what equilibrium will be established. More precisely, we would need to know what type of industry norms have been established in the history of the industry, what the ethical code is that the oligopolists refer to when they consider if their behavior is "allowable," and what conventions of behavior or industry institutions have evolved. In other words, although the information contained in cost and demand functions may be sufficient information upon which to model a newly born industry, if the industry is not new, but has a past, then the information available is greater than the information contained in the industry at its inception, because each firm has had an opportunity to observe each other's behavior over a period of time, and this common history contains a great deal of useful information upon which the firms can base their actions. Consequently, if the static game played by the oligopolists is a game of the prisoners' dilemma type and if the game is iterated, we can expect the firms in the industry to establish an industry code or convention of behavior that might determine an equilibrium in which the industry price is kept artificially high or might determine an extremely competitive mode of behavior for the oligopolists. The important questions from both the theoretical and policy point of view are these: Which convention of behavior can be expected to evolve? When can we expect industries to behave "competitively"? When can we expect them to collude? If they are behaving in what appears to be a collusive manner, how can we be sure whether their collusion is explicit or tacit? Some of these questions will concern us in Chapter 3. The point we are making here is that in prisoners' dilemma situations that are played repeatedly among a fixed set of players, we can expect some type of social institution to evolve in which both the behavior expected from all participants and the sanctions that are to be forthcoming for deviation are specified.

Inequality-preserving institutions: property rights and the status quo

There has been a great deal of interest recently among scholars in economics in the role and function of property rights [see, for example, Demsetz (1964), (1967)]. They assert that a well-functioning economy can exist only if a set of unambiguously defined property rights exist that detail the limits to which economic agents can use the goods in their possession. In addition, a great many market failures can be explained by a paucity of property rights in the use of common public property (such as air and sea), which leave agents' rights undefined. In a recent book James Buchanan (1975) states that it is necessary to explain how property rights emerge from a Hobbesian state of initial conflict and states that their existence is necessary if we are to carry on trade to any meaningful extent. Buchanan states:

The issue is one of defining the limits, and anarchy works only to the extent that limits among persons are either implicitly accepted by all or are imposed and enforced by some authority. In the absence of "natural" boundaries among individuals in the activities that they may undertake, there arises the need for a definitional structure, an imputation among persons, even if this structure, in and of itself, is arbitrary. The logical foundation of property lies precisely in this universal need for boundaries between "mine and thine." Escape from the world of perpetual Hobbesian conflict requires an explicit definition of the rights of persons to do things. [Buchanan 1975, p. 9]

In other words, what Buchanan is saying here is that the institution of property rights is a necessary condition for mutually beneficial trade because it allows people to coordinate their productive activities and avoid wasting time in "Hobbesian conflict," whose result is purely redistributive and not allocative. The fact that the rights assignment may be arbitrary and preserving of an unequal distribution of income merely reflects the fact that the equilibrium achieved with property rights is preferred by all agents to the state of conflict that would result if all property rights were removed, but not necessarily preferred by all agents to the state that might result under another set of property rights. The existence of property rights determines a noncooperative equilibrium to a social coordination problem, but not necessarily the only one.

To give a more precise structure to this discussion, let us consider the following abstract model of an agrarian society existing before the institution of property rights has been established. Assume a ranching community with two ranchers, A and B, and the two grazing pastures, 1 and 2. Assume that each pasture is on the top of a mountain and that the ranches are situated equally between the two pastures (Figure 2.2). Rancher A raises sheep and rancher B raises cattle, and it is common knowledge that pasture 1 has better grazing land than pasture 2. Each rancher would prefer to graze his herd in pasture 1 except that, if they tried to graze their herds there simultaneously, the land will be overgrazed and both herds would suffer. Consequently, each spring when it is time to graze the herds, each rancher must decide to move his herd up to either pasture 1 or pasture 2. Given the description of the situation, each spring the two-person coordination game shown by Matrix 2.6 is determined. From this

		Rancher B	
		Graze on pasture 1	Graze on pasture 2
Rancher A	Graze on pasture 1	2, 2	8, 4
	Graze on pasture 2	4, 8	2, 2

Matrix 2.6. The grazing game

matrix we see that if both ranchers bring their herds to the same pasture, they both experience low profits, whereas if they graze on separate pastures, they both benefit, although one will benefit more than the other. Clearly, if a system of property rights existed that specified who had the "right" to graze on pasture 1, the institution would be socially efficient, because the property right would function as a piece of information instructing each rancher how to behave (where to graze) at each iteration of the grazing game played each spring. Property rights evolve to solve this simple coordination problem.

Once property rights are created, however, in addition to functioning as a coordinating mechanism, they function to preserve the inequality of income

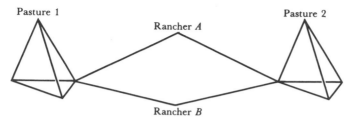

Figure 2.2. Property rights in an agrarian society.

they help create. They function as inequality-preserving institutions. To demonstrate how this happens, let us assume that the ranchers we have been observing suddenly die, both on the same day, and that their heirs take their place in the game. Now the heirs must also play the simple grazing game defined by Matrix 2.6, and from observing their parents, they are aware of the existing set of property rights and know that the other heir also knows that these property rights exist. Consequently, given this information, each rancher might be expected to respect these rights and play accordingly. However, as Buchanan points out, the existing set of property rights is arbitrary in that, although it does indeed determine a Pareto-optimal noncooperative equilibrium to the recurrent grazing game, it is not the only such solution. More precisely, it favors one of the ranchers at the expense of the other, and there is no reason to think that the disfavored party would necessarily accept this. Consequently, the disfavored rancher might try to upset the existing set of property rights by taking his herd to the "wrong" grazing land in the hope of convincing the other heir that he does not respect the current set of property rights, thereby hoping to force him to leave.

The important point, however, is that this attempt must fail if a social institution such as property rights is well defined, because, by definition, the institution would specify punishments for deviation by any agent, which in this case would result in the favored rancher's heir refusing to leave and continuing to graze on pasture 1 – his "rightfully assigned plot" – no matter what. As a result, property rights not only help solve a social coordination problem but in the process help to preserve the unequal distribution of income that is the result of the equilibrium solution to that problem. It is the policing provision of the property right that serves as an inequality-preserving institution.

Cooperative institutions: the emergence of the state

Although we have characterized organically created social institutions as evolving from the recurrent play of noncooperative games in normal form, it is still possible for institutions to arise organically or as if by an invisible hand in a cooperative game context. There is a problem of classification here, however, because if institutions are to be generated truly organically and not by conscious design, we might think that they would have to be only tacitly agreed or adhered to and not be the outcome of an explicit cooperative bargaining process in which binding contracts are possible. Despite this fact, Nozick (1975) demonstrates that it is possible, in a state-of-nature context, to explain the evolution or emergence of a minimal state that is created without individual or even group design. The existence of the state, as we will see, merely represents the equilibrium solution (the core solution) of a cooperative game and emerges from individual attempts at self-maximization. It is a result that no agent intended, but one that no agent or group of agents would rather do without. Its existence is unanimously accepted.

But how does the state actually evolve from a state of nature? According to Nozick the state emerges as the agents in society form protective associations to adjudicate disputes they have with each other and protect each other from outsiders. If there are any increasing returns to group size in the formation of these protective associations, one stable "grand protective association" will be formed to which all agents will belong and that would have the power to adjudicate all disputes. This grand protective association is what Nozick calls the "minimal state." Consequently, the agents need not sit down together with the explicit purpose of creating a state in order for it to emerge. It can be created unintentionally as the equilibrium outcome of individual protective behavior.

To understand this process, consider the following fictionalized model of Nozick's analysis. Assume a state of nature in which there exist N individuals who are identical in every way and have an initial endowment of M units of an all-purpose good which is such that all utility for all individuals is linear in this good. In other words, M units of this all-purpose good fall on each person in the society at the beginning of the analysis (which will contain only one period, for simplicity). Assume that N is an even number. When this manna falls, each person, because he is in a state of nature in which no property rights yet exist, must decide either to consume his manna in isolation or try to rob another agent's bundle so as to consume $2M$ units of the good minus a small theft cost of c. We assume in the analysis that there is only time enough to try to rob one person, so that each person must decide whom he will try to rob and commit c units of his M units for this purpose if he so decides. Finally, we will assume that since all agents are identical, the probability of successfully robbing another agent is equal to $\frac{1}{2}$ if the other agent prepares for the attack, and 1 if he does not. (It costs an agent d units to prepare for an attack with $d > c$.)

A state-of-nature theft game is then played as follows. In the beginning of the period, $N \times M$ units of manna fall on the N agents, so that each agent gets M units for himself. Then each agent i chooses one of N number $i = 0$, $1, \ldots, i - 1, i + 1, \ldots, N$, indicating which person he wants to try to rob, where 0 indicates a decision not to rob anyone and all other numbers indicate a decision to rob a particular agent. In addition, he decides whether or not to protect himself. If an agent robs another successfully, his final payoff is $2M$– assuming that no one attempted to rob him and he did not attempt to protect himself. Consequently, assuming that he attacks another agent and wins, his payoffs are $2M - c$ if he did not protect himself and was not robbed; $2M - c - d$ if he prepared for an attack, was attacked, and was successful in warding it off; and $M - c - d$ if he was attacked, prepared for it, and lost. If he did not attempt to rob anyone else, his payoffs are M if he did not prepare for an attack and was not attacked, 0 if he did not prepare and was attacked, and $M - d$ if he prepared for an attack and either warded it off successfully or was not attacked. The contingencies for any agent i in the game can be presented as follows:

	Rob and win	Rob and lose	Do not rob
Prepare for attack and either win or are not attacked	$2M - c - d$	$M - c - d$	$M - d$
Do not prepare and are not attacked	$2M - c$	$M - c$	M
Do not prepare and are attacked	$M - c$	$-c$	0
Prepare for attack and lose.	$M - c - d$	$-(c + d)$	$-d$

Now if we calculated the probability of each of these payoffs occurring, we can estimate the value of the game for player i by choosing that combination of actions (offensive and defensive) which yields the greatest expected return. To do this, assume that you are agent i and that the other $N - 1$ agents are deciding whether to rob anyone and, if so, whom. Because our analysis is cooperative, we must assume that each player must view the other $N - 1$ players as a coalition and must prepare himself against them *en masse*. Consequently, let us calculate whether they will attack him. First, we must assume that because the time period is short enough to allow only one attack, it will be efficient for the coalition of $N - 1$ to send only one attacker to rob the singleton player and therefore incur only one theft cost, c. If they attack, the probability of their winning is $\frac{1}{2}$ if he prepares and 1 if he does not. Their guaranteed minimal winnings from a robbery attempt is then

$$\min \left[(\tfrac{1}{2}(M - c) + \tfrac{1}{2}(-c); M - c) \right] = \tfrac{1}{2}(M - c) + \tfrac{1}{2}(-c)$$

which is positive as long as $M/2 > c$ (which we will assume is true). Consequently, the coalition of the remaining $N - 1$ players will always attack and try to rob the remaining player if he is alone. In addition, the singleton player will always rob one of the players in the coalition of $N - 1$ players, because his chances of winning are $\frac{1}{2}$ if the opponent defends himself and 1 if he does not. The guaranteed minimal winnings of the singleton player is then also

$$\min \left[(\tfrac{1}{2}(M - c) + \tfrac{1}{2}(-c); M - c) \right] = \tfrac{1}{2}(M - c) + \tfrac{1}{2}(-c)$$

which is again positive. Consequently, any player alone knows that he will be attacked and that he will attack one member of the coalition of $N - 1$. Knowing this, the single player will protect himself. We can then compute the value of the game for a player alone, because we know that he will protect himself and rob another player and that four possible compound events may occur, each with probability $\frac{1}{4}$. They can be represented as follows:

	Rob and win	Rob and lose
Attacked and win	$2M - c - d$	$M - c - d$
Attacked and lose	$M - c - d$	$-(c + d)$

With these four possible events and the corresponding probabilities, the value of a player acting alone in this game is

$$v(i) = \tfrac{1}{4}(2M - c - d) + \tfrac{1}{4}(M - c - d)$$
$$+ \tfrac{1}{4}(M - c - d) + \tfrac{1}{4}(-c - d) = M - c - d$$

Notice that the expected payoff to an individual player in a state of nature is less than it would be in a state in which each person has a right to consume the manna that fell on him and that right is protected by the state. In that case, his payoff would be M, which is greater than $M - c - d - (c, d > 0)$. But such a state does not exist, so that we might expect a group of agents to join together and form what Nozick calls a "protective association," agree not to rob each other, split the costs of common protection, and coordinate their attacks on the agents outside their association.[11]

Assuming that there are increasing returns to scale in the provision of protection [i.e., let $D_S = g(|S|)$ be the total cost of protection for a coalition with $|S|$ members and assume that $g(|1|) = d, g(|S + 1|) - g(|S|) > 0, [g(|S + 2|) - g(|S + 1|)] - [g(|S + 1| - g(|S|)] < 0]$, we can define the value of each protective association or coalition of agents as follows. Consider a protective association with S members, where $|S| < |N|/2$. ($|N|$ is the total number of agents in the economy.) From our calculations above, we know that it is always beneficial for members in association $N - S$ to try to rob each agent in S, because the expected value of each robbery attempt is $M - c -$

d (given self-protection) for each individual acting alone, so that the expected value of S robbery attempts for agency $N - S$ is $|S| [M - c] - g(|S|)$, which must also be greater than zero given the increasing returns to scale in the provision of protection. Consequently, the protective association S will provide protection for each agent and attempt to rob S agents in $N - S$. Because each agent in S can expect to be attacked, the expected value of the entire coalition is $v(S) = |S|(M - c) - g(|S|)$. However, because $g(|S|)$ is a concave function, we know that

$$\frac{v(S)}{|S|} > M - c - d$$

[since

$$\frac{v(S)}{|S|} = \frac{|S|(M - c) - g(|S|)}{|S|} = M - c - \frac{g(|S|)}{|S|} \quad \text{and} \quad \frac{g(|S|)}{|S|} < d]$$

or that it is individually rational for all agents in S to join the protective agency. In addition, for $|S| \leq |N|/2$ the function $v(S)$ defined over any such subset S is strictly convex.[12]

This implies that for protective agencies with $|S| \leq |N|/2$, there are increasing returns to protective agency size. When $|S| > |N|/2$, the situation becomes slightly different, because there are now more agents in the protective association than outside it. This creates a difference, because now only $|N| - |S|$ agents in S will be able to rob an agent in $N - S$ (there is a scarcity of victims). However, because all agents in the association may be robbed, all will have to be protected–as long as the expected return from protection is greater than the expected cost. Because only $|N| - |S|$ agents in S can be attacked by agents not in S, the value of a coalition with $|S|$ agents, where $|S| > |N|/|2|$, is

$$v(S) = [|N - S|] (M - c) + [|S| - (|N - S|)]M - g(|S|)$$

Finally, there is a size of coalition $|\tilde{S}|$, $|\tilde{S}| > |N|/2$, which is so great that the losses that would be incurred from robbery are so small that the agency would decide not to protect itself from the remaining small coalition $(N - S)$ but only to attack it and try to rob it. This would be true if $g(|S|) > (|N - S|/2)M$, where $|N - S|/2$ is the expected number of lost defenses that will occur when the remaining $|N| - |S|$ players attack coalition S and fight $|N| - |S|$ separate battles each with a $\frac{1}{2}$ probability of success, and M is the loss at each unsuccessful defense. $(|N| - |S|)/2$ is the expected value of a binomial variable. If we call such a number $|\tilde{S}|$, then

$$v(|S| \mid |S| \geq |\tilde{S}|) = [N - S] (M - c) - \left(\frac{N - S}{2}\right) M$$

As a result, the characteristic function for the state-of-nature theft game can be written as follows:

$$v(i) = M - c - d$$

$$v(S) = |S|(M - c) - g(|S|) \quad \text{for } S \le \frac{N}{2}$$

$$v(S) = (|N| - |S|)(M - c) + [|S| - (|N| - |S|)]M - g(|S|)$$
$$\text{for } S > \frac{|N|}{2} \quad \text{and} \quad g(|S|) < \left(\frac{|N| - |S|}{2}\right) M \quad \text{(i.e., } |S| < |\tilde{S}|)$$

$$v(S) = [|N| - |S|](M - c) - \left(\frac{|N| - |S|}{2}\right) M \quad \text{for } |S| \ge |\tilde{S}|$$

$$v(N) = nM$$

For $|S| \le |N|/2$, this function was shown to be convex, because the marginal contribution that each player added to the coalition was greater than the marginal contribution of all players added before him; that is, each player added a constant amount to the agency's revenue by attempting to rob a player in $N - S$ while reducing the average protection costs to all previous players in the coalition by an amount that increases as S gets larger. At $|S| = (|N|/2) + 1$, however, the marginal contribution of player $(|N|/2) + 1$ is less than the marginal contribution of player $N/2$, because there is no player in $N - S$ for player $(|N|/2) + 1$ to rob, and his addition to the coalition is merely the reduction in the protection costs attributable to him. Consequently, the characteristic function for the state-of-nature theft game is not necessarily convex throughout. Despite this fact, however, the game as we have specified it clearly has a nonempty core, which can be realized by an agreement among the players to form the grand coalition (or the grand protection agency including all players) and agree not to try to rob each other. Such an agreement will be supervised by the organizers of the protective association, who have been granted judicial and enforcement powers as part of the agreement to form the agency.

Because the game is symmetrical, one imputation that is always in the core if the core is nonempty is the imputation $x = (M_1, \ldots, M_i, \ldots, M_n)$. This imputation is achievable because, in forming the grand protective association, each player agrees not to rob the other and consequently there is no waste of resources on such things as theft costs and protection costs. In essence, this imputation gives each player a property right to consume the manna that falls on him, and as the manna falls equally, each player has a property right to consume $1/N$ of the total manna. This need not be the only imputation in the core, however; there may be imputations which, despite the symmetry of the game, give players unequal amounts of the manna to consume. This is equivalent to the protective agency agreeing to enforce an unequal distribution of income which is stable in that although income is not split equally, all players and groups of players would rather accept this distribution than abandon the grand protective agency and take their chances by themselves. Consequently, the institution of the property rights supporting this unequal distribution of income is yet another example of an inequality-preserving social institution, but an example that is found in a cooperative game context.

By now it should be obvious that the grand protective agency that all agents unanimously agree to create in order to enforce the derived property rights associated with the core of the game is nothing more than the state, and it is created by the agents *at the equilibrium* in that although the state emerges from the analysis, the players did not set out to create it at the beginning. Its creation emerges as part of the solution to the state-of-nature theft game, as do the set of property rights associated with it. These institutional values are then seen as being endogenous variables in the analysis and are not forced on the analysis at the outset. As a result, we have what Hayek describes as an institution created by human action but not by human design.

In the final analysis the state can be seen as an efficient institution that allows agents to achieve Pareto-optimal outcomes by assuring them of the sanctity of their property. This assurance allows them to avoid the costly defense and theft costs that would be incurred in the absence of the state, which have purely distributive properties for society as a whole.

2.3 Summary

In summation, this chapter has argued that if economics is going to study the evolution and function of social institutions, a straightforward state-of-nature approach may be useful. This approach would be one in which all equilibrium social institutions are solved for endogenously in the model and are outputs of the analysis and not inputs into it. We have described a wide variety of situations in which institutions evolve to help solve recurrent societal problems of either the coordination, prisoners' dilemma, or inequality-preserving types. Finally, through the inspiration of Robert Nozick, we have investigated a cooperative-game model of the emergence of the state as an endogenous institution and have shown it to be a property of the core of a state-of-nature theft game.

Although all the models presented here are rather abstract, my purpose was not to present a realistic analysis of any phenomenon as much as to present the type of situation from which social institutions emerge. Consequently, although I would not argue that any of the social institutions that I have discussed actually have emerged to solve the exact problem described, I would argue that they have arisen to solve a problem of that variety. In Chapter 3 a formal model of institution creation is presented, which depicts it as a Markovian diffusion process whose state space is the space of all possible norms and whose equilibria are the absorbing states of the process.

3 A mathematical theory of institution creation

BY SIMEON M. BERMAN AND ANDREW SCHOTTER

In this chapter I present a mathematical theory of institution creation. Being only *a* theory as opposed to *the* theory, it cannot be considered the only possible approach that one could take. However, it is my feeling that the model presented here does contain two elements that any successful theory of institution creation must contain. The first is a theory of norm creation and change which must be included in any theory that tries to depict the process of the creation of social institutions as we have defined them (i.e., as commonly adhered to regularities in behavior created to solve recurrent societal problems), because it is upon these norms that the regularities in behavior we are calling social institutions can be built. More precisely, we have defined social institutions or conventions as regularities (R) in the behavior of members of a population when they are agents in recurrent situations, Γ, which are such that:

1. Everyone conforms to R.
2. Everyone expects everyone else to conform to R.
3. Either everyone prefers to conform to R on condition that the others do if Γ is a coordination problem, in which case uniform conformity to R is a coordination equilibrium, or
4. If anyone ever deviates from R, it is known that some or all of the others will also deviate and the payoffs associated with the recurrent play of Γ using these deviating strategies are worse for all agents than is the payoff associated with R.

Now, notice that for a social institution or regularity R to be a well-functioning one, everyone must "expect everyone else to conform to R." It is my contention that the assurance that permits such an expectation is contained in the set of social norms that are developed by the society being investigated because, as we will see, social norms are informational devices that the agents of societies develop to help them place subjective probability estimates over each other's actions. For instance, the norm "honor among thieves" is a code or norm existing in societies that informs criminals what type of behavior can be expected from their colleagues. It gives them certain assurances as to how the others will behave if they are both caught and placed in a prisoners' dilemma situation. Consequently, it is upon these assurances that they build the social

52

convention of either confessing or not confessing. The norm, then, is the probabilistic informational basis upon which institutions are created and must be part of any full-fledged theory of institution creation.

Second, any theory of institution creation must not be deterministic and unique in its predictions. This is true because the exact institutional form that emerges from a recurrent problem is really a stochastic event, because for almost all problems of interest there are a variety of potential stable regularities that could be adhered to, and any theory that forces the analysis to prescribe only one as *the solution* must be arbitrary. In the theory presented here, however, we are able not only to predict the set of possible or potential equilibrium social institutions that can emerge from a given recurrent societal problem, but are able to place a probability distribution over the likelihood that one of them will actually be settled upon. This is done by depicting the process of institution creation as a stochastic or random process in which the equilibrium social institutions are the absorbing states. By an absorbing state we will mean a state in which the expectations of all of the players are such that they all expect the others to behave in a particular manner with probability equal to 1 and when they observe each others' behavior, that is exactly what they see happening. Consequently, which stable institutional arrangement emerges to solve a particular problem is a random event that depends crucially, as we will see, on the history of the play of the game and the process of norm creation.

There is what may be considered one drawback to the model presented here, however, and that is that it can only predict or describe the emergence of what may be called "uncorrelated" institutions, institutions in which the agents under investigation repeatedly choose the same action or strategy at each iteration of the game. Consequently, if we wanted to explain the evolution of the institution that governs what side of the road we are to drive on, our model would only be able to predict one in which every time someone chose to drive, he *always* drove either on the right or the left side of the road. It might be argued, however, that "correlated" institutions exist, which in this example would mean that players alternate their choices and drive on the right-hand side one day and on the left-hand side another day. Robert Aumann (1959) has discussed these types of institutions.

Although this may indeed be true, I would argue that it does not limit the applicability of our analysis, because correlated institutions can only evolve spontaneously or in an unplanned manner in the small-numbers case. In other words, it may be possible for two agents to tacitly create a correlated institution, but it is very unlikely that 200 and 20 million of them could. In fact, it is precisely because the coordination possibilities are so limited in large societies that uncorrelated institutions are so frequent. Consequently, the emergence of correlated institutions is, I would think, a small-numbers phenomenon, whereas the emergence of uncorrelated institutions is a large-numbers phenomenon. Because most major institutions involve large numbers, however, I feel that the analysis presented is not overly restrictive.

To explain this model, I will proceed in a two-stage manner. In the first part of this chapter, I will attempt to explain the relevant aspects of the theory in as nontechnical a manner as I can, by explaining it with reference to a two-person prisoners' dilemma situation. Here all of the salient aspects of the model will be explained in this simplified two-person world. Then, in the second part, the model will be generalized to an n-person society, while still analyzing primarily prisoners' dilemma games. It will formally be shown that the model described determines a unique stochastic process whose absorbing states are social institutions. It is my hope that a clear understanding of the model can be gotten by simply reading the first part of the chapter, and that the second part will be of interest only to the specialist. Consequently, for those readers who are not interested in the exact details of the model, nothing would be lost by simply reading the first part and then proceeding to Chapter 4.

Institution creation in a two-person world

3.1 Institution creation in a prisoners' dilemma world

As indicated in Chapter 2, social institutions, as we have defined them, are created to help agents in an economy solve recurrent prisoners' dilemma and coordination problems that reappear systematically in the economy. We have shown that these problems are associated with empirically significant phenomena such as the creation of money, property rights, the state, and conventions of war, even though these examples were presented in a highly stylized manner. However, to analyze these situations, we must rigorously define the exact problem these agents face. Technically, the problem is called a supergame problem, referring to a game derived by infinitely iterating a static game, which we will call the *constituent game* (Friedman 1977, Telser 1972).

To put some flesh on the analysis, assume that we are observing a two-person society in which the agents meet each other each period and must decide between one of two actions. For convenience, let us call action or strategy 1 the cooperative strategy and action or strategy 2 the noncooperative strategy. These strategies could, of course, be a low- and a high-price strategy for duopolistic firms in a market, or they could be choices of weapon systems for countries constantly fighting wars. Finally, assume that payoffs associated with any pair of strategy choices can be depicted as shown in Matrix 3.1. Notice that the game these agents play each period is a classic prisoners' dilemma game in which the set of strategies available for player 1 is $A_1 = (a_1^1, a_1^2)$ and the set available to player 2 is $A_2 = (a_2^1, a_2^2)$. The central feature of our analysis

		Agent 2	
		Strategy a_2^1 (cooperative)	Strategy a_2^2 (noncooperative)
Agent 1	Strategy a_1^1 (cooperative)	8, 8	0, 9
	Strategy a_1^2 (noncooperative)	9, 0	6, 6

Matrix 3.1. The constituent prisoners' dilemma game Γ

revolves around the fact that these agents know that they will face each other each period for a countably infinite number of time periods and that in deciding how they want to behave, they must take this fact into account. Taking this into account means recognizing that as time goes on, they will tacitly create a relationship with one another in which they learn what type of behavior they can expect from the other. In other words, a set of societal norms will be developed as each agent observes what the other does and upon these common observations a behavioral convention (or institutional rule) will be established. Once established, this convention, if it is an equilibrium convention, will prescribe behavior for our agents at each iteration of the constituent game. The solution to the problem will be institutionalized. The basic question is: If both cooperative and noncooperative conventions of behavior are possible equilibria for this particular recurrent prisoners' dilemma situation, which will actually emerge, and what factors determine this? These are the principal questions that we must answer in this chapter. We intend to do so by explaining that what finally evolves as *the* societal convention of behavior or social institution is very much a function of the history of the play of the supergame, because that will influence the type of norms that are established. These, in turn, will influence the actual convention that is built upon these norms.

3.2 Supergames

Before we can fully present our model, however, we must define what a supergame is and what an equilibrium convention of behavior or equilibrium institution is for such a game. To do this, consider the two-person prisoners' dilemma game depicted in Section 3.1 and denote it by the letter Γ. Γ is completely defined by the set of players, N, indexed $i = 1, 2$; the strategy sets for each player, $A_1 = (a_1^1, a_1^2)$ $A_2 = (a_2^1, a_2^2)$; and the payoff function for Γ, $U_i(b^k)$, $i = 1, 2$, defined by Matrix 3.1, where $b^k = (a_1^k, a_2^k)$, $k = 1, 2$. In this game there are four possible pairs of strategy choices: (a_1^1, a_2^1), (a_1^1, a_2^2), (a_1^2, a_2^1), and (a_1^2, a_2^2). We can denote them by the set B, where each element b^k in B is a pair of strategy choices that can be written as follows: $b^k = (a_1^k, a_2^k)$, $k = 1, 2$.

Matrix 3.1 tells each player what he can expect to receive in terms of utility for every pair of strategy choices $b^k = (a_1^k, a_2^k)$. In playing Γ, any player can either choose strategy 1, or choose strategy 2, or employ a mixed strategy $s_i = (s_i^1, s_i^2)$, where s_i^1, for instance, is the probability weight placed on the use of strategy 1 by player i. In other words, the player, when using a mixed strategy, does not choose either strategy 1 or strategy 2 but rather randomizes his choice by choosing strategy 1 with probability s_i^1 and strategy 2 with probability s_i^2. By introducing mixed strategies, the strategy sets of each player are increased from the sets $A_1 = (a_1^1, a_1^2)$ and $A_2 = (a_2^1, a_2^2)$, to the sets of vectors $S_1 = \{(s_1^1, s_1^2) \mid s_1^1 + s_1^2 = 1, s_1^1, s_1^2 \geq 0\}$ and $S_2 = \{(s_2^1, s_2^2) \mid s_2^1 + s_2^2 = 1, s_2^1, s_2^2 \geq 0\}$. In the game defined with these expanded strategy sets, the payoff function for any player can be written

$$U_i(s) = \sum_{a_i^k \in A_i} \sum_{a_j^k \in A_j} U_i(a_i^k, a_j^k)(s_i^k)(s_j^k), \qquad k = 1, 2$$

which is the expected utility that player i can contemplate when he chooses a mixed strategy $s_i = (s_i^1, s_i^2)$ and his opponent (player j) chooses $s_j = (s_j^1, s_j^2)$.

For this static game Γ, the question of interest is: Which strategy choices should either of our players make, and which pairs of strategies $s = (s_1, s_2)$ form equilibria for the game?

The problem we consider in this book is quite different, however, because our players play Γ an infinite number of times and as a result are forced to recognize the fact that the actions they take today are bound to influence the expectations that the other player will have about them in the future and hence the other player's future actions. The problem thus becomes richer and the strategic possibilities more complex.

To be more precise, in the supergame defined by the repeated play of Γ, each player will not simply choose one pure or mixed strategy from his possible sets of strategies; rather, he will have to choose a "mode of behavior" that will govern his actions over the entire infinite horizon of the game. One possible type of strategy for player 1 in our simple two-person prisoners' dilemma society can then be written in the following manner:

$$\sigma^1[a_1^1/a_2^1] = \begin{cases} a_{1_1} = a_1^1 & \\ a_{1_t} = a_1^1 & \text{if } a_{2_\tau} = a_{2\tau}^1, \quad \tau = 1, \ldots, t-1; \quad t = 2, 3, \ldots \quad (*) \\ a_{1_t} = a_1^2 & \text{otherwise} \end{cases}$$

This strategy instructs player 1 to play strategy a_1^1 as long as player 2 plays a_2^1 and to play a_1^2 in every period $t + 1$ onward if player 2 deviates in period t. In other words, player 1 is contemplating what may be called a cooperative mode of behavior in the game because he is willing to cooperate with player 2 and play a_1^1 as long as player 2 cooperates with him and plays a_2^1, but will punish him from period $t + 1$ onward if player 2 ever disappoints him. Strategy a_1^2 is the "policing" strategy. Notice that this is what may be called a "complete wrath" model because once a player double-crosses another, his punishment is eternal. Clearly, less extreme types of policing mechanisms are possible.

This type of supergame strategy is what we will call a supergame strategy of the type (*) and will be the only type of strategy we treat. It should be pointed out that I am certainly not the first person to investigate supergames involving these types of strategies. They have been studied extensively by Aumann (1959), Friedman (1977, chap. 8), and Telser (1972, chap. 4). Notice that this strategy $\sigma^1[a_1^1/a_2^1]$ for player 1 is completely indexed by the pair (a_1^1, a_2^1) because this completely defines the mode of behavior contemplated by player 1 (i.e., "I'll choose a_1^1 if you choose a_2^1"). We need not index the strategy by stating the policing strategy because in this prisoners' dilemma game this will always be strategy a_1^2, the noncooperative strategy. Each such supergame strategy is similarly indexed by one pair $b^k = (a_1^k, a_2^k)$ in Γ.

To finish our description of the supergame whose strategies are constrained to be of form (*), we must only note that the payoff to any player (say player 1) in the supergame is the present value of the discounted stream of utility that he would receive when he behaves according to one mode of behavior, σ^1, and his opponent another, σ^2:

$$\Pi_1 = \sum_{t=1}^{\infty} \alpha_1^{t-1} U_1(b_t^k) \tag{3.1}$$

where α_1 is the discount parameter for player 1, describing his preference for utility today versus utility tomorrow, and $b_t^k = (a_{1t}^k, a_{2t}^k)$ is the strategy pair that would be played in period t when the pair of behavior modes $\sigma = (\sigma^1, \sigma^2)$ is being used. An analogous payoff function is defined for player 2.

Thus, for each player in our simple two-person prisoners' dilemma society, we can define four supergame strategies of form (*), or modes of behavior that will constitute the players' strategy sets in the supergame, which we denote by L.

$$\Sigma^1 = (\sigma^1[a_1^1/a_2^1], \sigma^1[a_1^1/a_2^2], \sigma^1[a_1^2/a_2^1], \sigma^1[a_1^2/a_2^2]) \tag{3.2}$$
$$\Sigma^2 = (\sigma^2[a_2^1/a_1^1], \sigma^2[a_2^2/a_1^1], \sigma^2[a_2^1/a_1^2], \sigma^2[a_2^2/a_1^2]) \tag{3.3}$$

Consequently, when contemplating how they are going to behave over the course of their association with each other, each player can choose one of four possible modes of behavior or strategies. If player 1 chooses to behave according to $\sigma^1[a_1^1/a_2^1]$ (which is a cooperative mode of behavior, because he expects to play the cooperative strategy a_1^1 as long as player 2 plays his cooperative strategy a_2^1) and player 2 chooses to behave according to strategy $\sigma^2[a_2^1/a_1^1]$ (which is also a cooperative mode of behavior), then the cooperative "convention of behavior" $\sigma^{cooperative}(\sigma^1[a_1^1/a_2^1], \sigma^2[a_2^1/a_1^1])$ is defined in which both players tacitly agree to cooperate with the other as long as the other cooperates with him.

Similarly, if player 1 chooses to behave according to $\sigma^1[a_1^2/a_2^2]$ (which is a noncooperative mode of behavior, because he expects to play the noncooperative strategy a_1^2 as long as player 2 plays his noncooperative strategy a_2^2), then the noncooperative convention of behavior $\sigma^{noncooperative} = (\sigma^1[a_1^2/a_2^2], \sigma^2[a_2^2/a_1^2])$ is defined in which both players always behave noncooperatively.

Although these conventions seem logical enough, there are some more bizarre conventions that we can define which might not be as intuitive. For instance, say that player 1 chooses to behave according to $\sigma^1[a_1^1/a_2^2]$, which is certainly a mode of behavior that can be defined whether or not player 1 would ever follow it. This strategy says that player 1 will allow himself to be punished by playing a_1^1 as long as player 2 punishes him by playing a_2^2, but will play strategy a_1^2 if player 2 ever fails to punish him. Such odd behavior is clearly masochistic and hence we can call this the *masochistic mode of behavior*. Now say that player 1 chooses the masochistic mode $\sigma^1[a_1^1/a_2^2]$ and player 2 chooses $\sigma^2[a_2^2/a_1^1]$, which is a mode that says that player 2 will punish player 1 by choosing a_2^2 as long as player 1 cooperates and chooses a_1^1, but that if he ever deviates, he will choose a_2^2. In essence, this strategy leads player 2 to always play strategy a_2^2. We can call this strategy the *sadistic mode of behavior*, because player 2 is contemplating the infinite punishment of the cooperating player player 1. Hence $\sigma^{sadomasochistic} = (\sigma^1[a_1^1/a_2^2], \sigma^2[a_2^2/a_1^1])$ is what we call a sadomasochistic convention, in which player 2 is the sadist and player 1 the masochist and presents us with consistent, albeit odd, behavior. [Notice also that $\sigma^{sadomasochistic} = (\sigma^1[a_1^2/a_2^1], \sigma^2[a_2^1/a_1^2])$ is also a sadomasochistic convention, with player 1 being the sadist and player 2 the masochist.]

It should be pointed out, however, that these conventions could not emerge as equilibrium conventions in our prisoners' dilemma model because despite their names, the masochist in these conventions really does not like being punished and would not adhere to a convention in which he was continually being punished. Consequently, these terms are really misnomers, because typically a masochist is someone who enjoys being punished, which is not true in our model. It is therefore important not to be misled by these nametags.

In our two-person prisoners' dilemma society, a total of 16 conventions of behavior can be defined, each one consisting of a pair of modes of behavior–one for each player. The problem we face in this chapter is to present a theory that can be used to predict the exact equilibrium convention that will emerge from the game as the societal convention or institution governing behavior for these agents at each iteration of the problem, because such an equilibrium convention is exactly what we are calling a social institution. Before we can do this, however, we must define an equilibrium convention.

3.3 Equilibria in supergames: equilibrium conventions and institutions

To discover what an equilibrium convention of behavior is, consider the cooperative convention of behavior $\sigma^{\text{cooperative}} = (\sigma^1[a_1^1/a_2^1], \sigma^2[a_2^1/a_1^1])$, in which each player will play cooperatively (i.e., choose a_i^1) as long as the other does, but will punish the other by playing a_i^2 indefinitely if he deviates. Let α_1 and α_2 be the discount factors for the two players with $\alpha_i = 1/(1 + r_i)$, $i = 1, 2$, where r_i is the rate of time preference for player i. Now, this convention, or any other convention, will be an equilibrium convention if no player has any incentive to deviate from it and play a_i^2 in any period t. To discover if any such deviation is ever profitable, consider the strategy of deviating from strategy a_i^1 to a_i^2 for player i in period t, which will be denoted by $a_i^2(t)$. If this strategy is used, the following sequence of moves will be determined for player i: $(a_{i_1}^1, a_{i_2}^1, \ldots, a_{i_{t-1}}^1, a_{i_t}^2, a_{i_{t+1}}^2, \ldots)$. This is true because by deviating in period t to strategy 2, player i knows that the other player will punish him indefinitely by using strategy 2, against which a_i^2 is a best reply. Consequently, after the tth-period deviation, both players $i = 1, 2$ will use strategy a_i^2 in every period. As a result, the discounted present value of this tth-period deviation strategy for player i (which we can assume to be player 1 for convenience) is

$$\Pi_1(a_1^2(t)) = \sum_{\tau=1}^{t-1} \alpha_1^{\tau-1} U_1(a_1^1, a_2^1) + \alpha_1^{t-1} U_i(a_1^2, a_2^1) + \sum_{\tau=t+1} \alpha_1^{\tau-1} U_1(a_1^2, a_2^2) \tag{3.4}$$

To see if any such deviation is profitable, first notice that, since the game is stationary, the decision of whether to deviate is always the same at any time t, so that for simplicity we can assume that player 1 is contemplating a deviation in period 1 and we must discover the conditions under which this deviation would be profitable. Now, if player 1 does not deviate at all in period 1 (and hence not in any other period), his discounted payoff would be $U_1(a_1^1, a_2^1)/(1 - \alpha_1)$ under the cooperative convention, which is the discounted present value of infinitely receiving the payoff $U_1(a_1^1, a_2^1)$ when your discount factor is α_1 [it is the value of a perpetuity of $U_1(a_1^1, a_2^1)$]. However, if player 1 deviates in period 1, then although he would gain in utility by receiving $U_1(a_1^2, a_2^1)$ instead of $U_1(a_1^1, a_2^1)$ in that period [since $U_1(a_1^2, a_2^1) > U_1(a_1^1, a_2^1)$], he would receive the payoff $U_1(a_1^2, a_2^2)$ instead of $U_1(a_1^1, a_2^1)$ from period 2 onward and since $U_1(a_1^2, a_2^2) < U_1(a_1^1, a_2^1)$, this loss must be weighed against the one-period transitional gain. More precisely, the payoff from deviating in period 1 is

$$U_1(a_1^2, a_2^1) + \frac{\alpha_1 U_1(a_1^2, a_2^2)}{1 - \alpha_1} \tag{3.5}$$

and after some simple algebra we find that the payoff to the conforming strategy will be greater than the payoff to the deviating strategy if

$$\frac{\alpha_1(U_1(a_1^1, a_2^1) - U_1(a_1^2, a_2^2))}{1 - \alpha_1} > U_1(a_1^2, a_2^1) - U_1(a_1^1, a_2^1) \tag{3.6}$$

or

$$\alpha_1 > \alpha_1^* = \frac{U_1(a_1^2, a_2^1) - U_1(a_1^1, a_2^1)}{U_1(a_1^2, a_2^1) - U_1(a_1^2, a_2^2)} \tag{3.7}$$

What this expression tells us is that if the discount factor for player 1 is greater than some critical number α_1^*, $0 \leq \alpha_1^* \leq 1$, then no profitable deviation exists for player 1 and he will conform to the cooperative convention of behavior. A similar calculation can be made for player 2 and a critical α_2^*, $0 \leq \alpha_2^* \leq 1$ determined. Consequently, the cooperative convention $\sigma^{\text{cooperative}} = (\sigma^1[a_1^1/a_2^2], \sigma^2[a_2^1/a_1^1])$ will be an equilibrium convention if and only if $\alpha_1 \geq \alpha_1^*$ and $\alpha_2 \geq \alpha_2^*$.

    In our simple two-person prisoners' dilemma game, there are two stable conventions of behavior, which are the cooperative

$$\sigma^{\text{cooperative}} = (\sigma^1[a_1^1/a_1^2], \sigma^2[a_2^1/a_1^1])$$

and the noncooperative

$$\sigma^{\text{noncooperative}} = (\sigma^1[a_1^2/a_2^2], \sigma^2[a_2^2/a_1^2])$$

conventions. Consequently, whereas in the static prisoners' dilemma game only a noncooperative (a_1^2, a_2^2) equilibrium is possible, in the iteration of this game more strategic equilibrium possibilities are opened up. This is true for two reasons. One is that in the supergame there is a future in which deviating actions can be punished, and hence it is possible to police the cooperative convention and keep all players in line. Second, and this is the factor to be stressed here, in the supergame there is also a past, which offers data upon which the players can learn to trust each other and upon which a set of cooperative societal norms can be built. As was said before, these norms give the players the information they need to cooperate with each other. However, if they find by observing each others' past behavior that the other is not to be trusted, it is very likely that they will degenerate into a noncooperative convention. It is our job here to present a model that will allow an investigator to predict the likelihood of either of these occurring. Let us now turn our attention to this problem.

    From our analysis so far, we have a game Γ which is a prisoners' dilemma game represented by Matrix 3.1. It is this game that is going to be iterated a countably infinite number of times and will define the supergame that we will analyze. Now the set of strategies available for the players in Γ are $A_1 = (a_1^1, a_1^2)$ and $A_2 = (a_2^1, a_2^2)$, and if we restrict the supergame strategies available to them when the game is iterated to be of form (*), then the set of strategies from which they can choose is

$$\Sigma^1 = (\sigma^1[a_1^1/a_2^1], \sigma^2[a_1^1/a_2^2], \sigma^1[a_1^2/a_2^1], \sigma^1[a_1^2/a_2^2]) \tag{3.8}$$

and

$$\Sigma^2 = (\sigma^2[a_2^1/a_1^1], \sigma^2[a_2^2/a_1^1], \sigma^2[a_2^1/a_1^2], \sigma^2[a_2^2/a_1^2])$$

As a result, a game L is defined in which the set of strategies available to the players are Σ^1 and Σ^2 and the payoffs are the discounted utility streams that would result when any pair of strategies taken from Σ^1 and Σ^2, respectively, are chosen. In other words, game L is played as follows. Both players choose a mode of behavior or supergame strategy from each of their available sets (Σ^1 and Σ^2) that describes how they will behave into the infinite future, and hand these strategies to a referee, who plays out the game based on these strategies and awards payoffs. To demonstrate how we can pass from Γ to L, consider the game L derived from our present prisoners' dilemma game Γ when player 1 has a discount factor of $\alpha_1 = \frac{3}{4}$ and player 2 a discount factor $\alpha_2 = \frac{1}{2}$. The game L will then appear as shown in Matrix 3.2.

Player 2

	$\sigma^2[a_2^1/a_1^1]$	$\sigma^2[a_2^2/a_1^1]$	$\sigma^2[a_2^1/a_1^2]$	$\sigma^2[a_2^2/a_1^2]$
$\sigma^1[a_1^1/a_2^1]$	(32, 16)	18, 15	21.5, 15.5	18, 15
$\sigma^1[a_1^1/a_2^2]$	28.25, 11	0, 18	26, 14	0, 18
$\sigma^1[a_1^2/a_2^1]$	27, 6	(24, 12)	32, 0	(24, 12)
$\sigma^1[a_1^2/a_2^2]$	27, 6	(24, 12)	27, 6	(24, 12)

Player 1

Matrix 3.2. The Game L

The payoffs in this matrix are defined as follows. Assume that player 1 chooses $\sigma^1[a_1^1/a_2^1]$ and player 2 chooses $\sigma^2[a_2^1/a_1^1]$. These strategies state that player 1 will choose strategy a_1^1 as long as player 2 chooses a_2^1, and choose a_1^2 if player 2 ever deviates, and that player 2 will play a_2^1 as long as player 1 plays a_1^1 and will choose a_2^2 if he ever deviates. Because these strategies are consistent with each other, when they are given to the referee who plays L, he will continually play the pair (a_1^1, a_2^1) in each iteration of Γ. The payoffs are then $8/(1 - \frac{3}{4}) = 32$ for player 1 and $8/(1 - \frac{1}{2}) = 16$ for player 2, representing the discounted present value of the payoffs to the two players from the infinite plays of (a_1^1, a_2^1). If player 1 chooses strategy $\sigma^1[a_1^1/a_2^1]$ and player 2 chooses strategy $\sigma^2[a_2^1/a_1^2]$, then in period 1 player 1 will play a_1^1 and player 2 will play a_2^2. However, because as far as both players are concerned, both played deviating strategies in period 1, from period 2 onward the referee will play the pair (a_1^2, a_2^2). The payoffs in this case are

$$0 + \frac{\frac{3}{4}(6)}{1 - \frac{3}{4}} = 18$$

for player 1 and

$$9 + \frac{\frac{1}{2}(6)}{1 - \frac{1}{2}} = 15$$

for player 2. The other payoffs are defined analogously.

Notice that although Γ is a prisoners' dilemma game, the game L derived from it is not. In fact, there are no dominant strategies in L as there were in Γ. Also notice that L has five equilibrium points (all circled). Not all of these are observationally distinguishable, however. To understand what this means, consider any equilibrium point other than $(\sigma^1[a_1^1/a_2^1], \sigma^2[a_2^1/a_1^1])$ and $(\sigma^2[a_1^2/a_2^2], \sigma^2[a_2^2/a_1^2])$–the two "corner equilibrium points" in the matrix. For instance, consider the pair $(\sigma^1[a_1^2/a_2^1], \sigma^2[a_2^2/a_1^1])$ or any equilibrium point in Matrix 3.2 that has a check next to it. All of these equilibrium points yield the same payoff, $(24, 12)$. Even though, in terms of the payoff matrix, $(\sigma^1[a_1^2/a_2^1], \sigma^2[a_2^2/a_1^1])$ is an equilibrium point, the behavior specified by it is inconsistent. In other words, it instructs player 1 to use strategy 2 as long as player 2 uses strategy 1 and to use strategy 2 if he ever deviates. However, it simultaneously instructs player 2 to use strategy 2 as long as player 1 uses strategy 1 and to use strategy 2 if he ever deviates. Consequently, if these plans were followed in period 1, each player would choose strategy 2 causing the other to treat this act as a deviation, and from that period on both players would continue to choose strategy 2. As a result, when we observe these plans actually being used, we will be observing the repeated use of strategy 2 for all players [i.e., we will observe the repeated play of (a_1^2, a_2^2) in all periods]. The sequence of choices that are made in each period will then be indistinguishable from the sequence that would result if the consistent equilibrium pair $(\sigma^1[a_1^2/a_2^2], \sigma^2[a_2^2/a_1^2])$ were being used, which instructs each player to use strategy 2 as long as the other does. Behaviorally, to an outside observer, the play that results when the original pair of strategies is being used cannot be differentiated from the play that results when $(\sigma^1[a_1^2/a_2^1], \sigma^2[a_2^2/a_1^1])$ is being used. The problem existing then is that we cannot uniquely infer which modes of behavior are being followed by the players by observing their choices in each play of the supergame. When they are both following the strategy pair $(\sigma^1[a_1^2/a_2^1], \sigma^2[a_2^2/a_1^1])$, what we observe is behavior that is identical to what we would observe if they were both following $(\sigma^1[a_1^2/a_2^2], \sigma^2[a_2^2/a_1^2])$. Their true models of behavior are disguised by their actions, and even though $(\sigma^1[a_1^2/a_2^2], \sigma^2[a_2^2/a_1^1])$ is an equilibrium in game L, we will call it a *disguised equilibrium*. Our model will yield only undisguised equilibrium conventions as possible solutions.

To demonstrate that our analysis can also be applied to problems that arise when the recurrent societal problem is a coordination problem, as we will do in Chapter 4, consider the game shown by Matrix 3.3.

$$\Gamma = \begin{array}{c} & a_2^1 \quad\ a_2^2 \\ \begin{array}{c} a_1^1 \\ a_1^2 \end{array} & \left[\begin{array}{cc} 5,3 & 0,0 \\ 0,0 & 2,6 \end{array} \right] \end{array}$$

Matrix 3.3. Coordination game Γ

Notice that in coordination games there are no unique "policing strategies" as there are in prisoners' dilemma games, so that one would think that strategies of the (*) type could not be defined. This is not true, however. A supergame strategy of the (*) type for a player in a supergame defined by the infinite iteration of a coordination game could be defined, say for player 1, verbally as "I will choose strategy a_1^k, $k = 1, 2$, no matter what you do." This would mean that he would be saying "I will choose say strategy a_1^1 if you choose strategy a_2^1, but if you ever choose strategy a_2^2, I will choose strategy a_1^1 anyway." Consequently, you might say that in this simple coordination game, only two supergame strategies exist (i.e., "always choose a_1^{1}" or "always choose a_1^2," no matter what the other player does). To keep our notation consistent with the prisoners' dilemma situation described above, we will again define four supergame strategies of the (*) type, each of which can be denoted as follows:

$$\sigma^1[a_1^k/a_2^k] = \begin{cases} a_{11} = a_1^k & \text{if } a_{2\tau} = a_{2\tau}^k, & \tau = 1, \ldots, t-1 \\ a_{1t} = a_1^k & \text{otherwise} & t = 2, 3, \ldots \\ a_{1t} = a_1^k & & k = 1, 2 \end{cases}$$

Notice what this type of strategy implies. What it says is that player 1 will continue to choose strategy a_1^k, $k = 1, 2$, as long as player 2 chooses strategy a_2^k, $k = 1, 2$, but if player 2 ever deviates, player 1 will continue to choose strategy a_1^k. In other words, this strategy states that player 1 will choose strategy a_1^k no matter what player 2 does. This type of strategy is appropriate for a coordination game because, as we said above, by definition, coordination equilibria do not require policing strategy the way that cooperative prisoners' dilemma supergame equilibria do. To understand why, consider the following convention:

$$\sigma = (\sigma^1[a_1^1/a_2^1], \sigma^2[a_2^1/a_1^1])$$

Here both players decide to choose strategy 1 no matter what the other does. Notice that this convention requires no separate policing strategy because both players, given the other's mode of behavior, have no incentive to deviate in any period. To see why this is true, let us compare Matrices 3.4a and b. Say that

$$\begin{bmatrix} 8,8 & 0,9 \\ 9,0 & 6,6 \end{bmatrix} \quad \begin{bmatrix} 5,3 & 0,0 \\ 0,0 & 2,6 \end{bmatrix}$$

$$\text{(a)} \qquad\qquad \text{(b)}$$

Matrix 3.4. (a) Prisoners' dilemma game Γ (b) Coordination game Γ

it is period t in the prisoners' dilemma supergame and that the equilibrium cooperative convention of behavior is being followed:

$$\sigma^{\text{cooperative}} = (\sigma^1[a_1^1/a_2^1], \sigma^2[a_2^1/a_1^1])$$

If both players adhere to this convention in period t, they will both receive a payoff of 8 in that period. However, if either player deviated and played a_i^2 while the other adhered, he would receive a payoff of 9. Consequently, there are incentives for both players to deviate, and as a result the convention must specify a punishing or policing strategy that would specify punishments if either player succumbed to temptation and deviated. Now, consider the same convention if played in the coordination supergame $\sigma = (\sigma^1[a_1^1/a_2^1], \sigma^2[a_2^1/a_1^1])$. Here in period t, if both players adhered to the convention, then player 1 would receive a payoff of 5 in that period and player 2 would receive a payoff of 3. However, if either of them unilaterally deviate and choose strategy a_i^2, their payoff would drop to zero. Consequently, there is no incentive for either player to deviate from an equilibrium coordination supergame convention and hence no separate policing strategy is necessary. Each strategy polices itself.

Consequently, we can depict the strategy sets of our players in a recurrent coordination game again as

$$\Sigma^1 = (\sigma^1[a_1^1/a_2^1], \sigma^1[a_1^1/a_2^2], \sigma^1[a_1^2/a_2^1], \sigma^1[a_1^2/a_2^2])$$
$$\Sigma^2 = (\sigma^2[a_2^1/a_1^1], \sigma^2[a_2^2/a_1^1], \sigma^2[a_2^1/a_1^2], \sigma^2[a_2^2/a_1^2])$$

The game L to be derived from the recurrent play of this coordination game when the discount factor for player 1 (α_1) is $\frac{3}{4}$ and the discount factor for player 2 (α_2) is $\frac{1}{2}$ will appear as shown by Matrix 3.5. The payoffs here are easily derivable because positive payoffs result only when both players have a super-game strategy that prescribes that they choose the same strategy, so that any pair of strategies prescribing the joint use of strategy a_i^1, $i = 1, 2$, yields a discounted payoff of $5/(1 - \frac{3}{4}) = 20$ for player 1 and $3/(1 - \frac{1}{2}) = 6$ for

Player 2

$$
\begin{array}{c}
\hspace{3.5cm} \sigma^2[a_2^1/a_1^1] \quad \sigma^2[a_2^2/a_1^1] \quad \sigma^2[a_2^1/a_1^2] \quad \sigma^2[a_2^2/a_1^2]
\end{array}
$$

	$\sigma^2[a_2^1/a_1^1]$	$\sigma^2[a_2^2/a_1^1]$	$\sigma^2[a_2^1/a_1^2]$	$\sigma^2[a_2^2/a_1^2]$
$\sigma^1[a_1^1/a_2^1]$	(20, 6)	0, 0	(20, 6) ✓	0, 0
$\sigma^1[a_1^1/a_2^2]$	(20, 6) ✓	0, 0	(20, 6)	0, 0
$\sigma^1[a_1^2/a_2^1]$	0, 0	(8, 12) ✓	0, 0	(8, 12) ✓
$\sigma^1[a_1^2/a_2^2]$	0, 0	(8, 12) ✓	0, 0	(8, 12)

Player 1 appears at the left of the matrix.

Matrix 3.5. The game L

player 2, and any strategy yielding the joint use of strategy a_i^2, $i = 1, 2$ yields a discounted payoff of $2/(1 - \frac{3}{4}) = 8$ for player 1 and $6/(1 - \frac{1}{2}) = 12$ for player 2. All other discounted payoffs are zero. The equilibria are circled, and the disguised equilibria have checks next to them. Consequently, our analysis is also applicable to recurrent coordination games.

What we intend to do now is to use what we call a *static Bayesian solution procedure* to predict what equilibrium will emerge in the game L derived from the prisoners' dilemma game Γ. Consequently, it will be necessary for us to define what we mean by a static Bayesian solution procedure.

3.4 Static Bayesian solution procedures

Consider the game L described above, which is a finite game in normal form. If L were a one-shot static game with multiple equilibria, it would be reasonable to investigate various procedures that would prescribe behavior for each player in the game. John Harsanyi (1975) has opened the way for such investigations by defining what he calls the "tracing procedure," which is one of a class of solution procedures that we call static Bayesian solution procedures (SBSPs). To define what we mean by this term, let us first define what we shall call a norm [what Harsanyi (1975) calls a prior probability n-tuple].

Definition 3.1: A norm. In a two-person game L derived from a prisoners' dilemma game Γ where each player in L has four possible strategies, a norm is a pair of four-dimensional probability vectors $\mathbf{p} = (\mathbf{p}_1, \mathbf{p}_2)$, where $\mathbf{p}_1 = (p_1^1, p_1^2, p_1^3, p_1^4)$ represents the probability that player 2 places on player 1 using any one of his four supergame strategies in Σ^1, and $\mathbf{p}_2 = (p_2^1, p_2^2, p_2^3, p_2^4)$ is the probability that player 1 places on player 2 using any one of his four possible supergame strategies in Σ^2.

The pair $\mathbf{p} = (\mathbf{p}_1, \mathbf{p}_2)$ is a concise subjective statement of the type of behavior each player can expect from the other. This norm can reflect a wide variety of factors, but we will assume that the overriding factor determining what exact norm exists at any point in time will be the history of the play of the game under investigation and, as this history evolves, so will the existing norms.

A SBSP is a procedure that instructs each player how to behave in a given game L using only the information contained in the norm $\mathbf{p}$ and the payoff function of the game. More precisely, at any point in time t, given the norm $\mathbf{p}$ any player can choose to adhere to one of four modes of behavior. In addition, however, he can choose to randomize his choice and choose a mode of behavior at random with probabilities $\mathbf{s}_i = (s_i^1, s_i^2, s_i^3, s_i^4)$, $i = 1, 2$, $s_i \geq 0$, $\Sigma_{k=1}^4 s_i^k = 1$. This constitutes a mixed strategy for player i in the game L. A pair of such mixed strategies can be represented as $\mathbf{s} = (\mathbf{s}_1, \mathbf{s}_2)$, where $\mathbf{s}_1$ or $\mathbf{s}_2$ are four-dimensional vectors whose elements are nonnegative and sum to 1.

Definition 3.2: A static Bayesian solution procedure. A SBSP is a function $\mathcal{M}$ that for a given game L assigns a pair of mixed strategies $\mathbf{s} = (\mathbf{s}_1, \mathbf{s}_2)$ (one strategy for each player) to each norm $\mathbf{p} = (\mathbf{p}_1, \mathbf{p}_2)$.

In other words, a SBSP is a procedure that prescribes behavior for each player in a given game L based on the norm existing among the players. It prescribes behavior for each player conditional on the information available in the society, which we will assume is totally summarized by the norm $\mathbf{p}$.

This procedure is static because it prescribes behavior based only on the strategic description of the game L and on the norm $\mathbf{p}$ and contains no rules for changing behavior if the behavior prescribed by the procedure is not equilibrium behavior. These rules will be added by us.

There are many procedures that one would think of which would be considered SBSPs. For instance, one may define what Harsanyi (1975) defines as the "naive Bayesian solution procedure," which is a procedure that instructs each player to treat the other player as if he were using a mixed strategy equal to the probability vector defined by the norm and to maximize against that vector by choosing an optimal best-response mixed strategy. More simply, if you were player 1 in the game L and the norm existing was $\mathbf{p} = (\mathbf{p}_1, \mathbf{p}_2)$, you would choose that mixed strategy $\mathbf{s}_1 \in S_1$ (your strategy set) which maximized your payoff when expecting player 2 to play each of his four possible supergame strategies with probabilities equal to $\mathbf{p}_2 = (p_2^1, p_2^2, p_2^3, p_2^4)$. In short, the procedure will assign player 1 the mixed strategy s_1 for which

$$\max_{s_1 \in S_1} \Pi_1(s_1, \mathbf{p}_2)$$

is satisfied, and it will assign player 2 that mixed strategy for which

$$\max_{s_2 \in S_2} \Pi_2(s_2, \mathbf{p}_1)$$

is satisfied, where Π_1 and Π_2 are the supergame payoffs resulting when player 1 chooses mixed strategy s_1 and player 2 uses mixed strategy s_2.

In short, each player has total faith that the other will actually behave the way the norm predicts and chooses that mixed strategy which is a best response to this expectation. For a given norm $\mathbf{p}$, the naive Bayesian solution procedure is composed of a set of two one-person maximization problems, and if each person acted in this manner, each would be acting "optimally" if he believed that all information relevant for his strategy choice were summarized by the pair $\mathbf{p} = (\mathbf{p}_1, \mathbf{p}_2)$.

The pair $\mathbf{s} = (\mathbf{s}_1, \mathbf{s}_2)$ that results when each person acts in this manner is not necessarily an equilibrium for the game L, however, because although each $s_i \in S_i$ that is chosen is a best reply to $\mathbf{p}$, it is not necessarily a best reply to the strategy choice actually prescribed by the procedure. Another procedure that alleviates this problem and always prescribes equilibrium behavior for the players is the "tracing procedure" of Harsanyi. This procedure starts out by using the naive Bayesian solution procedure and then modifies the behavior prescribed until an equilibrium pair $s = (\mathbf{s}_1, \mathbf{s}_2)$ is chosen. In the tracing procedure, there is no divergence between what might be called "optimal" behavior and what is actually equilibrium behavior; they are both the same. The procedures we employ need not have this property, however, because our analysis does not rely on the one-time use of any solution procedure. It uses the same procedure over and over until equilibrium is reached. In other words, as we shall see, our analysis is not a static analysis that employs any given solution procedure once and only once in a given game L, but is a dynamic analysis in which the solution procedure employed is used repeatedly by the players at each point during the game. The behavior commonly observed is then used to alter the norm existing at the time and then, on the basis of the new norm, the solution procedure is used again. The process continues until the norm existing is such that the solution procedure being employed continually prescribes the same equilibrium strategy n-tuple that, when employed, changes the existing norm in such a way that the same equilibrium n-tuple is used again, and so on ad infinitum.

The type of SBSPs that are admissible for our analysis is quite general, but we do restrict them by requiring that if a norm $\mathbf{p}$ exists which leads each player to believe that all the other players will play their part in a particular equilibrium convention $\sigma^* = (\sigma^{*1}, \sigma^{*2})$ with probability equal to 1, then they will play their part in it also. This is basically a rationality assumption stating that if any player (say, player 1) feels that the other player will play σ^{*2} with probability 1, player 1 will play his best response σ^{*1} with probability 1. In addition, we require that this not be true for any convention $\sigma' = (\sigma'^1, \sigma'^2)$ if σ' is not an equilibrium. This can be summarized by the following definition.

Definition 3.3: A Bayesian best-response satisfactory SBSP A SBSP $\mathcal{M}$ is Bayesian-best-response-satisfactory if and only if whenever the norm **p** predicts that a certain equilibrium convention $\sigma^* = (\sigma^{*1}, \sigma^{*2})$ will be played with probability 1, each player i will play his part σ^{*i} with probability 1.

As we will see later, this condition guarantees that if the norms are such that all players have full certainty that a particular equilibrium convention of behavior is being followed, it actually will be adhered to and an equilibrium will be realized at that convention as all players' prior expectations are realized. Notice that the condition guarantees that if the convention under consideration is not an equilibrium convention, then even if all players expect it to be followed with probability 1, someone will deviate.

In the second part of the chapter, in the context of a diffusion process, we will place additional technical conditions on $\mathcal{M}$, but at present $\mathcal{M}$ can be quite general as long as it satisfies the condition of Bayesian best response satisfactoriness.

3.5 The analysis

At this point in our discussion, we have a game L that is a finite game in normal form and an unspecified SBSP $\mathcal{M}$. Consequently, if we could justify some pair of probability vectors (some norm), we could employ the procedure $\mathcal{M}$ on L to determine a pair of supergame strategies of the form (*). This pair would constitute two plans of action for the players in the recurrent play of Γ, and the pair chosen by $\mathcal{M}$ would be "optimal" given the norm. This is not what we intend to do, however, for two important reasons. First, although the pair chosen may be optimal in terms of $\mathcal{M}$, it may not determine an equilibrium pair, and if it does not, the choices made have no rational justification. More important, however, even if the pair chosen were an equilibrium (which would be the case if $\mathcal{M}$ were the tracing procedure), the analysis would be a static one employing a static solution procedure once and only once on a given game L with a fixed norm **p** of unknown origin. Our interests here are dynamic, however, in that although the solution procedure $\mathcal{M}$ may be a rational solution procedure for static one-shot games, the actual choice of the strategy n-tuple chosen by the procedure when observed by the players in a recurrent game will lead them, in Bayesian fashion, to change their initial prior probability beliefs from $\mathbf{p}^t = (\mathbf{p}_1^t, \mathbf{p}_2^t)$ in period t to $\mathbf{p}^{t+1} = (\mathbf{p}_1^{t+1}, \mathbf{p}_2^{t+1})$ in period $t + 1$. The true system is then dynamic, with the solution procedure being used as a rational solution procedure *at any time,* but in which the actual play of the game gives the players more information about each other, which, when plugged into the solution procedure, may lead to the same or different behavior.

To model this process, we proceed in a rather simple way. We assume that, for the moment, time is divided into discrete time units of equal length. At time period 0 each player must choose a supergame strategy $\sigma_k^i \in \Sigma^i$ based on the information available at that time about the other player. This information will be summarized by a pair of prior probability distributions $\mathbf{p} = (\mathbf{p}_1, \mathbf{p}_2)$, which we have called a norm. However, since in period zero there is no previous history to the game, there has been no opportunity for the players to learn about each other and no opportunity for any norms other than the degenerate "uniform" norm to be established in which each $\mathbf{p}_i$ is merely a uniform probability distribution. Under this uniform norm the probability with which player i in our simple two-person society will use any pure supergame strategy σ_k^i is simply $\frac{1}{4}$. In time period zero, then, it may make sense to employ procedure $\mathcal{M}$ on L using the uniform norm $\mathbf{p}^u = (\mathbf{p}_1^u, \mathbf{p}_2^u)$, and if we did, an "optimal" pair of strategy choices would be determined–optimal in terms of the information available at time period zero (the uniform norm) and the solution procedure $\mathcal{M}$. The players are then assumed to follow the dictates of that mixed strategy pair and choose one of their pure strategies with the prescribed probabilities. In other words, two independent experiments are performed determining two pure strategy choices.

After these two experiments have chosen a pair of supergame strategies or modes of behavior for the game, the players are assumed to follow the dictates of the pure strategies chosen and make the first move specified by these strategies. In other words, they take the first step specified by this strategy that actually specifies an infinite sequence of moves. This will result in a pair b^k of B being chosen by the players in period zero. In period 1, the players now have a one-period history and have observed the behavior of each other for period zero. In addition, we assume they know that all players have also observed the same history in period zero. In period 1, then, it is assumed that all the players reevaluate the plan of behavior they chose in period zero based on the information gained by observing each other's actions. More precisely, each player, using the same theory, is assumed to revise his initial period zero uniform prior probability distribution in an identical manner, so that in period 1 we have a new norm of behavior $\mathbf{p}^1$ established, which is again a pair of probability distributions, each one specifying the probability with which each player believes the other player will choose any one of his four pure strategies in L. Intuitively, each player tries to draw an inference from his period zero observation as to the mode of behavior–supergame strategy of form (*)–actually being followed by the other player, and these inferences are assumed to be drawn in an identical manner by both players. On the basis of this new norm, $\mathbf{p}^1$, the solution procedure $\mathcal{M}$ is employed once more in period 1 to define a pair of strategies in this period. This pair is chosen on the basis of the information available in period 1 as summarized in $\mathbf{p}^1$. This pair will specify two supergame strategies or two modes of behavior for the players. Again, each player is assumed in period 1 to take the first move specified, and as a result another pair b^k in B is chosen in period 1. The game now has a two-period history, and upon this new history a new norm is formed in exactly the same manner as it was in period zero and the process continues to period 2.

Consequently, our model is one in which the players continually choose plans of action in the form of supergame strategies based on the norm existing at that time and then take the first step specified by these plans. The information furnished by these mutual first steps is then incorporated into the game's history and a new norm created which, through solution procedure $\mathcal{M}$, leads to a new set of revised plans. A mutual first step is then taken in these revised plans, and the process continues until the first steps taken are repeatedly the same and constitute an equilibrium pair for game L. At this point an equilibrium is reached.

To formalize this, let H_1 be the set of four-dimensional probability vectors $\mathbf{p}_1 = (p_1^1, p_1^2, p_1^3, p_1^4)$, each describing a different subjective belief that player 2 might hold over player 1's actions in the game L, and let H^2 be a set describing the same beliefs of player 1 about player 2. More formally, H^1 and H^2 are what are called unit simplices because they are sets of vectors $\mathbf{p}_i = (p_i^1, p_i^2, p_i^3, p_i^4)$ which have the property that $p_i^k \geq 0$, $k = 1, 2, 3, 4$, and $\Sigma_{k=1}^4 p_i^k = 1$. When we take a pair of these vectors, one from H^1 and one from H^2 and put them together as $\mathbf{p} = (\mathbf{p}_1, \mathbf{p}_2)$, we have created a norm. Each simplex H^i appears as shown in Figure 3.1. The pyramid-shaped figure is the simplex and has the property that each point $\mathbf{p}_i = (p_i^1, p_i^2, p_i^3, p_i^4)$ is such that $p_i \geq 0$, $k = 1, \ldots, 4$, $\Sigma_{k=1}^4 p_i^k = 1$.

Notice that each corner of the simplex represents a belief by the other player that player i will use a particular supergame strategy with probability 1 and all other strategies with probability zero. Consequently, a probability vector associated with a corner point in the simplex represents a certain belief on the part of one player about the mode of behavior to be followed by the other. Points in the interior, such as $\mathbf{p}'$, represent beliefs in which the other player feels that there is a positive probability of player i using any one of his four possible strategies.

As stated above, at time period zero we assume that the uniform norm $\mathbf{p}^u = (\mathbf{p}_1^u, \mathbf{p}_2^u)$, in which $\mathbf{p}_1^u = (\frac{1}{4}, \frac{1}{4}, \frac{1}{4}, \frac{1}{4})$ $\mathbf{p}_2^u = (\frac{1}{4}, \frac{1}{4}, \frac{1}{4}, \frac{1}{4})$ exists. On the basis of this norm, the solution procedure $\mathcal{M}$ is employed, which specifies an n-tuple $s^0 = (s_1^0, s_2^0)$. The players each randomize in the manner prescribed by s^0 and make their separate choices of $\sigma^i \in \Sigma^i$. The resulting pair, $\sigma = (\sigma^1, \sigma^2)$, will prescribe a plan of action for each player, and it is assumed that each player takes the first step specified by this plan. This will result in a $b^k \in B$ chosen in period zero. However, when each player observes the pair b^k that appeared in period zero, he will take it as evidence that the convention of behavior indexed

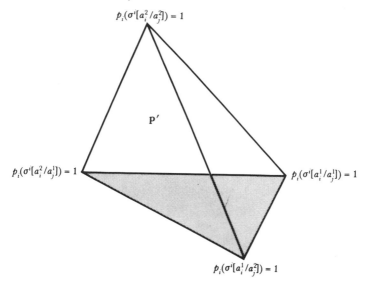

$p_i(\sigma^i[a_i^2/a_j^2]) = 1$

P'

$p_i(\sigma^i[a_i^2/a_j^1]) = 1$

$p_i(\sigma^i[a_i^1/a_j^1]) = 1$

$p_i(\sigma^i[a_i^1/a_j^2]) = 1$

Figure 3.1. The probability simplex for player i.

by that pair was adhered to in period zero. In other words, if as a result of using their period zero mixed strategies that were prescribed by $\mathcal{M}$, player 1 chose to follow the mode of behavior $\sigma^1[a_1^1/a_2^1]$, whose first step is to play a_1^1 in period zero, and player 2 chose $\sigma^2[a_2^1/a_1^1]$, whose first step is a_2^1, then since the pair $b^1 = (a_1^1, a_2^1)$ indexes a unique convention of behavior $\sigma = (\sigma^1[a_1^1/a_2^1], \sigma^2[a_2^1/a_1^1])$ (and consequently unique supergame strategies in Σ^1 and Σ^2), both players will take this observation as evidence that this mode of behavior was adhered to for one period.

To understand how these strategies are indexed by the pair $b^1 = (a_1^1, a_2^1)$, consider the strategy sets Σ^1 and Σ^2:

$$\Sigma^1 = (\sigma^1[a_1^1/a_2^1], \sigma^1[a_1^1/a_2^2], \sigma^1[a_1^2/a_2^1], \sigma^1[a_1^2/a_2^2])$$
$$\Sigma^2 = (\sigma^2[a_2^1/a_1^1], \sigma^2[a_2^2/a_1^1], \sigma^2[a_2^1/a_1^2], \sigma^2[a_2^2/a_1^2])$$

Notice that if the pair $b^1 = (a_1^1, a_2^1)$ is observed, this pair would index the strategy $\sigma^1[a_1^1/a_2^1]$ in Σ^1 and $\sigma^2[a_2^1/a_1^1]$ in Σ^2. Hence taken together, the observation created by observing that $b^1 = (a_1^1/a_2^1)$ is treated in the model as an observation of the convention $\sigma = (\sigma^1[a_1^1/a_2^1], \sigma^2[a_2^1/a_1^1])$. What the agents are then assumed to do is to increase the probability weight that they attach to their opponent's use of that strategy in the future by ϵ and decrease the probability that they will observe any other strategy by $\epsilon/3$. In other words, because both agents observe the same data and know that the other agent is also observing these data, then no matter how irrational what they observe may appear to be, we assume that if it occurred in the past, it is likely to occur again in the future;

and if it has not occurred, it is less likely. The basis upon which norms change in our model is then strictly historical. We allow no other basis upon which people can draw their inferences about one another. This procedure defines the following *norm updating rule*, which describes how norms are changed from period to period based on the information contained in the common observation of the players.

Definition 3.4: A norm-updating rule. If in any period t, $\mathbf{p}^t = (\mathbf{p}_1^t, \mathbf{p}_2^t)$ is the norm and if the pair $b^k \in B$ is observed in that period as a result of the SBSP, then because this pair b^k indexes a unique supergame strategy in each player's supergame strategy set Σ^i, we increase the probability weight in $\mathbf{p}_i^t$ attached to this player using that supergame strategy by ϵ and decrease the probability weight attached to the use of all other strategies by this player by $\epsilon/3$. These additions and subtractions will determine a new norm, $\mathbf{p}^{t+1} = (\mathbf{p}_1^{t+1}, \mathbf{p}_2^{t+1})$.

The explanation of this rule is quite simple. What it says is that the only information the players can be sure they all share is the information they obtain in common by observing the history of the game. Consequently, when they observe a pair $b^k = (a_1^k, a_2^k)$ associated with a supergame strategy $\sigma^i[a_i^k/a_j^k]$ in each player's strategy set, the mere fact that this pair has occurred establishes the convention of behavior associated with it, in which each player plays $\sigma^i[a_i^k/a_j^k]$ as part of the game's history. Because it has happened in the past, we increase the probability weight associated with it in each player's simplex by ϵ. In essence, the players are saying that if it happened before, it can happen again. The weight attached to any particular supergame strategy in a given player's strategy set at time t is then simply proportional to the number of times the pair b^k associated with it was observed in the play of the game from period zero to period $t - 1$.

This assumes that the basis upon which players create beliefs about each other (create norms or trust) depends *solely* upon the common history of the game. All relevant information is contained in the game's history, which they themselves generate as they play. In essence, all players act as if what is probable in the future is equivalent to what was observed in the past.

Because we start out at the uniform norm and transform each probability distribution of each player in an identical manner, the norms generated, $\mathbf{p} = (\mathbf{p}_1, \mathbf{p}_2)$, have the property that $\mathbf{p}_1^t = \mathbf{p}_2^t$ for all $t = 1, 2, \ldots$. In other words, each probability vector for each player is identical throughout the analysis, and the norm existing at any time is a pair of identical probability vectors. Although this may seem restrictive and can clearly be relaxed, it does greatly simplify our analysis, because it allows us to represent the norm $\mathbf{p} = (\mathbf{p}_1, \mathbf{p}_2)$, which is a pair of vectors, as one single vector $\mathbf{p}_i \in H^i$, because all vectors are identical. Consequently, we will be working with one vector $\mathbf{p}_i$ instead of a pair of vectors, and the set of all norms will be represented by one representative simplex W.

Using this fact, we can illustrate our model very simply. Consider the two-person 2×2 game presented in Matrix 3.1. Here the pure strategy set for player 1 was $A_1 = (a_1^1, a_1^2)$ and the pure strategy set for player 2 was $A_2 = (a_2^1, a_2^2)$. As we demonstrated, this game yields game L, in which

$$\Sigma^1 = (\sigma^1[a_1^1/a_2^1], \sigma^1[a_1^2/a_2^1], \sigma^1[a_1^1/a_2^2], \sigma^1[a_1^2/a_2^2])$$
$$\Sigma^2 = (\sigma^2[a_2^1/a_1^1], \sigma^2[a_2^1/a_1^2], \sigma^2[a_2^2/a_1^1], \sigma^2[a_2^2/a_1^2])$$

Letting

$$\mathbf{p}_1 = (p_1(\sigma^1[a_1^1/a_2^1]), p_1(\sigma^1[a_1^1/a_2^2]), p_1(\sigma^1[a_1^2/a_2^1]), p_1(\sigma^1[a_1^2/a_2^2])$$
$$\mathbf{p}_2 = (p_2(\sigma^2[a_2^1/a_1^1]), p_2(\sigma^2[a_2^1/a_1^2]), p_2(\sigma^2[a_2^2/a_1^1]), p_2(\sigma^2[a_2^2/a_1^2])$$

(3.9)

we can represent both H^1 and H^2 as a three-dimensional simplex. This is illustrated in Figure 3.2.

Since all movement within H^1 and H^2 is identical, let us concentrate on H^1. Looking at H^1, we notice that each corner of the simplex represents a subjective probability vector held by player 2 about player 1, in which he thinks player 1 will play a certain supergame strategy (follow a certain mode of behavior) with probability 1. For instance, at point A player 2 feels that player 1 will play $\sigma^1[a_1^1/a_2^1]$ with probability 1. Every other point in H^1 represents a different subjective belief.

To investigate the dynamics of the model, assume that at time t the existing norm can be represented by point G. At G each player will use $\mathcal{M}$ to determine an "optimal" mixed strategy $s_i = (s_i^1, s_i^2, s_i^3, s_i^4)$ for himself–each player's s_i may, of course, be different. Given the resulting pair of mixed strategies, we can define the probability that any pair b^k will be observed in period t when the players use these mixed strategies to make their choices, as follows. Let

$$s = \left\{ \begin{bmatrix} s^1(\sigma^1[a_1^1/a_2^2]) \\ s^1(\sigma^1[a_1^1/a_2^1]) \\ s^1(\sigma^1[a_1^2/a_2^1]) \\ s^1(\sigma^1[a_1^2/a_2^2]) \end{bmatrix} \begin{bmatrix} s^2(\sigma^2[a_2^2/a_1^1]) \\ s^2(\sigma^2[a_2^1/a_1^1]) \\ s^2(\sigma^2[a_2^2/a_1^1]) \\ s^2(\sigma^2[a_2^2/a_1^2]) \end{bmatrix} \right\}$$

(3.10)

For example, $s^1(\sigma^1[a_1^1/a_2^2])$ states the weight that player 1 will give to the supergame strategy (or mode of behavior), instructing him to play strategy 1 as long as his opponent (player 2) plays strategy 2 and take an appropriate noncooperative action if he deviates. Once a particular supergame strategy is chosen with these probabilities, each player is assumed to take the first step specified by this strategy. Consequently, the probability that player 1 chooses a supergame strategy whose first step is a_1^1 is $\Sigma_{j=1}^2 s^1(\sigma^1[a_1^1/a_2^j])$ and the probability that he chooses a supergame strategy whose first step is a_1^2 is $\Sigma_{j=1}^2 s^1(\sigma^2[a_1^2/a_2^j])$. The probability that player 2 chooses strategy a_2^1 is $\Sigma_{i=1}^2 s^2(\sigma^2[a_2^1/a_1^i])$, and the probability that he chooses strategy a_2^2 is $\Sigma_{i=1}^2 s^2(\sigma^2[a_2^2/a_1^i])$.

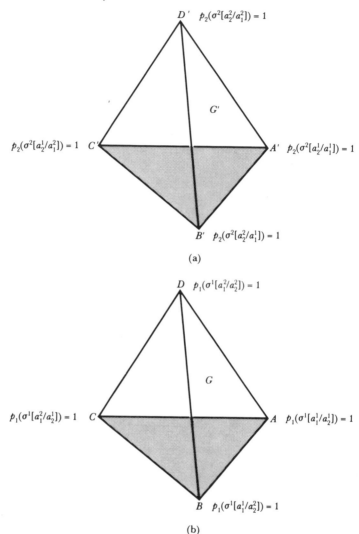

Figure 3.2. The probability simplices H^1 and H^2.

Consequently, at the end of period t, the probability of observing any pair $b^k \in B$ of strategies under $\mathbf{s} = (\mathbf{s}_1, \mathbf{s}_2)$ is

$$q(a_1^1, a_2^1) = \left[\sum_{j=1}^{2} s^1(\sigma^1[a_1^1/a_2^j]) \cdot \sum_{i=1}^{2} s^2(\sigma^2[a_2^1/a_1^i]) \right] \tag{3.11}$$

$$q(a_1^1, a_2^2) = \left[\sum_{j=1}^{2} s^1(\sigma^1[a_1^1/a_2^j]) \cdot \sum_{i=1}^{2} s^2(\sigma^2[a_2^2/a_1^i]) \right] \tag{3.12}$$

$$q(a_1^2, a_2^1) = \left[\sum_{j=1}^{2} s^1(\sigma^1[a_1^2/a_2^j]) \cdot \sum_{i=1}^{2} s^2(\sigma^2[a_2^1/a_i^1]) \right] \qquad (3.13)$$

$$q(a_1^2, a_2^2) = \left[\sum_{j=1}^{2} s^1(\sigma^1[a_1^2/a_2^j]) \cdot \sum_{i=1}^{2} s^2(\sigma^2[a_2^2/a_i^1]) \right] \qquad (3.14)$$

Consequently, the probability of observing any pair of strategies b^k can be constructed from the information contained in the "optimal" pair of mixed strategies dictated by the solution procedure $\mathcal{M}$. The history that evolves is stochastic, or what we will call "strategically stochastic," because there is a positive probability that at any time a variety of pairs $b^k \in B$ will be observed and these probabilities are dictated by the pair of mixed strategies used by the players. When a pair is chosen, however, the weights in each H^i are changed in the exact manner specified by the norm-updating rule. In other words, the information given by $\mathbf{s} = (\mathbf{s}_1, \mathbf{s}_2)$ at any time t is sufficient to calculate the probability that the norm $\mathbf{p}^t$ will move by ϵ in the ith direction (i.e., toward the ith corner of the simplex), away from any corner $j \neq i$ by $\epsilon/3$. If the equilibrium mixed strategies are completely mixed, the vector $\mathbf{p}_i$ has a positive probability of moving in any direction (i.e., toward any corner of the simplex). In addition, because the pure strategy played by one's opponent is a stochastic event, the actions taken by the players may not fulfill their expectations; in other words, their opponent may not play a complementary role in the convention of behavior envisioned by the player under investigation. Such unfulfilled expectations generate disequilibrium states.

Because of the manner in which we update our norm, when the vector $\mathbf{p}_1 \in H^1$ is at point B (Figure 3.2b), which indicates that player 2 feels that player 1 will play strategy $\sigma^1[a_1^1/a_2^2]$ with probability 1, the vector $\mathbf{p}_2 \in H^2$ will be at point B', which indicates that player 1 feels that player 2 will use strategy $\sigma^2[a_2^2/a_1^1]$ with probability 1, which is complementary to $\sigma^2[a_1^1/a_2^2]$ in the pair $\sigma = (\sigma^1[a_1^1/a_2^2], \sigma^2[a_2^2/a_1^1])$. Consequently, when we are at the point B in simplex H^1, we are in a state that says that the convention $\sigma = (\sigma^1[a_1^1/a_2^2], \sigma^2[a_2^2/a_1^1])$ is expected to occur with probability 1, because we are simultaneously at point $B \subset H^1$ and $B' \subset H^2$. We can then redraw the simplex H^1 by placing at the corners the conventions of behavior associated with those points and realizing that when we are at those points, the conventions of behavior denoted are expected to occur with probability 1. This is done in Figure 3.3, and we call the resulting simplex the representative simplex W. Consequently, by construction at any time during the analysis $p_1^i = p_2^i$, we can actually represent the state space of our model by one representative three-dimensional simplex, which we denote by W. We need operate only on that simplex, always realizing, however, that all of the other norm probability vectors are identically placed in their respective simplices and always keeping in mind the proper interpretation of the corner points.

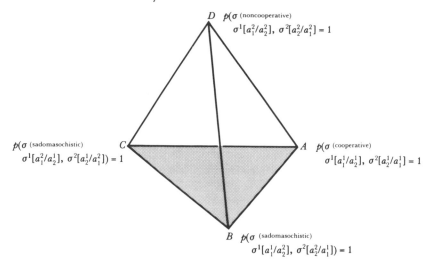

Figure 3.3. The representative simplex W.

As a result, the process depicted is one in which the norm existing among the players moves from state to state in a random manner, where the probabilities of transition from one state to the next are dictated by the optimal mixed strategies prescribed by the SBSP being used. The exact random walk defined and its limiting diffusion process will be defined in the second part of the chapter. The question for us now is where equilibrium will be reached.

3.6 Equilibria

To investigate the equilibria of the process or its absorbing states, let us consider Figure 3.3 and interpret the corner points. In this game, as in all games of this type, the corner points of the simplex correspond to the state of common belief among the players that each of the others will follow a particular convention of behavior with probability 1. However, any one of these conventions, if it happened to be an equilibrium convention, would be an undisguised equilibrium convention. For instance, in the simplex generated by our prisoners' dilemma game, corner A corresponds to a cooperative convention of behavior in which both players agree to use strategy 1 (cooperate) in every period if the other player does, whereas corner D corresponds to a noncooperative convention in which both players choose strategy 2. Corners C and B represent what we call sadomasochistic conventions, because they are conventions (such as point B) in which player 1 (the masochist) agrees to cooperate with player 2 (use strategy 1) as long as player 2 double-crosses him, and player 2 (the sadist) agrees to double-cross player 1 as long as he cooperates. If either player fails to play his part, strategy two is resorted to. Clearly, such odd conventions are not equilibrium conventions in our game L and will not appear as absorbing states in our stochastic process either.

To investigate the equilibria of our model, assume that at time period t the state of the process is at $p^t \in W$, which is an interior point of the simplex. Since we are in the interior, some $b^k \in B$ will be observed in period t, and as a consequence we will move by ϵ in the direction associated with this pair and away from all the other corners by $\epsilon/3$. The corner that we move toward is determined stochastically as a result of the two random experiments defined by the pair of mixed strategies $\mathbf{s} = (\mathbf{s}_1, \mathbf{s}_2)$ dictated by $\mathcal{M}$ given $\mathbf{p}^t$. However, because the probabilities determining movement are the result of the mixed strategies employed by the players, we call the model "strategically stochastic." Consequently, as long as we are in the interior of the simplex, the existing norm will not be stationary and will move in the direction of some corner of the simplex. Such an interior point, then, could not be an equilibrium point. Now assume that p^t is a corner point, say corner C (or D), which is not associated with an equilibrium convention in L. From our assumption of Bayesian best response satisfactoriness, for $\mathcal{M}$, all of the players cannot be instructed by $\mathcal{M}$ to choose the strategies associated with the convention of behavior associated with the convention of behavior associated with point C. Since at least one player will deviate from this convention, we will observe some pair $b^k \in B$ not associated with this convention, and in period $t + 1$ the norm will move from point C either into the interior of the simplex or to a point along the boundary, depending on what was observed. Consequently, corner points such as C not associated with equilibria in L are not stationary norms and are not equilibria for our model. The same logic can be used to demonstrate that all points on the boundary of the simplex cannot define equilibria for the model either. However, let us look at a corner point associated with an undisguised equilibrium point of L. These are points A and B in Figure 3.3. If the process arrived at point A, each player expects the other to cooperate with him as long as he also cooperates, and each knows that he will be punished if he deviates. Since this is an equilibrium pair of strategies and we are at a corner point in which each player expects the other to play his part in this convention with probability 1, $\mathcal{M}$ will instruct each player to conform to this convention. Consequently, we will observe the strategy pair (a_1^1, a_2^1) appearing in period t, and by the norm-updating rule we would want to increase the weight attached to the equilibrium pair $(\sigma^1[a_1^1/a_2^1], \sigma^2[a_2^1/a_1^1])$ by ϵ and decrease all others by $\epsilon/3$. However, because we are already at a corner point of the simplex, this is impossible, so that we will keep the norm unchanged. In other words, we cannot make it any more probable that $\sigma = (\sigma^1[a_1^1/a_2^1], \sigma^2[a_2^1/a_1^1])$ will be the convention followed, because we already expect it to be followed with probability 1 and our observation merely confirms this belief. As a result, in period $t + 1$ we will have

$p^{t+1} = p^t$, and since $\mathcal{M}$ is stationary, the pair $(\sigma^1[a_1^1/a_2^1], \sigma[a_2^1/a_1^1])$ will be chosen again in period $t + 1$. Even more important, if the state of the process ever reaches the points A or B, the conventions associated with those corner points will be followed ad infinitum. Consequently, we say that the process is absorbed at those corner points and the conventions of behavior associated with them become "institutionalized."

In summary, interior points and boundary points (other than absorbing points) cannot be equilibria in this model because given these norms, the observed behavior of the agents will lead them to update their norms and always move from interior or nonabsorbing boundary norms toward some corner of the norm simplex. Hence these interior or nonabsorbing boundary points cannot be stationary points in the model. The regularity of behavior that results is what Lewis (1969) calls a "social convention" and what we are calling a "social institution." It represents a regularity of behavior that will be used by the agents to govern their behavior at each occurrence of the prisoners' dilemma game defined and is such that:

1. Everyone conforms to this regularity (because it is an equilibrium).
2. Everyone expects everyone else to conform to it (because the norm supporting this convention leads all players to think that the other will also conform).
3. If anyone ever deviates from the convention or regularity, it is known that some or all of the others will also deviate, and the payoffs associated with the recurrent play of Γ using these deviating strategies are worse for all agents than the payoff associated with R (this is the definition of an equilibrium institution).

Our model has as its equilibria, then, exactly the types of regularities in behavior that we have defined as social institutions.

As a result of this discussion, we can state the following proposition without proof.

Proposition 3.1. A norm $p^* \in W$ is a stationary norm and the convention $\sigma^* = (\sigma^{*1}, \sigma^{*2})$ associated with $p^* \in W$ through $\mathcal{M}$ is an equilibrium convention of behavior if and only if p^* is a corner point of W associated with some undisguised equilibrium of L. (See page 63 for a definition of undisguised equilibrium.)

Corner points such as p^* will represent the absorbing points of the Markov process to be explained in the second part of the chapter.

It may have struck the reader that the notion of an absorbing point in our model (and the equilibrium behavior associated with it) is similar to the notion of rational expectations equilibrium. This is indeed true. Notice what our equilibrium says. If the norm p^* is in the corner of the representative simplex W associated with an equilibrium convention, each player expects the other to choose the mode of behavior associated with that corner with probability 1. Let us say that the norm is such that each player expects the cooperative convention $\sigma^{\text{cooperative}} = (\sigma^1[a_1^1/a_2^1], \sigma^2[a_2^1/a_1^1])$ to be adhered to with probability 1. Consequently, player 1 would expect player 2 to play $\sigma^2[a_2^1/a_1^1]$ with probability 1, and player 2 would expect player 1 to play $\sigma^1[a_1^1/a_2^1]$ with probability 1. However, if player 1 expects player 2 to play $\sigma^2[a_2^1/a_1^1]$ with probability 1, he will play $\sigma^1[a_1^1/a_2^1]$ with probability 1, whereas if player 2 expects player 1 to play $\sigma^1[a_1^1/a_2^1]$ with probability 1, he will play $\sigma^2[a_2^1/a_1^1]$. Hence we will observe player 1 playing $\sigma^1[a_1^1/a_2^1]$ with probability 1 and player 2 playing $\sigma^2[a_2^1/a_1^1]$, which is exactly what both players expected to observe. Hence the actions of the players consistently reinforce the beliefs of the players and our equilibrium notion has the self-fulfilling characteristic typical of all rational expectations equilibria.

3.7 Summary

In this part of Chapter 3, I have tried to demonstrate that the process of institution creation can be meaningfully represented as a supergame in which the equilibrium conventions of behavior or social institutions that emerge are built upon norms of behavior created as the history of the game being played unfolds. The important point to be made, and the one that makes this approach unique, is that the social institution that is actually created to solve the recurrent prisoners' dilemma game described is a stochastic event, and that if history could be repeated, a totally different convention could be established for the identical situation. The point is that the set of institutions existing at any point in time is really an accident of history and that what exists today could have evolved in a very different manner. All that we know about the institutional history of a society is what happened, not what could have happened.

Finally, with reference to the actual model proposed in this chapter, it is clear that it is quite general, if not too general. In fact, it is more a framework into which various models of this phenomenon can be placed, because a wide variety of specific models can be created using our framework simply by specifying different SBSPs as descriptions of behavior and norm-updating rules and investigating the results obtained. The level of generality used so far, however, has the advantage of not committing us to any one SBSP. In the second part of this chapter we demonstrate that our model, when used in conjunction with *any* SBSP that satisfies a minimal set of criteria, yields a unique stochastic diffusion process governing the emergence of norms for any given game and that this process has a unique solution. When this is completed, we offer an example that applies our theory to a specific coordination problem, demonstrating exactly what type of diffusion process results. Our analysis will continue to be restricted to problems of the prisoners' dilemma variety, except when we consider the coordination problem.

The general case

In this part of the chapter we generalize and formalize the analysis presented in the first part. In doing this, however, it will be necessary to repeat some of the material presented there. I apologize to the reader for these repetitions, but I do feel that they are necessary if the material presented here is to be coherent. The major way in which this part differs from the earlier material is that we present an analysis for an arbitrary number of players and formally demonstrate how the model defines a unique random walk model whose limiting behavior defines a stochastic diffusion process. (This was not attempted earlier; only an intuitive explanation was offered.) It is then demonstrated that we can define the probability of the process being absorbed at any equilibrium convention by solving a particular partial differential equation defined by the process. In addition, the process defined allows us to calculate what the expected first passage time to absorption is for any equilibrium convention of behavior. In other words, we can actually calculate how long a given society faced with a particular recurrent problem would take to tacitly settle upon a given social convention as a guide to behavior. This is significant for government policy, however, because if a Pareto-optimal equilibrium convention of behavior exists and if the expected first passage time to this convention is extremely long, a case could be made for the government's intervening and creating this institution explicitly, because the societal losses created at the suboptimal disequilibrium, which would persist for an extremely long time, may justify such interventions. Consequently, the question of relevance is not only which equilibrium convention will be established but how long one could expect to wait until a particular one is.

In the remainder of the chapter I present some game-theoretical notation and definitions, then the model described in the first part of the chapter, and then demonstrate formally how the model determines a unique random walk whose limiting behavior defines a continuous stochastic process. The method of defining the limiting probability distribution over these equilibrium conventions is shown to be equivalent to solving a partial differential "diffusion equation," and the first-passage-time problem is shown to be solved by solving a particular partial differential equation determined by the model.

3.8 Background preliminaries

Consider a game Γ with n players indexed $i = 1, \ldots, n$. Let each player have a finite strategy set A_i with K_i pure strategies denoted by $a_i^1, \ldots, a_i^k, \ldots,$

$a_i^{K_i}$. Following the notation of Harsanyi (1975), if player i has K_i pure strategies, then let

$$K = \prod_{i=1}^{n} K_i$$

$$\overline{K}_i = \prod_{j \neq i} K_j = K/K_i$$

K is then the total number of pure strategy n-tuples available in the game and $\overline{K}_i$ is the total number of $n - 1$ tuples that player i can contemplate when he views the actions of all the other players in the game. We can number these n-tuples consecutively as

$$b^1, \ldots, b^k, \ldots, b^K$$

The set of all possible n-tuples will be called B and $B = A_i \times \cdots \times A_n$. In addition, we can assume that the $\overline{K}_i$ possible $(n - 1)$-tuples of players other than player i can also be numbered consecutively as $c_i^1, \ldots, c_i^k, \ldots, c_i^{K_i}$. The set of all $\overline{K}_i$ $(n - 1)$-tuples of the form c_i^k will be called C_i. Consequently, $C_i = A_1 \times \cdots \times A_{i-1} \times \cdots \times A_{i+1} \times \cdots \times A_n$.

A "mixed strategy" for player i ($i = 1, \ldots, n$) takes the form of a probability vector s defined over i's pure strategies as follows: $s_i = (s_i^1, \ldots, s_i^k, \ldots, s_i^{K_i})$, where s_i^k are probability weights assigned by s_i to each of its pure strategies $a_i^1, \ldots, a_i^k, \ldots, a_i^{K_i}$. The set S_i of all mixed strategies available to player i is called a strategy set. S_i is then a $(K_i - 1)$-dimensional simplex satisfying the conditions

$$s_i^k \geq 0 \qquad k = 1, \ldots, K_i$$

$$\sum_{k=1}^{K_i} s_i^k = 1$$

The set $S = S_1 \times \cdots \times S_n$ will be called the strategy space of game Γ. A particular element of S can be written in the form $s = (s_i, \bar{s}_i)$, where $\bar{s}_i = (s_1, \ldots, s_{i-1}, s_{i+1}, \ldots s_n)$ is a particular strategy $n - 1$-tuple used by all of the players in Γ except i. Finally, let $U_i(b^k)$ be the payoff to player i when the n-tuple $b^k = (a_1^k, \ldots, a_i^k, \ldots, a_n^k)$ is chosen. Then if the n-tuple of mixed strategies $s = (s_1, \ldots, s_n)$ is chosen, the expected payoff to player i or $U_i(s)$ can be defined as

$$U_i(s) = \sum_{a_1^k \in A_1}, \ldots, \sum_{a_n^k \in A_n} U_i(a_1^k, \ldots, a_i^k, \ldots, a_n^k) \times (s_1^k)$$
$$\times \cdots \times (s_i^k) \times \cdots \times (s_n^k), \qquad i = 1, \ldots, n$$

As a result of this notation, Γ can be defined as follows.

Definition 3.5: The game Γ. A finite game Γ can be defined as a triple $\Gamma = (S; U_i(s), i = 1, \ldots, n; N)$, where

(a) $S = S_1 \times \cdots \times S_n$

(b) $U_i(s) = \sum\limits_{a_i^k \in A_1}, \ldots, \sum\limits_{a_n^k \in A_n} U_i(a_1^k, \ldots, a_i^k, \ldots, a_n^k) \times (s_1^k)$

$$\times \cdots \times (s_i^k) \times \cdots \times (s_n^k).$$

(c) $N = \{i/i = 1, \ldots, n\}.$

Now, assume that Γ is going to be played repeatedly by the same set of players a countably infinite number of times and that the final payoff to any player i in this "supergame" will be equal to the discounted present value of the payoffs to i at each iteration. Whereas for each player i a strategy for Γ will consist of a choice of some $s_i \in S_i$, when Γ is iterated a supergame strategy for player i will consist of an initial action a_{i_1} in period 1, a function that chooses a_{i_2} as a function of all of the actions in the first period, $\rho_{i_2}(b_1)$, $b_1 = (a_{1_1}, \ldots, a_{i_1}, \ldots, a_{n_1})$; a function that chooses a_{i_3} as a function of b_1 and b_2, $\rho_{i_3}(b_1, b_2)$; and so on. A supergame strategy for player i, σ^i, may then be written as $\sigma_i = (a_{i_1}^k, \rho_{i_2}(b_1), \rho_{i_3}(b_1, b_2), \ldots, \rho_{i_t}(b_1, \ldots, b_{t-1}))$. Now, if α_i $(i = 1, \ldots, n)$ is the discount parameter for player i expressing his preference for utility today versus utility tomorrow, the supergame payoff to player i is

$$\Pi_i = \sum_{t=1}^{\infty} \alpha_i^{t-1} U_i(b_t^k), \qquad i = 1, \ldots, n$$

(i.e., the present discounted value of all future payoffs in Γ). Call this supergame $\mathscr{S}$.

Although the types of supergame strategies described above are rather general, we investigate next a specific simple type of supergame strategy that we call a pure supergame strategy of form (*). To describe what this type of strategy is, it is best to restrict ourselves (for expository purposes) to the analysis of supergames that iterate constituent games of the prisoners' dilemma type (although our analysis could also be applied to supergames defined by iterating static coordination games, as discussed previously). These will be games in which a unique pure strategy Nash equilibrium exists for Γ in dominant strategies whose associated payoffs are not Pareto-optimal. In addition, for these games there exist payoffs associated with other pure strategy n-tuples that are not equilibrium payoffs but are Pareto-superior to the payoffs associated with the Nash equilibrium of the game. A typical example of such a game is the classic prisoners' dilemma game [Kurz's (1977) "game of altruism" is another example].

For these games we can define the following type of supergame strategy:

$$\sigma^i[a_i^m/c_i^m] = \begin{cases} a_{i_1} = a_i^m \\ a_{i_t} = a_i^m \\ a_{i_t} = a_i^{nc} \end{cases} \text{if } c_{i_\tau} = c_i^m, \quad \tau = 1, \ldots, t-1; \quad t = 2, 3, \ldots \cdot \quad (*)$$

where a_i^{nc} is the noncooperative equilibrium strategy for player i.

This strategy instructs player i to choose strategy a_i^m in the first period and then to continue to choose strategy a_i^m as long as the other $n - 1$ players choose c_i^m. If in any period, t, any other player $j \neq i$ deviates, that deviation will be punished by player i from period $t + 1$ onward by the repeated use of a_i^{nc}.

If the constituent game that is to be iterated is not of the prisoners' dilemma variety, there would not be a unique policing strategy such as a_i^{nc} for each player. Hence a different policing strategy may have to be used for each proposed mode of behavior for any player. Although this may conceivably be quite complex, it could still be achieved and would still yield a finite set of supergame strategies that could be used to define game L. Rather than enter into this more complex situation, we will stick with prisoners' dilemma constituent games except for some quick examinations of supergames defined by iterating coordination games (see page 22), which are also rather easy to deal with. This is not a restriction for us, however, because we are concerned only with the evolution of institutions created to solve exactly these two categories of problems—prisoners' dilemma and coordination problems.

To continue, let $b^m = (a_i^m, c_i^m)$. Then, if each player followed the supergame strategy $\sigma^i[a_i^m/c_i^m]$, we could denote this n-tuple as $\sigma(b^m) = (\sigma^1[a_1^m/c_1^m], \ldots, \sigma^n[a_n^m/c_n^m])$. In short, $\sigma(b^m)$ is a convention of behavior in which each player agrees to play a_i^m in each period if the other $n - 1$ players play $c_i^m = (a_1^m, \ldots, a_{i-1}^m, a_{i+1}^m, \ldots, a_n^m)$ and each will choose a_i^{nc} if anyone deviates. This strategy arises naturally from this type of constituent game because the game Γ has nonequilibrium n-tuples of pure strategies whose associated payoffs are Pareto-superior to the payoffs associated with the Nash equilibrium but which must be policed, because by being nonequilibrium payoffs, there is an incentive for at least one player to deviate, and this incentive must be dissuaded. Consequently, the supergame strategy involves a policing mechanism.

To discover what a supergame equilibrium strategy is, let $a^{nc} \in B$ be the noncooperative equilibrium pure strategy n-tuple for Γ, and assume that the payoff associated with a^{nc} in Γ is not Pareto-optimal. Consider the strategy n-tuple $\sigma(b^m)$ of type (*) defined above. To see whether $\sigma(b^m)$ is a supergame noncooperative equilibrium, let us consider a deviation from $\sigma(b^m)$ for player i. If he were to deviate in any period, say period t, and deviate by using strategy a_i^k in period t, all players would use their noncooperative strategy $a_j^{nc}, j \neq i$, from period $t + 1$ onward–to which player i would have to respond with a_i^{nc}, because this is the best reply to $\bar{a}_i^{nc}, = (a_i^{nc}, \ldots, a_{i-1}^{nc}, a_{i+1}^{nc}, \ldots, a_n^{nc})$. The period t deviation strategy for player i, $a_i^k(t)$, determines the following sequence of moves for him:

$$a_i^k(t) = (a_{i_1}^m, a_{i_2}^m, \ldots, a_{i_{t-1}}^m, a_{i_t}^k, a_{i_{t+1}}^{nc}, a_{i_{t+2}}^{nc}, \ldots) \tag{3.15}$$

and the payoff to such a strategy is

$$\sum_{\tau=1}^{t-1} \alpha_i^{\tau-1} U_i(b^m) + \alpha_i^{t-1} U_i(a_i^k, c_i^m) + \sum_{\tau=t+1}^{\infty} \alpha_i^{\tau-1} U_i(b^{nc}) \tag{3.16}$$

where $b^{nc} = (a_1^{nc}, \ldots, a_n^{nc})$. If $\sigma(b^m)$ is to be noncooperative equilibrium strategy for the supergame, no such deviation can be profitable or $\sigma^i[a_i^m/c_i^m]$ must be a best response to $\bar{\sigma}^i(b^m) = (\sigma^1[a_1^m/c_1^m], \ldots, \sigma^{i-1}[a_{i-1}^m/c_{i-1}^m], \sigma^{i+1}[a_{i+1}^m/c_{i+1}^m], \ldots, \sigma^n[a_n^m/c_n^m])$. To see if any such profitable deviation exists for player i, let us first make clear that if player i is going to deviate in period t when he expects $\bar{\sigma}^i(b^m)$ to be played by all of the $n - 1$ other players, his optimal deviation must be such as to maximize $U_i(a_i, c_i^m)$. Let us denote this a_i as a_i^k. Since our game Γ is stationary and not dependent on time, we can consider a deviation in period 1 as the relevant time t, because any calculation there is relevant for $t > 1$. Consequently, the payoffs to i under a_i^m and $a_i^k(1)$ are:

$$\frac{U_i(b^m)}{1 - \alpha_i}$$

and

$$U_i(a_i^k, c_i^m) + \frac{\alpha_i U_i(b^{nc})}{1 - \alpha_i} \tag{3.17}$$

respectively, and a_i^m determines a greater payoff to player i than $a_i^k(1)$ if

$$\frac{\alpha_i(U_i(b^m) - U_i(b_i^{nc}))}{1 - \alpha_i} > U_i(a_i^k, c_i^m) - U_i(b^m) \tag{3.18}$$

or

$$\alpha_i^* > \frac{U_i(a_i^k, c_i^m) - U_i(b^m)}{U_i(a_i^k, c_i^m) - U_i(b^{nc})} \tag{3.19}$$

Since the right-hand side of (3.19) is always less than 1, no profitable deviation exists for player i for any values of α_i between $\alpha_i^* \leq \alpha_i \leq 1$, and if the set of discount parameters $\alpha = \{\alpha_i\}$, $i = 1, \ldots, n$, is such that (3.19) holds for all $i = 1, \ldots, n$, then $\sigma(b^m)$ is a noncooperative supergame equilibrium.

Our object here is to investigate which noncooperative pure strategy equilibrium of the form (*) will evolve in the repeated play of Γ if several such equilibria exist. The point is that when a fixed set of players repeatedly play the same game over and over (as do oligopolists in markets or countries fighting wars), they develop conventions of behavior or institutional rules that govern their behavior in these situations. These conventions are equivalent to supergame equilibria because they specify behavior for each player in each iteration of Γ, and this behavior is stable in the supergame sense. The exact convention or institution that emerges cannot, of course, be determined a priori because it will depend on the history of play of the game: as the game is iterated, the players will learn about each other, develop trust, and so on. We call this process the process of "norm creation" and will see that the types of norms developed will be of major importance in determining which convention will evolve in a game.

The fact that we consider only supergame strategies of a very simple type might be considered a shortcoming of the analysis, but we do not feel that it is. It is our belief that if a convention of behavior is to be workable, it must be easy to understand and to follow. Hopelessly complex conventions are therefore less likely to be followed. Consequently, because conventions in our framework are societal or institutional rules of thumb, it is unlikely that the rules would be too complex. Studying a simple one should therefore be a step in the right direction.

From this discussion we see that supergame strategies of form (*) have a very convenient characteristic for notational purposes. They can be completely defined by an n-tuple of pure strategies in Γ. In other words, we can write a supergame strategy for player i as $\sigma^i[a_i^m/c_i^k]$, which could be read: player i will choose pure strategy a_i^m as long as all other players choose the $(n-1)$-tuple c_i^k and will play a_i^{nc} if anyone deviates. We do not include a_i^{nc} in the notation; because a_i^{nc} is unique, it is known which noncooperative strategy will be resorted to if any player deviates.

Let $\sigma = (\sigma^1, \ldots, \sigma^i, \ldots, \sigma^n)$ be an n-tuple of supergame strategies for the supergame. Each supergame strategy for each player can be characterized by a different n-tuple in Γ, so each player has a total of

$$K = \prod_{i=1}^{n} K_i$$

supergame strategies of form (*) (if we assume that each supergame strategy for each player will be policed by one and only one punishing strategy). Each can be written as $\sigma_1^i, \ldots, \sigma_k^i, \ldots, \sigma_K^i$. Consequently, $\tilde{K} = K^n$ possible n-tuples of supergame strategies can be formed and we can order them consecutively as $d_1, \ldots, d_k, \ldots, d_{\tilde{K}}$. These n-tuples have very specific meanings. Each player's strategy constitutes a particular "mode of behavior" or plan for him to follow in the supergame and prescribes the actions he will take, conditional on the actions of others. Together, they constitute a particular convention of behavior, and the question we ask is: If many of these conventions could constitute a stable noncooperative equilibrium, which one would evolve?

To further our analysis, let Σ^i denote the set of all K pure supergame strategies of form (*) that can be defined for player i, $i = 1, \ldots, n$. Each pure supergame strategy of form (*) for player i constitutes a plan of action for i in the supergame. For each n-tuple $d_k^i = (\sigma^i, \bar{\sigma}^i)$, where $\bar{\sigma}^i = (\sigma^1, \ldots, \sigma^{i-1}, \sigma^{i+1},$

$\ldots, \sigma^n)$, we can define a payoff vector $\Pi(d_k) = (\Pi^1, \ldots, \Pi^n) \in R^N$, where $\Pi^i(\sigma^i, \bar{\sigma}^i) = \Pi^i(d_k)$ describes the payoff to player i when all n players behave according to $d_k = (\sigma^i, \bar{\sigma}^i)$. The payoffs are defined by

$$\Pi^i(d_k) = \sum_{t=1}^{\infty} \alpha_i^{t-1} U_i(b_t^k) \tag{3.20}$$

where $b_t^k = (a_{1t}^k, \ldots, a_{nt}^k)$ is the n-tuple of pure strategies in Γ defined by d_k in period t. As a result, an n-person game L in normal form can be defined in which the strategy space is $\Sigma = \Sigma^1 \times \cdots \times \Sigma^n$, and the payoff functions are Π_i, $i = 1, \ldots, n$. This game is then a game in normal form in which the strategies are supergame strategies of the form (*) and the payoffs discounted sums that would result if a referee were to play out the game after receiving a particular n-tuple d_k of supergame strategies. Finally, if the players use mixed strategies in deciding upon a strategy $\sigma_k^i \in \Sigma^i$, then let $s = (s_1, \ldots, s_n)$ be an n-tuple of such mixed strategies and define the payoff to player i under such an n-tuple as

$$\Pi^i(s) = \sum_{\sigma_k^1 \in \Sigma^1}, \ldots, \sum_{\sigma_k^n \in \Sigma^n} \Pi^i(\sigma_k^1, \ldots, \sigma_k^i, \ldots, \sigma_k^n)(s_1^k) \times \cdots$$
$$\times (s_i^k) \times \cdots \times (s_n^k) \tag{3.21}$$

This derived game L whose pure strategies are supergame strategies of form (*) can be defined as follows.

Definition 3.6: The game L. The finite game L can be defined by a triple $L = (\Sigma; \Pi^i, i = 1, \ldots, n; N)$, where

(a) $\Sigma = \Sigma^1 \times \cdots \times \Sigma^n$.

(b) $\Pi^i(s) = \sum_{\sigma_k^1 \in \Sigma^1}, \ldots, \sum_{\sigma_k^n \in \Sigma^n} \Pi^i(\sigma_k^1, \ldots, \sigma_k^i, \ldots, \sigma_k^n)(s_1^k) \times \cdots$
$$\times (s_i^k) \times \cdots \times (s_n^k).$$

(c) $N = \{i \mid i = 1, \ldots, n\}$.

Earlier in the chapter we described how one can generate the game L from a particular game Γ (see Matrices 3.1, 3.2, 3.3, and 3.5) and demonstrated the basics of the model by describing the way in which the model defines a set of norms that change depending upon the history of the game. Before we proceed any further here, however, let us pause and formally state some definitions that generalize concepts introduced less rigorously in the first part of the chapter.

Definition 3.7: A norm. A norm $\mathbf{p} = (\mathbf{p}_1, \ldots, \mathbf{p}_n)$ is an n-tuple of K-dimensional prior probability vectors in which each vector $\mathbf{p}_i = (\mathbf{p}_i^1, \ldots, \mathbf{p}_i^K)$ represents the probability that all players except player i place upon player i choosing any one of his K pure supergame strategies in L.

Definition 3.8: A static Bayesian solution procedure (SBSP). A SBSP is a function

$$\mathcal{M}(\mathbf{p}, L) \to S = \prod_{i=1}^{n} S_i$$

where

(a) $\mathbf{p}$ is an n-tuple of K-dimensional prior probability vectors $\mathbf{p} = (\mathbf{p}_1, \dots, \mathbf{p}_i, \dots, \mathbf{p}_n)$, $p_1 \in H^1, \dots, p_n \in H^n$, which we will call a norm.
(b) S is the mixed strategy space of the game.
(c) L is the game L.

Definition 3.9: A norm-updating rule. In any period t, if $\mathbf{p}^t = (\mathbf{p}_1^t, \dots, \mathbf{p}_i^t, \dots, \mathbf{p}_n^t)$ is a point of H, and if the n-tuple $b^k \in B$ is observed by the players as a result of using the solution procedure, the point $\mathbf{p}_i^{t+1}$ in each player's simplex H^i is related to $\mathbf{p}_i^t$ as follows. The coordinate of $\mathbf{p}_i^{t+1}$ corresponding to the supergame strategy indexed by $b^k \in B$ is obtained from the corresponding coordinate of $\mathbf{p}_i^t$ by the addition of a fixed constant ϵ; all other coordinates of $\mathbf{p}_i^{t+1}$ are obtained from those of $\mathbf{p}_i^t$ by the subtraction of $\epsilon/(K - 1)$.

Given these definitions and our discussion in the first part, we are now in a position to formally study how the model presented there generates a random walk in the space of norms.

3.9 The random walk model for our analysis

In the next several sections it will be shown that our model can be represented by a random walk in the representative simplex of norms we have called W. We will see that the random walk can, after appropriate scaling of the time and state variables, be approximated by a well-studied stochastic diffusion process in the simplex. The partial differential equation that characterizes the diffusion process is then used to obtain the probability distribution of absorption at the various equilibria of the original supergame, as well as the expected first passage time to these equilibria.

From the construction of the earlier model, in which each of the n players plays according to the movement of an n-tuple $\mathbf{p} = (\mathbf{p}_1, \dots, \mathbf{p}_n)$ in n simplices, the movement within each simplex is identical to that in every other. Therefore, we simplify matters by investigating only movement within one representative simplex, which we have called W. Thus the state of our model at a particular time is a probability distribution $\mathbf{p} = (p_1, \dots, p_K)$ on K points, where the p_i's are nonnegative real numbers whose sum is 1. Any p_i represents the belief that a particular supergame strategy, indexed by some b^k in B, will be followed.

However, since movement within all simplices is identical, if player i has a particular probability of acting according to a particular supergame strategy, all other players have the same probability, so the corresponding points in the various simplices are identical.

The model operates as follows. If the current state is $\mathbf{p}$, each player employs the SBS procedure $\mathcal{M}$, which prescribes a mixed strategy $s_i = (s_1, \ldots, s_K)$ for his use; consequently, n mixed strategies are chosen. Using these mixed strategies, each player chooses a supergame strategy from the K that are available to him in the game L and then takes the first step in executing this strategy. Consequently, we observe the occurrence of one play of some particular n-tuple b^k in B of the constituent game Γ. Since each supergame strategy of the form (*) is indexed by a different b^k, each player considers the observation of b^k as evidence that the particular supergame n-tuple, or convention of behavior, was adhered to by all n players for one period. Using a norm-updating rule, the players will then change $\mathbf{p}$ to $\mathbf{p}'$. Because the particular b^k that is actually observed is randomly chosen according to the mixed strategies specified by $\mathcal{M}$, we can think of the process as one moving from state to state on the basis of successive random experiments whose probability laws are determined by these mixed strategies.

More formally, the state of our model at a particular time is a probability distribution $\mathbf{p} = (p_1, \ldots, p_K)$ on K points. The individual moves in the model are executed in the following random manner. If the current state is $\mathbf{p}$, a random experiment is performed, and, in accordance with its outcome, the state moves to a new point $\mathbf{p}'$, which is also a K-component probability vector. The probability distribution for the latter random experiment is determined only by the current state $\mathbf{p}$ through $\mathcal{M}$ and the norm-updating rule, and is independent of the history of states visited before the current state $\mathbf{p}$. Under this assumption the successive states of the model form a Markov chain whose state space is included in the closed representative simplex in a $(K-1)$-dimensional subspace, $W = \{(p_1, \ldots, p_K), p_i, \geq 0 \; \Sigma_i \, p_i = 1\}$. The successive states are assumed at time points indexed by the variable $t, t = 0, 1, 2, \ldots$.

The state at time t is a random K-component vector that we denote as

$$\mathbf{X}(t) = (X_i(t), i = 1, \ldots, K)$$

The conditional probability that the state $\mathbf{p}'$ is visited at time $t + 1$, given that $\mathbf{p}$ is the state at time t, is denoted

$$P\{\mathbf{X}(t + 1) = \mathbf{p}' | \mathbf{X}(t) = \mathbf{p}\} \tag{3.22}$$

It is assumed to be independent of t, so that the Markov chain is homogeneous in time. The conditional probability (3.22) is known as the transition probability function of the chain.

Let us now describe the law of transition from state to state. There are n

players in the game, each having K available actions, of which he chooses exactly one on each play. A *convention of behavior* is a behavioral prescription that assigns one mode of behavior or supergame strategy $\sigma^i \in \Sigma^i$ to each player. Thus, if the players are identified with the integers $1, \ldots, n$ and the strategies for each player with the integers $1, \ldots, K$, then a convention of behavior is represented as an n-tuple of integers selected from among each player's set Σ^i, indexed $1, \ldots, K$, which assigns a strategy choice for each player.

The SBS procedure is executed in the following way. Each player has a mixed strategy determining a probability distribution defined over the set of K available strategies. This induces a probability distribution on the set of K strategies of each player in the game L. From this we can calculate the conditional probability, given the current norm $\mathbf{p}$, of observing a specified convention of behavior as indicated by the actual occurrence of some b^k. This is done by means of the SBS procedure. Indeed, the latter defines an n-tuple of mixed strategies $\mathbf{s} = (s_1, \ldots, s_n)$ for each $\mathbf{p}$. This determines a probability distribution over the set of the K strategy choices of player h. The latter makes a choice of strategy and takes the first step on it, choosing some a_h^k in A_h in that period. The event that player h chooses a strategy whose first step dictates the choice $a_h^k = j$ is defined as the event that, as a result of using the mixed strategy prescribed by $\mathcal{M}$, player h chooses a supergame strategy whose first step prescribes the choice $a_h^k = j$. The induced probability distribution is denoted $(g_{h,j}, j = 1, \ldots, K_h)$, where the latter is defined as

$$q_{h,j} = \text{probability that player } h \text{ chooses a supergame strategy whose}$$
$$\text{prescribed first step is } j, \qquad h = 1, \ldots, n, j = 1, \ldots, K_h \quad (3.23)$$

(where K_h is the cardinality of A_h in Γ). This probability depends on the current state $\mathbf{p}$, so we write $q_{h,j} = q_{h,j}(\mathbf{p})$.

Each player selects a strategy in accordance with the appropriate distribution (3.23). The result of these n random experiments is an n-tuple of integers, each one selected from among $(1, \ldots, K_h)$, or, equivalently, a one-period observation of a particular convention of behavior. The n individual random experiments are assumed to be mutually independent (for a given value of $\mathbf{p}$); thus the probability that n-tuple $b^k = (j_1, \ldots, j_n)$ is observed is the product of probabilities,

$$\prod_{h=1}^{n} q_{h,j_h}(\mathbf{p})$$

Our representative simplex has K corner points, where the first is of the form $(1, 0, \ldots, 0)$, the second of the form $(0, 1, \ldots, 0)$, $\ldots$, and the Kth of the form $(0, \ldots, 1)$. These represent the set of norms in which all other $n - 1$ players believe that the player whose simplex we are observing will use a particular supergame strategy indexed by the n-tuple $b^k \in B$ with probability

1 and all others with probability 0. However, since we are at the same point in each player's simplex, each corner point represents a commonly held belief that the convention of behavior defined by the common adherence to the strategy indexed by $b^k \in B$ in each player's strategy set Σ^i in L will be followed with probability 1. This was depicted in Figure 3.3.

Now order the n-tuples $b^k \in B$ by the index $i = 1, \ldots, K$. If $(j_1, \ldots, j_n)$ is the ith n-tuple in this ordering, we denote the probability of the latter as

$$Q_i(\mathbf{p}) = \prod_{h=1}^{n} q_{h,j_h}(\mathbf{p}) \tag{3.24}$$

$\{Q_i(\mathbf{p}), i = 1, \ldots, K\}$ is a probability distribution on the set of n-tuples.

The rules of transition are as follows. Let $\mathbf{p}$ be the state at time t. An n-tuple is observed at random according to the probability distribution $\{Q_i(\mathbf{p})\}$. Each n-tuple indexes a distinct supergame strategy of the form (*). If the selected n-tuple is of index i, the state $\mathbf{p}'$ at time $t + 1$ is the K-component vector such that

$$p'_i = p_i + \epsilon, \qquad p'_j = p_j - \frac{\epsilon}{K - 1}, \qquad j \neq i \tag{3.25}$$

where $\epsilon > 0$ is an arbitrary small positive number, fixed over time. In other words, the component of $\mathbf{p}$ in the direction of the ith corner $(0, \ldots, 0, 1, 0, \ldots, 0)$ of W is increased by ϵ, and all other components are reduced by equal amounts $\epsilon/(K - 1)$. This rule holds as long as $\mathbf{p}'$ is actually in the simplex, but is modified if the point $\mathbf{p}'$ is actually outside W. We defer the description of this modification.

It follows from the description above that $\mathbf{X}(t)$, $t = 0, 1, \ldots$ is, in fact, a homogeneous Markov process in W. By a suitable choice of ϵ, the state space may be taken to be finite; indeed, the states can be restricted to K-tuples in W whose coordinates are integer multiples of $\epsilon/(K - 1)$. (This does not restrict the smallness of ϵ.) We call $\mathbf{X}(t)$ a random walk because the process moves from a state $\mathbf{p}$ only to another state $\mathbf{p}'$ which is relatively close to it.

Let $\mathbf{X}(t + 1) - \mathbf{X}(t)$ be the vector difference representing the displacement of the state that is the result of the play at time t. It follows from (3.25) that the components of the displacement vector are of the form

$$X_i(t + 1) - X_i(t) = \epsilon \qquad \text{for some } i$$
$$X_j(t + 1) - X_j(t) = \frac{-\epsilon}{K - 1} \qquad \text{for all } j \neq i \tag{3.26}$$

Therefore, the law of transition is determined by the distribution of the random index i for which (3.26) holds. According to (3.24), this distribution is $\{Q_i(\mathbf{p})\}$. It follows that the transition probability function can be expressed in terms of $\{Q_i(\mathbf{p})\}$.

For the purpose of identifying the limiting diffusion process for the given random walk, we compute the mean vector and product moment matrix of $\mathbf{X}(t + 1) - \mathbf{X}(t)$. According to (3.24) and (3.26), $X_i(t + 1) - X_i(t)$ assumes the values ϵ and $-\epsilon/(K - 1)$ with conditional probabilities $Q_i(\mathbf{p})$ and $1 - Q_i(\mathbf{p})$, respectively; hence

$$E[X_i(t + 1) - X_i(t) | \mathbf{X}(t) = \mathbf{p}] = \epsilon \left[Q_i(\mathbf{p}) - \frac{1 - Q_i(\mathbf{p})}{K - 1} \right] \tag{3.27}$$

Similarly, we find that

$$E[(X_i(t + 1) - X_i(t))^2 | \mathbf{X}(t) = \mathbf{p}] = \epsilon^2 \left[Q_i(\mathbf{p}) + \frac{1 - Q_i(\mathbf{p})}{(K - 1)^2} \right] \tag{3.28}$$

If $i \neq j$, the product $(X_i(t + 1) - X_i(t))(X_j(t + 1) - X_j(t))$ assumes two possible values:

$$\frac{\epsilon^2}{(K - 1)^2} \quad \text{with probability } 1 - Q_i(\mathbf{p}) - Q_j(\mathbf{p})$$

$$-\frac{\epsilon^2}{(K - 1)} \quad \text{with probability } Q_i(\mathbf{p}) + Q_j(\mathbf{p})$$

Indeed, the former is assumed if neither index i nor index j is selected, and the latter is assumed if either i or j is selected. It follows that the product moment of the displacement is

$$E[(X_i(t + 1) - X_i(t))(X_j(t + 1) - X_j(t)) | \mathbf{X}(t) = \mathbf{p}]$$
$$= \frac{\epsilon^2}{(K - 1)^2} [1 - KQ_i(\mathbf{p}) - KQ_j(\mathbf{p})] \tag{3.29}$$

We summarize the content of this section by stating that any SBS procedure $\mathcal{M}$ and any norm-updating rule uniquely determine a Markov chain that has the form of a random walk. The payoff function of the game Γ influences the procedure $\mathcal{M}$, which, in turn, determines the transition probabilities of the chain.

3.10 Absorption and first passage times: assumptions for our model

According to the definition of the law of transition in (3.25), the observed state $\mathbf{X}(t)$ constantly changes as long as it moves within the interior of W sufficiently far from the boundary. According to our description of the model in Section 3.6, this may no longer be true when $\mathbf{X}(t)$ reaches the boundary of the simplex, particularly the corner points. A state $\mathbf{p}$ is said to be an *absorbing* state if $\mathbf{X}(t)$ cannot move from $\mathbf{p}$ once it has reached it: $P\{\mathbf{X}(t + 1) = \mathbf{p}' | \mathbf{X}(t) = \mathbf{p}\} = 0$ for $\mathbf{p}' \neq p$. In the opposite case, where $P\{\mathbf{X}(t + 1) = \mathbf{p}' | \mathbf{X}(t) = \mathbf{p}\} > 0$ for some $\mathbf{p}' \neq \mathbf{p}$, $\mathbf{p}$ is not absorbing and $\mathbf{X}(t)$ must eventually move from it. In our model all interior points of W are not absorbing; however, some of the corner points are absorbing.

Let these corner points be denoted

$$\mathbf{e}_1 = (1, 0, \ldots, 0), \quad \mathbf{e}_2 = (0, 1, 0, \ldots, 0), \quad \ldots, \quad \mathbf{e}_K = (0, \ldots, 0, 1) \qquad (3.30)$$

Suppose that there is a positive integer $k \leq K$ such that $\mathbf{e}_1, \ldots, \mathbf{e}_k$ are absorbing and $\mathbf{e}_{k+1}, \ldots, \mathbf{e}_K$ are not absorbing. Suppose also that the rules of the model have been specified not only at all interior points $\mathbf{p}$ whose distance from the boundary of W ensures that the points $\mathbf{p}'$ in (3.25) are also in W, but also at all other points at the boundary or near it. The rules for transition from the latter points may be arbitrary except that they are required to satisfy the following two conditions:

1. They are nonabsorbing except for $\mathbf{e}_1, \ldots, \mathbf{e}_k$.
2. The state $\mathbf{p}'$ cannot be reached in one step from $\mathbf{p}$ if the distance between the two points is greater than $\epsilon(1 + (K - 1)^2)^{1/2}$. [The latter is the distance between successive states that are both in the interior of W; see (3.25).]

Condition 1 is implied by our condition of Bayesian best response satisfactoriness, imposed on $\mathcal{M}$.

Condition 2 restricts the size of the steps prescribed by the norm-updating rule. Two mathematical problems of interest in the model are:

1. *The absorption probability problem:* Find the probability that the process ultimately reaches the point $\mathbf{e}_j$ (and remains there), $j = 1, \ldots, k$.
2. *The expected first-passage-time problem:* Let N represent the first value of t for which $\mathbf{X}(t) = \mathbf{e}_j$, for some $1 \leq j \leq k$. Find $E(N)$, the expected value of N.

Because there are finitely many states in the chain, we may arrange them in a finite sequence $\mathbf{p}_1, \ldots, \mathbf{p}_m$, where m is the number of states. Let $\mathbf{p} = (P_{ij})$ be the $m \times m$ matrix whose entries are the transition probabilities (3.22):

$$P_{ij} = P\{\mathbf{X}(t + 1) = \mathbf{p}_j \mid X(t) = \mathbf{p}_i\}$$

For convenience the states are ordered so that $\mathbf{p}_j = \mathbf{e}_j$, $j = 1, \ldots, k$.

3.11 Absorption and first passage times: general results

A state $\mathbf{p}_h$ is called *transient* if, given that the process is currently at $\mathbf{p}_h$, the probability of ultimately returning to $\mathbf{p}_h$ is less than 1. A necessary and sufficient condition for the state to be transient is that

$$\sum_{n=1}^{\infty} P_{h,h}^{(n)} < \infty \qquad (3.31)$$

where $P_{i,j}^{(n)}$ is the entry (i, j) of the power $\mathbf{P}^n$ of $\mathbf{P}$ (see Feller 1968, chap. 15). The states $\mathbf{p}_1, \ldots, \mathbf{p}_k$ are clearly not transient because they are absorbing states.

Let $f_{h,j}$ be the probability that starting from a transient state $\mathbf{p}_h$, the process is eventually absorbed in $\mathbf{p}_j$, $j = 1, \ldots, k$. Then, for each j, $(f_{h,j})$ satisfies the system of equations

$$f_{h,j} = \sum_{\{i:\ p_i \text{ is transient}\}} \mathbf{P}_{h,i} f_{ij} + \mathbf{P}_{h,j} \tag{3.32}$$

This system always has a nonnegative solution, and the probabilities $(f_{h,j})$ form the minimal nonnegative solution (see Feller 1968, chap. 15). If $\mathbf{p}_h$ is transient, let m_h denote the conditional expected value of N (the first passage time into the set of absorbing states) starting from $\mathbf{p}_h$. Then m_h satisfies the linear system

$$m_h = 1 + \sum_{\{i:\ p_i \text{ transient}\}} P_{hi} m_i \tag{3.33}$$

(see Parzen 1962, chap. 6).

In particular, if all the nonabsorbing states are transient, then with probability 1 the process will eventually enter one of the absorbing states starting from any nonabsorbing state, and the expected first passage times are defined for all the latter states.

By means of systems (3.32) and (3.33), the absorption and first-passage-time problems can, with sufficient patience and computational resources, be explicitly solved. However, this approach does not exploit the special character of our Markov process–that it is a random walk–so that the successive displacements are small. In the next several sections we associate our random walk with an approximating diffusion process and then show that the absorption and first-passage-time problems are identical with problems involving the solution of classical diffusion equations. Consequently, the mathematical prerequisites for the next two sections are greater than those previously encountered.

3.12 The limiting diffusion process

The magnitude of the displacement $\mathbf{X}(t + 1) - \mathbf{X}(t)$ is, in the Euclidean metric in K-space, proportional to ϵ; indeed, by the formula for that metric, we have

$$\|\mathbf{X}(t + 1) - \mathbf{X}(t)\|^2 = \epsilon^2 + \frac{\epsilon^2}{(K - 1)^2}$$

By a limiting process well known in probability theory we will scale the process by reducing the time between successive steps from 1 to ϵ^2, and then let $\epsilon \to 0$. The random walk $\mathbf{X}(t)$, $t = 0, 1, \ldots$, becomes a Markov process $\mathbf{X}(t)$ with a continuous time parameter $t \geq 0$ and with continuous sample functions. Such a process is known as a *diffusion* process. Under very general conditions the characteristics of interest in the random walk (absorption probabilities and expected first passage times) converge in the appropriate sense to the corresponding characteristics of the diffusion process. The characteristics of the latter are identified as solutions of certain partial differential equations; therefore, the solutions of such problems in our model are similarly identified as solutions of such equations. In this way we establish a direct correspondence between our model and well-established models in probability theory and physics. One of the benefits of this correspondence is that the computational methods that are available to solve such partial differential equations for the physicist can now be used by the economist. We expect to illustrate the use of such methods in forthcoming publications.

Our present program in this section will be to identify the class of diffusion processes that arise as limits of the scaled random walk of our model for $\epsilon \rightarrow 0$. A rigorous formulation and proof of a theorem stating the convergence of our random walk to a diffusion process is a very technical matter and would be of possible interest only to the specialist in probability theory. This falls in the domain of the subject of *weak convergence* of measures on separable metric spaces, which has been actively studied for the past several decades [see Billingsley (1968)]. We will not attempt such a proof; instead, we will show only that a certain class of diffusion processes may be obtained in a natural manner as a result of passage to the limit for $\epsilon \rightarrow 0$. The parameters of the diffusion process are obtained directly from the parameters of the model. It will also be shown that the limiting diffusion process is of a well-known and relatively simple form. Finally, we show how the absorption and first-passage-time problems are solved for the diffusion process.

Let $\mathbf{X}(t)$, $t \geq 0$, be a diffusion process assuming values in a Borel set in K-space. In our case this set is W. If $\mathbf{x}$ is a point in W, B is a Borel subset of W, and $t > 0$, the transition probability for the passage from $\mathbf{x}$ at time $h > 0$ into the set B at time $t + h$ is defined as

$$P(t, \mathbf{x}, B) = P[\mathbf{X}(t + h) \in B \,|\, \mathbf{X}(h) = \mathbf{x}] \tag{3.34}$$

and is independent of h. Under general conditions it is well known that the function of $K + 1$ variables

$$u(t, x_1, \dots, x_K) = P(t, \mathbf{x}, B), \qquad \mathbf{x} = (x_1, \dots, x_K)$$

satisfies the backward diffusion equation

$$\frac{\partial u}{\partial t} = \sum_{i=1}^{K} m_i(\mathbf{x}) \frac{\partial u}{\partial x_i} + \frac{1}{2} \sum_{i,j=1}^{K} A_{ij}(\mathbf{x}) \frac{\partial^2 u}{\partial x_i \partial x_j} \tag{3.35}$$

where $m_i(\mathbf{x})$ and $A_{ij}(\mathbf{x})$, $i, j = 1, \dots, K$, are specified functions on W. Under appropriate regularity conditions on m_i and A_{ij}, and suitable boundary conditions on u, (3.35) has a unique solution that determines P in (3.34). Under such circumstances the structure of the diffusion process is determined by the given forms of m_i and A_{ij}. The vector $\mathbf{m}(\mathbf{x}) = (m_i(\mathbf{x}), i = 1, \ldots, K)$ is the vector of *coefficients of drift*. The component $m_i(\mathbf{x})$ is defined as the mean rate of displacement of the ith component of the process at the point $\mathbf{x}$:

$$m_i(\mathbf{x}) = \lim_{h \to 0} \frac{1}{h} E[(X_i(t + h) - X_i(t)) | \mathbf{X}(t) = \mathbf{x}] \tag{3.36}$$

The matrix $(A_{ij}(\mathbf{x}), i, j = 1, \ldots, K)$ is the matrix of *coefficients of diffusion*. The element A_{ij} is the product moment displacement rate of the ith and jth components:

$$A_{ij}(\mathbf{x}) = \lim_{h \to 0} \frac{1}{h} E[(X_i(t + h) - X_i(t))(X_j(t + h)$$
$$- X_j(t)) | \mathbf{X}(t) = \mathbf{x}] \tag{3.37}$$

In considering the diffusion process in the simplex W or the polyhedron V in (3.30), we use the symbol $\mathbf{p}$ for the state (as in Section 3.9) in place of $\mathbf{x}$, so that m_i and A_{ij} are functions of $\mathbf{p}$: $m_i = m_i(\mathbf{p})$ and $A_{ij} = A_{ij}(\mathbf{p})$. The term ϵ^2 is introduced as the length of the time interval between successive plays of the game L, and the variable ϵ is introduced in the family of conditional probability distributions in (3.24):

$Q_i(\mathbf{p}, \epsilon) =$ probability of a step of length ϵ in the direction of the ith
$\qquad\qquad\qquad\qquad$ convention given the current state $\mathbf{p}$ (3.38)

We identify the displacements of the random walk with those of the limiting diffusion process, and calculate m_i and A_{ij} using the limits obtained from (3.27), (3.28), and (3.29) in (3.36) and (3.37). Put $h = \epsilon^2$ in (3.36); then, according to (3.27), we have

$$\lim_{\epsilon \to 0} \frac{1}{\epsilon^2} E[X_i(t + \epsilon^2) - X_i(t) | \mathbf{X}(t) = \mathbf{p}] \tag{3.38}$$
$$= \lim_{\epsilon \to 0} \frac{KQ_i(\mathbf{p}, \epsilon) - 1}{(K - 1)}, \qquad i = 1, \ldots, K$$

Let us assume that the latter limit exists and is finite, and denote it as

$$m_i(\mathbf{p}) = \lim_{\epsilon \to 0} \frac{KQ_i(\mathbf{p}, \epsilon) - 1}{\epsilon(K - 1)} \tag{3.39}$$

The finiteness of the latter limit implies, in particular, that

$$\lim_{\epsilon \to 0} Q_i(\mathbf{p}, \epsilon) = \frac{1}{K} \tag{3.40}$$

This signifies that the mean displacement is locally nearly the same in all K directions, which is a condition of local isotropy. It also follows from (3.39) and the fact that Q_i is a probability distribution that

$$\sum_{i=1}^{K} m_i(\mathbf{p}) = 0 \tag{3.41}$$

We derive $A_{ij}(\mathbf{p})$ in a similar manner. According to (3.28) and (3.40), we have

$$\lim_{\epsilon \to 0} \frac{1}{\epsilon^2} E\{(X_i(t + \epsilon^2) - X_i(t))^2 | \mathbf{X}(t) = \mathbf{p}\}$$

$$= \lim_{\epsilon \to 0} \{Q_i(\mathbf{p}, \epsilon) + \frac{1}{(K-1)^2} [1 - Q_i(\mathbf{p}, \epsilon)]\} = \frac{1}{K-1}$$

Thus, according to definition (3.37), we find that

$$A_{ii}(\mathbf{p}) = \frac{1}{K-1} \tag{3.42}$$

According to (3.29) and definition (3.37), we have for $i \neq j$,

$$A_{ij}(\mathbf{p}) = \lim_{\epsilon \to 0} \frac{1}{\epsilon^2} E[(X_i(t + \epsilon^2) - X_i(t))(X_j(t + \epsilon^2) - X_j(t)) | \mathbf{X}(t) = \mathbf{p}]$$

$$= \lim_{\epsilon \to 0} \frac{1}{(K-1)^2} [1 - KQ_i(\mathbf{p}, \epsilon) - KQ_j(\mathbf{p}, \epsilon)]$$

Thus, by (3.40), we have

$$A_{ij}(\mathbf{p}) = -\frac{1}{(K-1)^2}, \qquad i \neq j \tag{3.43}$$

It follows from (3.42) and (3.43) that the matrix of diffusion coefficients does not depend on $\mathbf{p}$ and is also of a particularly simple form: the elements on the diagonal are all equal to $1/(K-1)$ and those off the diagonal are equal to $-1(K-1)^2$. If we write the diffusion equation (3.35) with the state variables (p_i) in the place of (x_i), we obtain

$$\frac{\partial u}{\partial t} = \sum_{i=1}^{K} m_i(\mathbf{p}) \frac{\partial u}{\partial p_i} + \frac{1}{2(K-1)} \sum_{i=1}^{K} \frac{\partial^2 u}{\partial p_i^2} - \frac{1}{2(K-1)^2} \sum_{i \neq j} \frac{\partial^2 u}{\partial p_i \partial p_j} \tag{3.44}$$

We note that $(m_i(\mathbf{p}), i = 1, \ldots, K)$ is the only unspecified set of functions in (3.44). These functions can, in principle, be computed in terms of the limiting properties of the updating rule. Suppose, as above, that we introduce the variable ϵ in the family of probability distributions (3.23): $q_{h,j} = q_{h,j}(\mathbf{p}, \epsilon)$. Then (3.44) becomes

$$Q_i(\mathbf{p}, \epsilon) = \prod_{h=1}^{n} q_{h,j_h}(\mathbf{p}, \epsilon) \tag{3.45}$$

so $m_i(\mathbf{p})$ is determined by this through (3.39). For example, suppose that there exist numbers $w_{h,j}(\mathbf{p})$, $h = 1, \ldots, n, j = 1, \ldots, m$, such that

$$\lim_{\epsilon \to 0} \frac{K^{1/n}q_{h,j}(\mathbf{p}, \epsilon) - 1}{\epsilon} = w_{h,j}(\mathbf{p}) \tag{3.46}$$

If $Q_i(\mathbf{p}, \epsilon)$ is given by (3.45), then (3.39) is satisfied with

$$m_i(\mathbf{p}) = \sum_{h=1}^{n} \frac{w_{h,j_h}(\mathbf{p})}{K - 1} \tag{3.47}$$

3.13 Transformation of the coordinate system

There are two unrelated complications involving the diffusion process with the diffusion equation (3.44). The first is that the equation is not recognizable as that of a familiar diffusion process. The second is that the state space is restricted to a subset of a $(K - 1)$-dimensional hyperplane, so that it does not move freely in K dimensions. It is mathematically fortuitous that these two problems can be solved together by means of a suitable transformation of the system of coordinates. This is an orthogonal transformation that is used in one of the fundamental methods of classical statistics. By means of this transformation, W is mapped onto a simplex W' in $(K - 1)$-dimensional space and, at the same time, the matrix (A_{ij}) of diffusion coefficients is transformed into a multiple of the identity of order $K - 1$, augmented by 0s to a $K \times K$ matrix. In the new coordinate system we recognize the diffusion process as the "$(K - 1)$-dimensional Wiener process with drift" [see Dynkin (1965)].

Now we describe the transformation in detail. Let $R = (r_{ij})$ be a real orthogonal $K \times K$ matrix such that the last row is the vector with equal components $1/\sqrt{K}$. Such a matrix defines a linear transformation of K-space in the usual way: if $\mathbf{x}$ is a point with coordinates (x_i), then $R\mathbf{x}$ is a point with coordinates $\Sigma_j r_{ij}x_j$, $i = 1, \ldots, K$. The simplex W may be described as the convex hull of the K points $\mathbf{e}_1, \ldots, \mathbf{e}_K$, defined in Section 3.10. Let W' be the image of W under the linear transformation R; then W' is the convex hull of the K images $R\mathbf{e}_1, \ldots, R\mathbf{e}_K$. By the definition of the matrix R, we have

$$r_{Kj} = \frac{1}{\sqrt{K}}, \qquad j = 1, \ldots, K \tag{3.48}$$

It follows from the definition of matrix multiplication that the vectors $R\mathbf{e}_1$, $\ldots$, $R\mathbf{e}_K$ represent the column vectors of R; furthermore, (3.48) implies that the last entry of each column vector is $1/\sqrt{K}$; therefore, W lies in the $(K - 1)$-dimensional subspace of points $(x_1, \ldots, x_K)$ such that $x_K = 1/\sqrt{K}$.

As an example of such a matrix R in four dimensions, we mention the matrix

$$
\begin{bmatrix}
\dfrac{1}{\sqrt{2}} & -\dfrac{1}{\sqrt{2}} & 0 & 0 \\[2mm]
\dfrac{1}{\sqrt{6}} & \dfrac{1}{\sqrt{6}} & -\dfrac{2}{\sqrt{6}} & 0 \\[2mm]
\dfrac{1}{\sqrt{12}} & \dfrac{1}{\sqrt{12}} & \dfrac{1}{\sqrt{12}} & -\dfrac{3}{\sqrt{12}} \\[2mm]
\dfrac{1}{2} & \dfrac{1}{2} & \dfrac{1}{2} & \dfrac{1}{2}
\end{bmatrix}
\tag{3.49}
$$

In the following lemma, the diffusion equation (3.44) is transformed in accordance with the transformation R.

Lemma 3.1: Let R' be the transpose of R, and define $\mathbf{x} = R\mathbf{p}$, $\mathbf{p} \in W$. Let $M_h(\mathbf{x})$, $h = 1, \ldots, K - 1$, be the functions given by the relations

$$
M_h(\mathbf{x}) = \sum_{i=1}^{K} m_i(R'\mathbf{x})r_{hi}, \qquad h = 1, \ldots, K - 1
\tag{3.50}
$$

If u in (3.44) is considered to be a function of t and $x_1, \ldots, x_K$ (where the latter are functions of $p_1, \ldots, p_K$), then u satisfies

$$
\frac{\partial u}{\partial t} = \sum_{h=1}^{K-1} M_h(\mathbf{x}) \frac{\partial u}{\partial x_h} + \frac{K}{2(K - 1)^2} \sum_{h=1}^{K-1} \frac{\partial^2 u}{\partial x_h^2}
\tag{3.51}
$$

Proof. See the appendix to this chapter.

Equation (3.51) is the diffusion equation for the diffusion process in $(K - 1)$-space known as the Wiener process with drift coefficient vector $(M_h(\mathbf{x}))$. According to the definition of the drift coefficient vector in (3.36), $M_h(\mathbf{x})$ is the mean rate of displacement of the component of index h at the point $\mathbf{x}$. The matrix of diffusion coefficients in (3.51) is $K/(K - 1)^2$ times the identity of order $K - 1$. In the particular case where $M_h(\mathbf{x})$ is identically equal to 0 for $h = 1, \ldots, K - 1$, the diffusion process reduces to the ordinary Wiener process in $K - 1$ dimensions.

The result of this mathematical discussion is that the class of diffusion processes which arise as limits of the random walk for our model consists of processes with a diffusion equation that can be transformed into the canonical forms (3.51) or (3.52). The only arbitrary functions in the equations are (M_h). Under appropriate boundary conditions on u and suitable regularity conditions on the functions M_h, (3.51) and (3.52) have unique solutions that represent the transition probability functions of the corresponding processes. The general description of such conditions forms the core of much of the modern theory of diffusion processes, and it is certainly beyond the scope of the current investigation [see Dynkin (1965)]. However, in Section 3.14 we propose a simple set of boundary conditions suitable for certain examples and show how they can be used in solving the diffusion equation. Finally, we mention that the most general and usable regularity condition on the drift function M_h is that they be bounded on the closure of the state space and satisfy a uniform Hölder condition. The latter means that there exists a positive finite B such that $|M_h(\mathbf{x}) - M_h(\mathbf{x}')| \leq B\|x - x'\|$ for all $\mathbf{x}$ and $\mathbf{x}'$ and indices h (see Dynkin 1965, vol. I, p. 4).

3.14 Application of the theory of diffusion processes to the solution of supergame problems

Having completed the identification of our model with a diffusion process we now consider the formulation and solutions of the problems in our model in the framework of diffusion theory. The diffusion equation, and, in particular, the coefficients of drift and diffusion, describe the behavior of the process in the interior of W. To complete the description of the process, we also have to define the behavior of the process at the boundary of W. (The same is true for the process of rank k in V.) We would like to describe a set of boundary conditions for our diffusion process that reflect reasonable conditions for the original supergame.

One of the remarkable results of the modern theory of diffusion processes is that the behavior of the process at the boundary is one of only a few possible types: stopping, absorption, reflection, diffusion along the boundary, and the various combinations of these [see Dynkin (1965, vol. I, p. 7)]. This result is due to Feller (1952, 1957) in the one-dimensional case, and to Wentzell (1959, 1960) in the K-dimensional case, for $K \geq 2$.

Now we shall describe a class of boundary conditions that we will assume for the diffusion process in W representing our supergame. Let us assume that the process is of full rank. (The discussion for a process of partial rank is similar.) Suppose that the k corner points $\mathbf{e}_1, \ldots, \mathbf{e}_k$ are absorbing, for some k, $1 \leq k \leq K$; and that $\mathbf{e}_{k+1}, \ldots, \mathbf{e}_K$ are not absorbing.

We modify the simplex W in a small neighborhood of each of its absorbing corner points. Let $S_1, \ldots S_k$ be spheres centered at $\mathbf{e}_1, \ldots, \mathbf{e}_k$, respectively, and of small radii $r_1, \ldots, r_k$. The simplex is modified by the excision of the absorbing points and all points of W within the corresponding spheres; thus the intersections $S_1 \cap W, \ldots, S_k \cap W$ form part of the boundary of the modified simplex. We assume that:

1. All points of the boundary that belong to one of the spheres $S_1, \ldots, S_k$ are absorbing points. Absorption at the sphere centered at $\mathbf{e}_j$ signifies that the process terminates with the selection of the convention of behavior correspond-

ing to e_j, $j = 1, \ldots, k$. The introduction of the spherical boundary around each absorbing point has the interpretation that the process terminates at the convention associated with that corner if the norm **p** comes sufficiently close to the corresponding absorbing point. The mathematical purpose of the introduction of the spherical boundary is to ensure that the absorbing point can, in fact, be reached from the other points in the interior of the simplex. Indeed, without this kind of boundary, the corner points are not necessarily accessible from the interior, and the process wanders indefinitely in the interior of the region.

2. At all other points of the boundary of the modified simplex, the process has probability 1 of returning to the interior of the region. In other words, the process is sure to remain "alive" at such points.

These boundary conditions are illustrated in Figure 3.4 for a two-dimensional simplex.

These two boundary conditions can be satisfied by imposing some relatively simple conditions on the SBS procedure $\mathcal{M}$. In fact, if we impose two mild conditions on the SBS procedure $\mathcal{M}$, the diffusion process associated with our supergame model will, under technical mathematical conditions on the scaling of the random walk, also satisfy the two boundary conditions stated above. These two conditions on $\mathcal{M}$ are:

Condition 1: δ-ball sufficiency. Let e^* be a vertex of W corresponding to a pure strategy equilibrium point σ^* of L. There exists a small number $\delta > 0$ such that every point **p** of W within the ball of e^* of radius δ is mapped by $\mathcal{M}$ onto σ^*.

This condition means that $\mathcal{M}$ instructs the players to use a particular pure equilibrium strategy as soon as the players all believe that the latter strategy is *very likely* to be used (i.e., very close to 1). This is a natural stochastic continuity condition and is related to the discs shown in Figure 3.4. In short, it states that if all players feel "almost certain" that a particular equilibrium convention of behavior σ^* will be followed, they will indeed follow it. (In this book we do not attempt to discuss the technical mathematical conditions on the scaling of the random walk.)

Condition 2: Nonequilibrium positiveness. For all i in N and for all norms of distance at least δ from any of the corners $e_1, \ldots, e_K$, the s_i specified by $\mathcal{M}$ for any player i has all positive components.

This signifies that for any player, and for any norm outside the spheres S_1, $\ldots, S_K$, the SBS procedure prescribes a positive probability to *every* pure strategy. (The probabilities assigned to some of these may be, of course, very small.)

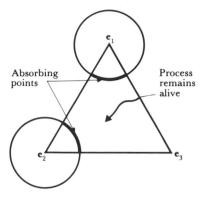

Figure 3.4. A class of boundary conditions for the supergame diffusion.

This condition guarantees that, at all norms not in any of the spheres, the process will "stay alive." The interpretation of this condition is that unless a convention has been established as *the* convention of behavior for a particular situation, in which case all players are almost certain that it will be followed by all others, there is always a positive probability that any player will follow any given mode of behavior. If you wish, you may interpret these small but positive probabilities as mistake probabilities, stating that there is always a finite (although small) probability of any player acting irrationally if no equilibrium convention of behavior has been established.

As noted in our description of the original model, the initial state is the point in W with equal coordinates $1/K$. (We note that the image of this point under the transformation R is the point whose first $K - 1$ coordinates are equal to 0 and whose Kth coordinate is $1/\sqrt{K}$. See the appendix to this chapter.) The problems to be solved are the diffusion analogues of the corresponding problems described for the random walk in Section 3.11:

1. *The absorption probability problem.* Determine the distribution of the position of the terminal state of the game over the absorbing parts of the boundary. In particular, find the probabilities of absorption on $S_1, \ldots,$ S_k, respectively.
2. *The expected-first-passage-time problem.* Determine the expected time to reach one of the spheres from the initial state.

In Section 3.11 these problems were solved for the finite Markov chain by setting up systems of linear equations and identifying the solutions of these systems as the corresponding absorption probabilities and expected first passage times. The procedure is similar for the diffusion process: here the system of linear equations is replaced by a partial differential equation obtained from the diffusion equation.

Next, we briefly sketch the well-known method of solving these problems. Let G be a domain in K-dimensional space and let G' be its boundary. Suppose that G' can be decomposed into three disjoint sets A, B, and C. Let $X(t)$, $t \geq 0$, be a diffusion process in $G \cup G'$ with the diffusion equation (3.44). Suppose that A and B have disjoint closures, so that they are mutually separated by some open set. Let $f(\mathbf{x})$ be the probability that the process starting at x reaches the set A before it reaches B; then $f(\mathbf{x})$ *satisfies the partial differential equation obtained from (3.45) by setting the right-hand member equal to 0:*

$$\sum_{i=1}^{K} m_i(\mathbf{x}) \frac{\partial f}{\partial x_i} + \frac{1}{2} \sum_{i,j=1}^{K} A_{ij}(\mathbf{x}) \frac{\partial^2 f}{\partial x_i \partial x_j} = 0 \qquad (3.52)$$

with the boundary condition

$$f(\mathbf{x}) = 1, \quad \mathbf{x} \in A, \qquad f(\mathbf{x}) = 0, \quad \mathbf{x} \in B \qquad (3.53)$$

Let $f_j(\mathbf{x})$, $j = 1, \ldots, k$, be the probability that the process, starting at a point $\mathbf{x}$ in the interior of the state space, is absorbed at the corresponding sphere S_j, $j = 1, \ldots, k$. Setting $A_j = W \cap S_j$ and $B_j = W \cap (\cup_{i \neq j} S_i)$, we find that $f_j(x)$ satisfies (3.52) with the boundary condition (3.53).

The boundary condition (3.53) is generally not sufficient to ensure a unique solution of (3.52) because it does not specify the behavior of f on the remaining portion C of the boundary. The boundary condition on C is specified by the assumed properties of the process on that set. For example, if we assume that the process is reflected along the normal at all points of C, the additional boundary condition for (3.52) is

$$\frac{\partial f}{\partial n}(\mathbf{x}) = 0, \quad \mathbf{x} \in C \qquad (3.54)$$

where $\partial f / \partial n$ is the derivative in the normal direction.

Suppose, again that G is a domain in K-space and that G' is a portion of the boundary of G that is absorbing. We also assume that the process, starting from any point $\mathbf{x}$ in G, is sure to be ultimately absorbed at some point of G'; then $g(\mathbf{x})$ *satisfies the partial differential equation obtained from (3.35) by setting the right-hand member of (3.35) equal to* -1:

$$\sum_{i=1}^{K} m_i(\mathbf{x}) \frac{\partial g}{\partial x_i} + \frac{1}{2} \sum_{i,j=1}^{K} A_{ij}(\mathbf{x}) \frac{\partial^2 g}{\partial x_i \partial x_j} = -1 \qquad (3.55)$$

with the boundary condition

$$g(\mathbf{x}) = 0, \quad \mathbf{x} \in G' \qquad (3.56)$$

As for (3.52), the condition (3.56) is generally not sufficient to ensure a unique solution unless G' forms the complete boundary of G.

A precise discussion of (3.52) and (3.55) may be found in Dynkin (1965, p. 5).

3.15 An example

In this section we demonstrate explicitly how one goes from the analysis of the supergame to the diffusion process with its diffusion equation.

Consider the following simple coordination game, which will be iterated by two players:

$$\Gamma = I \begin{bmatrix} \alpha_1, B_1 & 0, 0 \\ 0, 0 & \alpha_2, B_2 \end{bmatrix}, \qquad \alpha_1, \alpha_2, B_1, B_2 > 0$$

Now we can define four supergame strategies for each player in this game as follows:

$$\Sigma^1 = (\sigma^1[a_1^1/a_2^1], \sigma^1[a_1^1/a_2^2], \sigma^1[a_1^2/a_2^1], \sigma^1[a_1^2/a_2^2])$$
$$\Sigma^2 = (\sigma^2[a_2^1/a_1^1], \sigma^2[a_2^2/a_1^1], \sigma^2[a_2^1/a_1^2], \sigma^2[a_2^2/a_1^2])$$

in which, say, strategy $\sigma^i[a_i^1/a_j^1]$ states that player i will choose strategy a_i^1 as long as player j chooses strategy a_j^1 and if j ever deviates, he will choose strategy a_i^1, meaning that he will choose strategy a_i^1 no matter what j does. Now, let us assume that since the players only received positive payoffs when they both choose the same strategy, the static Bayesian solution procedure dictates that for any $\mathbf{p} \in W$ (a three-dimensional unit simplex with four corner points), each player chooses between behaving according to $\sigma^i[a_i^1/a_j^1]$ and $\sigma^i[a_i^2/a_j^2]$, $i = 1$, 2, only (i.e., puts positive probability weight only on the strategies associated with the undisguised equilibria points of L). Consequently, if we index the players by $h = 1, 2$ and the two supergame strategies that they will put positive weight on as $j = 1, 2$, we can define $q_{h,j}$ as the probability defined by the static Bayesian solution procedure dictating that player h use strategy j. Before specifying a specific functional form for the static Bayesian solution procedure that would define $q_{h,j}$ at each $\mathbf{p} \in W$, let us start more generally by stating that the weight attached to the choice of supergame strategy $j = 1, 2$ by player $h = 1, 2$ is a function, $w_{h,j}$, of the norm $\mathbf{p} = (p_1, p_2, p_3, p_4) \in W$ denoted $w_{h,j}(p_1, p_2, p_3, p_4)$ such that the probability defined is

$$q_{h,j} = \tfrac{1}{2}(1 + \epsilon w_{h,j}) \tag{3.57}$$

Without loss of generality we can take ϵ to be so small that $\epsilon w < 1$. Since $q_{h,1} = 1 - q_{h,2}$, $h = 1, 2$, we write $w_1 = w_{11}$, $w_2 = w_{21}$, and the probabilities in (3.57) may be written as

$$
\begin{aligned}
q_{11} &= \tfrac{1}{2}(1 + \epsilon w_1) \\
q_{12} &= \tfrac{1}{2}(1 - \epsilon w_1) \\
q_{21} &= \tfrac{1}{2}(1 + \epsilon w_2) \\
q_{22} &= \tfrac{1}{2}(1 - \epsilon w_2)
\end{aligned}
\tag{3.58}
$$

For simplicity, define the four undisguised conventions as $(1, 1)$, $(2, 2)$, $(1, 2)$, and $(2, 1)$, respectively, where, for example, $(1, 1)$ represents the convention in which player 1 chooses $\sigma^1[a_1^1/a_2^1]$ while player 2 chooses $\sigma^2[a_2^1/a_1^1]$, or

$$(1, 1) = \sigma(a_1^1, a_2^1) = (\sigma^1[a_1^1/a_2^1], \sigma^2[a_2^1/a_1^1])$$

The four vertices of the simplex W represent norms of behavior in which the players expect these conventions to be followed with probability 1 and can be written as

$$\begin{aligned}
\mathbf{e}_1 &= (1, 0, 0, 0)\\
\mathbf{e}_2 &= (0, 1, 0, 0)\\
\mathbf{e}_3 &= (0, 0, 1, 0)\\
\mathbf{e}_4 &= (0, 0, 0, 1)
\end{aligned}$$

respectively. The functions $m_i(p_1, p_2, p_3, p_4)$ represent the coefficients of drift in the direction of $\mathbf{e}_i$, $i = 1, 2, 3, 4$. By applying (3.36) to the specific form (3.58), we obtain

$$\begin{aligned}
m_1 &= \tfrac{1}{3}(w_1 + w_2)\\
m_2 &= -\tfrac{1}{3}(w_1 + w_2)\\
m_3 &= \tfrac{1}{3}(w_1 - w_2)\\
m_4 &= \tfrac{1}{3}(w_2 - w_1)
\end{aligned} \tag{3.59}$$

Now let R be the matrix (3.49). The images of $\mathbf{e}_1, \ldots, \mathbf{e}_4$ (in the three-dimensional subspace) are the points $\mathbf{f}_i$ with coordinates

$$\mathbf{f}_1 = \begin{bmatrix} \dfrac{1}{\sqrt{2}} \\[2mm] \dfrac{1}{\sqrt{6}} \\[2mm] \dfrac{1}{\sqrt{12}} \end{bmatrix} \quad \mathbf{f}_2 = \begin{bmatrix} -\dfrac{1}{\sqrt{2}} \\[2mm] \dfrac{1}{\sqrt{6}} \\[2mm] \dfrac{1}{\sqrt{12}} \end{bmatrix} \quad \mathbf{f}_3 = \begin{bmatrix} 0 \\[2mm] -\dfrac{2}{\sqrt{6}} \\[2mm] \dfrac{1}{\sqrt{12}} \end{bmatrix} \quad \mathbf{f}_4 = \begin{bmatrix} 0 \\[2mm] 0 \\[2mm] -\dfrac{3}{\sqrt{12}} \end{bmatrix} \tag{3.60}$$

respectively. The functions M_h obtained from (m_i) by means of the transformation (3.50) are

$$M_1 = \left(\frac{\sqrt{2}}{3}\right)(w_1 + w_2)$$

$$M_2 = \left(\frac{2}{3\sqrt{6}}\right)(w_2 - w_1) \tag{3.61}$$

$$M_3 = \left(\frac{2}{3\sqrt{3}}\right)(w_1 - w_2)$$

The variables x_1, x_2, and x_3 defined in Section 3.13 are obtained from the p's by applying the matrix (3.49).

Let us now make this more specific by defining the exact static Bayesian solution procedure to be used by both players that will define the $w_{h,j}$ functions specified in (3.58).

The state space of the process is the simplex W whose corner points are associated with the four conventions $(1, 1)$, $(2, 2)$, $(1, 2)$, and $(2, 1)$. Now it is obvious from Γ that the only supergame equilibria are the conventions $(1, 1)$ and $(2, 2)$, and let us denote the corners of W associated with these points as e_1 and e_2. Consequently, place small spheres of radius δ at these points, and from the assumption of δ-ball sufficiency we know that absorption occurs when one or the other of these spheres is reached. Let Π_1 and Π_2 be the payoffs to player 1 in game L at conventions $(1, 1)$ and $(2, 2)$, respectively (the undisguised equilibrium conventions). Similarly, let χ_1 and χ_2 be the payoffs to player 2 in L at these same conventions. What we are going to assume is that at any norm $p \in W$ the static Bayesian solution procedure instructs each player to give positive weight only to supergame strategies associated with the undisguised equilibrium conventions $(1, 1)$ and $(2, 2)$ and that the probability weights attached to these strategies depend only on the payoffs to be derived at these conventions and the distance of the norm from the corners associated with them (i.e., e_1 and e_2), measured in the Euclidean metrics. It is like a gravity procedure with attracting points at e_1 and e_2. This static Bayesian solution procedure will define the functions w_1 and w_2 that specify the q's in (3.58).

Let us assume that

$$w_1 = \frac{\Pi_1}{\Pi_1 + \Pi_2} (\|p - e_2\|^2 - \|p - e_1\|^2) \tag{3.62}$$

$$w_2 = \frac{\chi_1}{\chi_1 + \chi_2} (\|p - e_2\|^2 - \|p - e_1\|^2) \tag{3.63}$$

Put $\Pi = \Pi_1/(\Pi_1 + \Pi_2)$ and $\chi = \chi_1/(\chi_1 + \chi_2)$; then it follows directly from the definition that

$$w_1 = 2\Pi(p_1 - p_2) \tag{3.64}$$
$$w_2 = 2\chi(p_1 - p_2)$$

It follows from (11.16) that

$$(m_i) = \tfrac{2}{3}(p_1 - p_2) \begin{bmatrix} \Pi + \chi \\ -\Pi - \chi \\ \Pi - \chi \\ -\Pi + \chi \end{bmatrix} \tag{3.65}$$

Since $p = R'x$, we find that

$$p_1 - p_2 = \sqrt{2}x_1 \tag{3.66}$$

Therefore, it follows from (3.61) and (3.64) that the M-functions are

$$M_1(\mathbf{x}) = \frac{4}{3} (\Pi + \chi)x_1$$

$$M_2(\mathbf{x}) = \frac{4\sqrt{2}}{3\sqrt{6}} (\chi - \Pi)x_1 \tag{3.67}$$

$$M_3(\mathbf{x}) = \frac{4\sqrt{2}}{3\sqrt{3}} (\Pi - \chi)x_1$$

so that these are functions of x_1 alone. This is not surprising. Indeed, the two equilibrium points in the transformed simplex, $\mathbf{f}_1$ and $\mathbf{f}_2$ in (3.60), differ only in the sign of their first coordinates. The diffusion equation (3.51) assumes the particular form

$$\frac{\partial u}{\partial t} = \frac{4}{3} (\Pi + \chi)x_1 \frac{\partial u}{\partial x_1} + \frac{4\sqrt{2}}{3\sqrt{6}} (\chi - \Pi)x_1 \frac{\partial u}{\partial x_2}$$

$$+ \frac{4\sqrt{2}}{3\sqrt{3}} (\Pi - \chi)x_1 \frac{\partial u}{\partial x_3} + \frac{2}{9} \left(\frac{\partial^2 u}{\partial x_1^2} + \frac{\partial^2 u}{\partial x_2^2} + \frac{\partial^2 u}{\partial x_3^2} \right) \tag{3.68}$$

which is all that need be solved to calculate the absorption probabilities of our model. Although an analytic solution does not exist for this particular partial differential equation, a numerical solution can be found and the desired absorption probabilities calculated for every set of parameter values.

Appendix: Details of the proof of Lemma 3.1 and associated results

Let R be a real orthogonal $K \times K$ matrix with $R = (r_{ij})$. Let R' be the transpose; then $RR' = I$ (identity), so that

$$\sum_{k=1}^{K} r_{ik}r_{jk} = \delta_{ij} \qquad \text{(Kronecker delta)} \tag{3.69}$$

If the last row has equal components $1/\sqrt{K}$, that is,

$$r_{Kj} = \frac{1}{\sqrt{K}}, \qquad j = 1, \ldots, K \tag{3.70}$$

then it follows from (3.69) and (3.70) that

$$\sum_{j=1}^{K} r_{ij} = 0, \qquad i = 1, \ldots, K - 1 \tag{3.71}$$

Put $\mathbf{x} = (x_1, \ldots, x_K)$ and $\mathbf{p} = (p_1, \ldots, p_K)$; suppose that $\mathbf{x} = R\mathbf{p}$ defines an orthogonal transformation of the variables; then $\partial x_h/\partial p_i = r_{hi}$. According to the chain rule for partial derivatives, we have

$$\frac{\partial u}{\partial p_i} = \sum_{h=1}^{K} \frac{\partial u}{\partial x_h} r_{hi} \tag{3.72}$$

$$\frac{\partial^2 u}{\partial p_i \partial p_j} = \sum_{h,k=1}^{K} \frac{\partial^2 u}{\partial x_h \partial x_k} r_{hi} r_{kj}, \qquad i,j = 1, \ldots, K \tag{3.73}$$

Equation (3.69) implies that $\mathbf{p} = R'\mathbf{x}$, so that (3.72) implies that

$$\sum_{i=1}^{K} m_i(\mathbf{p}) \frac{\partial u}{\partial p_i} = \sum_{h=1}^{K} \left[\sum_{i=1}^{K} m_i(R'\mathbf{x}) r_{hi} \right] \frac{\partial u}{\partial x_h} \tag{3.74}$$

The term of index $h = K$ on the right-hand side of (3.74) is equal to 0. Indeed, (3.70) implies that

$$\sum_{i=1}^{K} m_i(R'\mathbf{x}) r_{Ki} = \frac{1}{\sqrt{K}} \sum_{i=1}^{K} m_i(R'\mathbf{x})$$

which, by (3.41), is equal to 0.

If we put $i = j$ in (3.73) and sum over i, we obtain

$$\sum_{i=1}^{K} \frac{\partial^2 u}{\partial p_i^2} = \sum_{h,k=1}^{K} \frac{\partial^2 u}{\partial x_h \partial x_k} \left[\sum_{i=1}^{K} r_{hi} r_{ki} \right]$$

and the latter, according to (3.69), is equal to $\sum_{i=1}^{K} \partial_2 u / \partial x_i^2$; therefore,

$$\sum_{i=1}^{K} \frac{\partial^2 u}{\partial p_i^2} = \sum_{i=1}^{K} \frac{\partial^2 u}{\partial x_i^2} \tag{3.75}$$

which is the well-known result that the Laplacean is invariant under orthogonal transformations.

Let us now substitute the value for r_{Ki} [from (3.70)] on the right-hand side of (3.73):

$$\sum_{h,k=1}^{K} \frac{\partial^2 u}{\partial x_h \partial x_k} r_{hi} r_{kj} + \frac{1}{\sqrt{K}} \sum_{h=1}^{K-1} \frac{\partial^2 u}{\partial x_h \partial x_K} r_{hi}$$
$$+ \frac{1}{\sqrt{K}} \sum_{k=1}^{K-1} \frac{\partial^2 u}{\partial x_K \partial x_k} r_{kj} + \frac{1}{K} \frac{\partial^2 u}{\partial x_K^2}$$

Fix j, and sum over $i \neq j$; then, according to (3.71), the sum is equal to

$$- \sum_{h,k=1}^{K-1} \frac{\partial^2 u}{\partial x_h \partial x_k} r_{hj} r_{kj} - \frac{1}{\sqrt{K}} \sum_{h=1}^{K-1} \frac{\partial^2 u}{\partial x_h \partial x_K} r_{hj}$$
$$+ \frac{K-1}{\sqrt{K}} \sum_{k=1}^{K-1} \frac{\partial^2 u}{\partial x_K \partial x_k} r_{kj} + \frac{K-1}{K} \frac{\partial^2 u}{\partial x_K^2}$$

Now sum over $j = 1, \ldots, K$; then, according to (3.69) and (3.71), the sum is equal to

$$-\sum_{h=1}^{K-1} \frac{\partial^2 u}{\partial x_h^2} + (K-1)\frac{\partial^2 u}{\partial x_K^2}$$

It follows that

$$\sum_{i,j=1,i\neq j}^{K} \frac{\partial^2 u}{\partial p_i \partial p_j} = -\sum_{h=1}^{K-1} \frac{\partial^2 u}{\partial x_h^2} + (K-1)\frac{\partial^2 u}{\partial x_K^2} \tag{3.76}$$

By the remark following (3.74) and by direct substitution from (3.74), (3.75), and (3.76) into (3.44), we find that the latter equation assumes the form (3.51).

In section 3.14 it was noted that if $\mathbf{p}$ is the point with equal coordinates $1/K$, then its image $R\mathbf{p}$ is the point whose first $K-1$ coordinates are equal to 0 and whose Kth coordinate is $1/\sqrt{K}$. This follows directly by application of (3.70) and (3.71).

4 Information and social institutions

At this point in our discussion we have defined the type of problem whose solution requires the creation of a social institution and have discussed the actual process of institution creation by depicting it as a Markovian diffusion process whose absorbing points coresond to stable social institutions. This discussion has begged some very important questions: What function do social and economic institutions serve that could not be fulfilled in their absence? Exactly why are they efficient, if indeed they ever are?

The answer that we give is simple. Social and economic institutions are informational devices that supplement the informational content of economic systems when competitive prices do not carry sufficient information to totally decentralize and coordinate economic activities. More precisely, we see that although prices convey information concerning the relative scarcity of social resources and thereby create an incentive system for agents to economize, social institutions convey information about the expected actions of other agents when these actions are not perfectly coordinated by prices and consequently create incentives for such coordinated activity. In addition, we see that institutions tend to "codify memory" for the agents in the economy and thereby transform the game they are playing from a game of imperfect recall into one that has what we will call *institution-assisted perfect recall*. This transformation allows a considerable amount of informational efficiency, in that it permits the agents in the economy to employ stationary behavioral strategies in their play of the game and such strategies are highly efficient informationally. This will be accomplished by referring to a simple model of a two-person two-good Edgeworth barter economy. With the help of this model we hope to present all of the salient aspects of the problem.

Before we do this, however, let us pause briefly and investigate some properties of games in extensive form, because this information will come in handy later.

109

4.1 Games in extensive form

Games are abstract sets of rules constricting behavior and defining payoffs for players in a given situation of strategic interdependence. Consequently, a formal description of a game must consist of several components. First, we must, of course, know the set of agents called "players" who will be participating in the game. Let N be the set of players and index N as $i = 0, 1, 2, \ldots, n$, where 0 indicates the player called "chance" and $i = 1, 2, \ldots, n$ indicates what we will call "personal" players. Once the players are identified, however, the rules of the game should define the sequence of moves or, put differently, the rules should specify whose turn it is to take an action and the set of alternative actions available to him at each of his moves. In addition, since chance is a player, the rules should specify when chance moves, the set of alternatives available to him, and the probability with which any of the alternatives that he could determine could result. For example, in poker the rules dictate who is allowed to bid, call, ask for cards, raise, and so on, and these rules are defined unambiguously. In addition, because the first move in any honest card game is a shuffle and a deal, chance is assumed to make the first move. With an honest deck we can determine what the probability is that any given set of hands is dealt, using only the rules of classical probability. Consequently, the alternatives of the chance player (the set of hands he could determine) at his move are clearly stated together with the associated probabilities.

Two more pieces of information are needed, however, before a game can be considered to be fully described. First the rules of the game must define the information available to any player at any one of his moves. In other words, they must specify what a player knows about the previous moves of the other players when it is his turn to choose an alternative. If he knows all previous moves, including chance moves, the game is one of "perfect information," whereas if he is ignorant of any past move or set of moves, the game is one of "imperfect information." For example, chess is a game of perfect information since all moves are made in the open and in plain view of each player. Consequently, when it is a given player's turn to move, he knows all previous moves that have taken place before him, including his own. Poker, however, is not a game of perfect information because the very first move of the game (the chance deal move) is secret. In other words, when a player moves in poker he does not know the very first move of the game (the hands dealt to his opponents). Finally, the abstract collection of rules being discussed becomes a game when a set of outcomes are associated with each sequence of alternatives chosen by the players at their moves and a set of n utility payoffs are associated with each outcome. In other words, a game is fully described when each player's turn to move is unambiguously known, the set of alternative actions available to him at each move is defined, the information at his disposal when he moves is specified, and a set of payoffs is associated with each sequence of alternatives. When

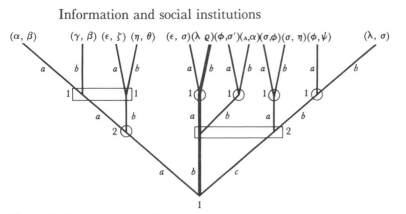

Figure 4.1. A game in extensive form.

all of this information is available, the situation under investigation can be called a game in extensive form.

There is a convenient way to represent a game in extensive form and that is to depict it as a connected graph with a distinguished vertex or a *game tree*. To do this, consider the game tree describing a two-person game shown in Figure 4.1. This game tree completely defines a two-person game. It is composed of a set of nodes called moves, in which each node is indexed by the player whose turn it is to act at that node. Consequently, the set of all nodes is partitioned into "player sets," each indexed by a player and indicating that at these nodes it is a particular player's turn to act. The arcs eminating from a given node indicate the alternatives available to the player whose turn it is to move. For instance, in this game player 1 moves first and has three alternatives to choose from. After he has chosen, player 2 moves and must choose one of two alternatives. Then player 1 moves again, at which point he has only two alternatives to choose from, and finally, depending on the path of the play of the game, a payoff is associated with each terminal vertex or node of the tree. As a result, the tree indicates the moves, alternatives, and payoffs of the game.

In addition, notice that the set of nodes indexed by player 2's index is subpartitioned into two sets containing one and two nodes, respectively. The elements of this subpartition are called the "information sets" for player 2 and indicate the information available to him at his move. This is done very simply. Notice that if player 1 chose alternative *a*, then by circling the node at the end of arc *a* alone, we indicate that player 2 knows unambiguously what player 1 did on his previous move. However, if player 1 chooses alternative *b* or *c*, then by jointly circling the nodes at ends of these arcs we indicate that player 2 cannot distinguish when *b* or *c* was chosen. He cannot differentiate which node in that information set he is at and therefore has imperfect information when it is his turn to move. Similarly, at player 1's second move, the information sets are such that if he chooses *a* on his first move, he will not be able to distinguish

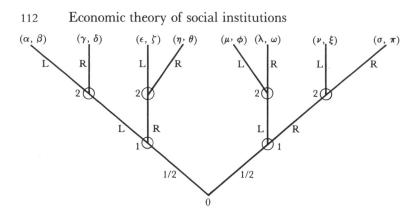

Figure 4.2. A game of perfect information.

whether player 2 chose alternative *a* or *b* at his first move but is able to distinguish what player 2 did at his second move if he himself chose *b* or *c* to start the game. The dark line through the game tree indicates one "play" of this game, which emanates from the starting point and ends at a terminal node. It depicts the sequence of alternatives chosen at the various information sets and associates a utility pair to each terminal node corresponding to a separate sequence. The association of a payoff pair with each sequence of alternative choices is represented as a payoff function for the game.

From our description of a player's information set it should be obvious that if all information sets of players consist of one node and one node only, then when any player moves he knows exactly where he is on the game tree and consequently knows all the moves made by all players (including chance and himself) before him. Consider Figure 4.2. Here chance moves first and has a 50:50 chance of taking one of two actions. Player 1, in full knowledge of chance's move, chooses left or right; then player 2, in full knowledge of both the chance player and player 1, makes his move. As a result of these three moves, a payoff is determined. Because the information sets are single-element sets, the game is one of perfect information, which means that at any player's information set, he knows all of the moves made prior to his. If all information sets are not single-element information sets, the game is one of imperfect information.

In this chapter we are concerned with a different type of informational distinction, which will be of vital importance for a full understanding of the role of social institutions. This distinction is one between games of "perfect recall" and games of "imperfect recall." A game of perfect recall is merely one in which whenever a player makes a move, he remembers all of *his* previous moves, although he may be uncertain about the previous moves of the other players. In games of imperfect recall, when a player moves he may not be able

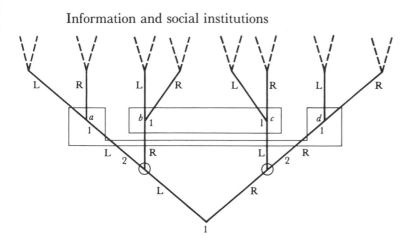

Figure 4.3. A game of imperfect recall.

to remember one or more of his own previous moves. In other words, games of perfect and imperfect recall refer to how much a player remembers about *his own* previous actions in the game, whereas games of perfect and imperfect information consider not only if a player remembers what he himself did but also what all other players did. Consequently, all games of imperfect recall are automatically games of imperfect information (because information about one's own past moves is imperfect), but the converse need not be true, because all players may have perfect knowledge about themselves but still be ignorant of how others have chosen to move in the past. To illustrate this point, let us consider Figure 4.3. Notice that at player 1's second move he is unable to distinguish what he did at his first move because the information sets at that move contain nodes that could have been reached by either an L move or an R move at move 1.

It may seem odd that a player can have periodic amnesia when playing a game and systematically forget what he himself did previously. Although this would indeed be odd for individual players, it is natural if the players we are observing are actually teams of agents in which each agent moves at a different information set of the player of which he is a member. Clearly, if the players find it hard to communicate, it may be that the player is not fully informed about his own past behavior. The standard example here is the situation that exists in bridge in which a player (composed of two partners) periodically forgets the cards held by one of his team members when it is his turn to play. The signaling aspect of information sets in games of imperfect recall is singularly appropriate here.[1] For our institutional problem, it will be natural to think of societies or temporal economies as teams of nonoverlapping generational agents. Consequently, in that context questions of perfect and imperfect recall naturally arise, because we must ask what generations of agents who are alive today remember the actions of their predecessors.

For the reader who is not totally familiar with game theory, it must seem odd that we have spent a considerable amount of time talking about games and have not yet mentioned the word "strategy" at all. To rectify this, we can define a strategy as a complete plan of action for a player in a game that dictates behavior for every possible contingency that he may come upon in playing a game. More precisely, it defines a particular alternative choice for each information set he may arrive at in the game. For example, in Figure 4.1 one particular strategy for player 1 may be described as follows: "choose a on the first move and b on the second move." Each such complete plan of action is called *pure strategy*. More formally, a strategy for player i is a function that assigns to each of i's information sets one of the arcs which follows a representative node of that set. If the set of such pure strategies is finite, we may call it A_i and index each strategy in this set as $a_i^1, \ldots, a_i^k, \ldots, a_i^{K_i}$. In some situations or games an unambiguously best or *dominant strategy* may not exist for a player. Such a strategy, if it existed, would be one for which the payoff from using it is higher than it would be from using any other strategy, no matter what the other players do.

When this is not true, a player may want to employ what is called a *mixed strategy*, one that does not uniquely specify one plan of action or pure strategy to follow, but tells the player first to use a random device to choose a pure strategy for himself and then employ the strategy chosen. More formally, a mixed strategy for player i with a pure strategy set A_i is a probability distribution $s^i = (s^i(a_i^1), \ldots, s^i(a_i^k), s^i(a_i^{K_i}))$, where $s^i(a_i^k)$ is the probability with which player i will use pure strategy a_i^k and where $s^i(a_i^k) \geq 0$ for all $a_i^k \in A_i$, $\sum_{k=1}^{K_i} s^i(a_i^k) = 1$. Consequently, in devising a mixed strategy a player must first construct all possible pure strategies or plans, assign a probability to each one, perform a random experiment with these probability weights, and then play the pure strategy that is chosen by the random experiment. The construction of such a strategy then involves a great amount of computation and information storage and can be classified as a *global strategy*, in the sense that it is constructed by giving probability weights to a set of pure strategies which are themselves plans of action specifying behavior for a player over the entire length of the game tree.

More information-efficient types of strategies do exist, however. One of these, called a *behavioral strategy*, if used, can drastically cut down on the amount of information storage and retrieval needed in the computation of strategies. The idea behind a behavioral strategy is quite simple. Unlike a mixed strategy, which assigns a probability distribution to each global pure strategy, a behavioral strategy simply assigns a probability distribution to each local information set which defines the probability weight that the player will use in deciding upon any one of his alternative actions at that set. In other words, to use a behavioral strategy a player need not compute all possible pure strategies and then assign a probability weight to each one; he need only choose one distribution for each of his information sets, which is a much simpler task.

To illustrate this point, let us consider an example given by Owen (1968). Say that a player is given a card from a deck of 52 cards; after seeing his card, he has a choice of either passing or betting a fixed amount. The total number of pure strategies conceivable is 2^{52}, because there are 52 cards and two alternatives to choose from once each card is picked. The set of mixed strategies is then of dimension $2^{52} - 1$, because mixed strategies are all points in a unit simplex, and these have a dimension of one less than the set they are defined over. A behavioral strategy, however, simply gives the probability of betting (a number between 0 and 1) with each hand. Hence there are only 52 such strategies. Finally, a behavioral strategy is a *stationary behavioral strategy* if the probability distributions defined for each information set are invariant with respect to the history of the game up until that set. They are ahistorical. In this chapter we see that economic agents will be able to employ these information-efficient stationary behavioral strategies once the proper set of social institutions is created and that by allowing economic agents to use such strategies, social and economic institutions take on their societal efficiency.

The question that logically arises at this point is: Why, if behavioral strategies are so much simpler and more efficient to compute, would anyone ever want to use a cumbersome mixed strategy? The answer is very simple. Every mixed strategy may not be realizable through the use of behavioral strategies. In other words, there may exist games in which it is optimal to use a particular mixed strategy, and that mixed strategy may not be reproducible by the player if he limits himself to only behavioral strategies.

To illustrate this point and to point out the circumstances under which such problems arise, consider the game tree presented by Owen (1968) and shown here as Figure 4.4. In this game player 1's pure strategies are LL, LR, RL, and RR. A mixed strategy is a four-dimensional probability vector $x = (x_1, x_2, x_3, x_4)$ specifying the probability with which player 1 will use any of his four pure strategies. A behavioral strategy in this game is a pair of two-dimensional probability vectors $(y_1, 1 - y_1), (y_2, 1 - y_2)$, where y_1 is the probability of moving left at move 1 and $1 - y_1$ is the probability of moving right and similarly for y_2 and $1 - y_2$ at move 2. Notice that for any choice of y_1 and y_2 a mixed strategy is determined in which the probabilities of LL, LR, RL, and RR are given as follows: $(y_1)(y_2), (y_1)(1 - y_2), (1 - y_1)(y_2)$, and $((1 - y_1)(1 - y_2))$, respectively. Now this game is a zero-sum game, since whatever amount one player wins, the other player loses. In such games, "optimal" strategies exist in the sense that there are strategies, called *mini-max strategies,* which guarantee players a certain minimal amount regardless of what the other

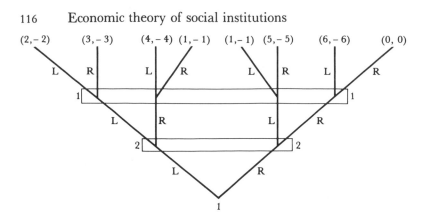

Figure 4.4. Behavioral and mixed strategies in games with imperfect recall.

player or players do. In this game an optimal mixed strategy exists and can be written as follows: $(0, \frac{5}{7}, \frac{2}{7}, 0)$. Clearly, no matter what values are chosen for y_1 and y_2 in a player's behavioral strategy, he will never be able to replicate this mixed strategy; consequently, such an optimal mixed strategy is not realizable through the use of behavioral strategies.

The import of this discussion, then, is that there are circumstances in which players may have to use mixed strategies because, although informationally cumbersome, results are obtainable from using them which are not achievable from behavioral strategies. But under what circumstances is this not true? In other words, for which types of games can any mixed strategy be realized through the use of behavioral strategies and the consequent informational saving realized? The answer is that if the game under investigation is a game of perfect recall, any mixed strategy can be reproduced by using an appropriate behavioral strategy.

To illustrate this point, let us consider Figure 4.5, which is identical to Figure 4.4 except that the information sets are drawn differently. In contrast to the game pictured in Figure 4.4, this game is a game of perfect recall. The set of pure strategies for player 1 is again LL, LR, RL, and RR, whereas a mixed strategy is again a four-dimensional vector (x_1, x_2, x_3, x_4). Now in this game, player 1 has three information sets instead of two. This is true because he can now distinguish at move 2 what move he made at move 1. A behavioral strategy is then composed of three two-dimensional probability vectors $(y_1, 1 - y_1)$, $(y_2, 1 - y_2)$, and $(y_3, 1 - y_3)$, where y_1, y_2, and y_3 are the probability weights attached to moving left at any of player 1's information sets labeled A, B, and C, respectively, in the diagram. Notice, however, that the mixed strategy $(0, \frac{5}{7}, \frac{2}{7}, 0)$ (or any other mixed strategy for that matter) can now be achieved by setting $y_1 = \frac{5}{7}$, $y_2 = 0$, $1 - y_1 = \frac{2}{7}$, $1 - y_2 = 1$, $y_3 = 1$, and $1 - y_3 = 0$. Such a result will be true for any game and any mixed strategy as long as the game is one of perfect recall. Consequently, if games have perfect recall, any

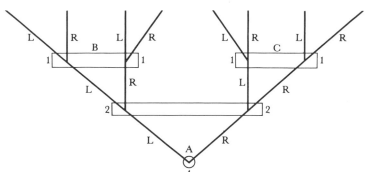

Figure 4.5. Behavioral and mixed strategies in games with perfect recall.

global mixed strategy can be achieved by a more inexpensive set of local behavioral strategies and, as a result, we may expect behavioral strategies to be used.

The relationship among mixed strategies, behavioral strategies, and games of perfect recall is summarized in the following theorem of Kuhn's, which is rephrased to suit our purposes.

Theorem 4.1 (Kuhn 1953).[2] In every extensive form game with perfect recall, a realization equivalent behavioral strategy can be found for every mixed strategy of a real player i.

Here "realization equivalent" means that under both the behavioral and the mixed strategies mentioned in the theorem, there is an identical probability for player i of playing any given pure strategy.

The concept of a behavioral strategy has an interesting relationship to economics in that if we depict each player in an n-person game in extensive form as being composed of a set of agents, each agent being active at a distinct information set of the larger player, then behavioral strategies for this team are equivalent to a set of decentralized plans of action in which each agent has a card with the appropriate behavioral strategy written on it that will dictate the choices to be made at his information set, and these plans can be carried out individually by the active agents locally at their information sets without regard to what has happened elsewhere on the game tree. Consequently, a similar informational saving that results when decentralized pricing mechanisms are used in economies can be achieved by individual players when viewed as teams, if they employ behavioral strategies.

This fiction of representing individual players as teams of agents each one active at a different information set of the player will be a very useful one for us when we discuss the informational efficiency of social institutions. Reinhard Selten (1975) has called such constructs "games in agent normal form," which we shall define simply as games in which each player is composed of a set of agents each of which is active at one information set. The agent has a choice of any alternative defined at that information set, and the payoff to any agent is identical to the final payoff received by the player whose team he is on. As such, these players qualify as "teams" in the Marschak–Radner (1972) sense.

4.2 Institutions and information

To motivate our discussion of the informational aspects of social and economic institutions, let us refer to an article written by F. A. Hayek (1945) entitled "The Use of Knowledge in Society." In this article, Hayek describes the perfectly competitive economy as an information system in which a vector of competitive prices transmits information of a global type, reflecting the societal scarcity of resources to a set of informationally specialized agents. Upon receiving this information, agents maximize individually, and if certain assumptions are met at the equilibrium, the resulting trades are Pareto-optimal. However, can the informational content of an economy always be summarized merely by a price vector that under certain very restricted conditions is sufficient to allow a set of economic agents to achieve a Pareto-optimal state, or does it include more? It is our main argument that economies contain an information network far richer than that described by a price system. This network is made up of a whole complex of institutions, rules of thumb, customs, and beliefs that help to transfer a great deal of information about the anticipated actions of agents in the economy when those actions cannot be decentralized by prices or when price mechanisms are too costly to administer.

These mechanisms, even in the face of such phenomena as externalities and nonconvexities, transfer the information that allows the economy to achieve a Pareto-optimal state. Our argument, then, is that in the face of phenomena that are "not nice" in the neoclassical sense, as economies evolve they develop rules of thumb, norms, institutions, and so on, that will transfer the information necessary to coordinate the activities of economic agents in a decentralized Pareto-optimal manner. Institutions are then information mechanisms that supplement the information contained in competitive prices and consequently allow what we will call institution-assisted decentralization.

To illustrate exactly what we are talking about, let us consider the most simple textbook-variety two-person two-good neoclassical Edgeworth-box barter economy and discuss the information requirements that are sufficient to coordinate economic activity in a decentralized manner.

Game 4.1: The strictly convex barter game

Consider a barter economy with two traders, a_1 and a_2, each of whom have the utility functions depicted in Figure 4.6 by strictly convex indifference curves. Assume that the initial endowments of the traders are represented by

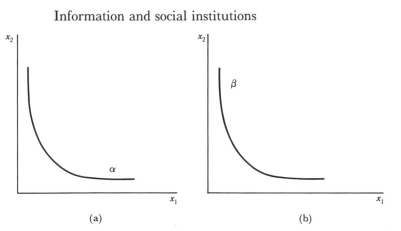

Figure 4.6. Preferences and endowments in the strictly-convex barter game: traders of type 1; traders of type 2.

the points α and β, where α represents the endowment of a trader of type 1 and β the endowment of a trader of type 2. If the economy were treated as a static neoclassical exchange problem, the Edgeworth box diagram shown in Figure 4.7 would completely describe the allocation problem under consideration. The way the model works is as follows. A fictitious auctioneer is posited whose job it is to announce price vectors that will act as parameters for the agents in the economy who will take these prices as given and maximize their utility on the basis of them, subject to a wealth constraint dictated by their initial endowment. Such a price vector is represented by the line pp'. Notice that at the price vector pp' announced by the auctioneer there exists an allocation that simultaneously maximizes each consumer's utility while satisfying the budget constraint:

$$I = p_1 w^1_{x_1} + p_2 w^1_{x_2} = p_1 x^{*1}_1 + p_2 x^{*1}_2$$
$$I = p_1 w^2_{x_1} + p_2 w^2_{x_2} = p_1 x^{*2}_1 + p_2 x^{*2}_2$$

where
$w^1_{x_1}$ = trader 1's initial endowment of good x_1
$w^1_{x_2}$ = trader 1's initial endowment of good x_2
$w^2_{x_1}$ = trader 2's initial endowment of good x_1
$w^2_{x_2}$ = trader 2's initial endowment of good x_2
$x^{*1}_1, x^{*1}_2, x^{*2}_1, x^{*2}_2$ = equilibrium amounts of good x_1 and x_2 going to traders 1 and 2, respectively

As is usually stated, this economy can be *completely coordinated* in a decentralized manner by the prices represented by the line pp'. This is all the information needed to reach point E, which is a Pareto-optimal allocation given the endowment (α, β). Consequently, the information content of this economy consists totally of prices, and the institutional framework of the model (which is posited at the outset and represented by a fictitious auctioneer) is sufficient to achieve a Pareto-optimal allocation. All agents' behavior is completely coordinated by prices.

The world we live in, however, is not static. It cannot be represented well by a static model that exists in hypothetical time with no past and no future. Rather, we have argued, it is an evolutionary world in which social agents recurrently face strategic situations and must devise rules of thumb or modes of behavior to handle them. To represent this fact in our simple model, let us divide each trader into an infinite number of agents indexed $a_{1t} = a_{11}, a_{12},$ ... and $a_{2t} = a_{21}, a_{22}, \ldots$, and divide time into periods of equal length indexed $t = 1, 2, \ldots$. Each agent on a given team will have an identical utility function and an identical initial endowment. Consequently, all agents on team 1 will have a utility function identical to the one depicted in Figure 4.6a with initial endowment α, and all agents on team 2 will have utility functions identical to the one depicted in Figure 4.6b and have an initial endowment of β. The payoff to any agent is equivalent to the team's final payoff, which can be considered to be the discounted present value of the stream of infinite team-member payoffs.

The model will work as follows. Each agent on each team will be given an index indicating the time period during which he will be active. Consequently, a_{1t} will be the agent on team 1 who will be active during period t, and a_{2t} will be the agent on team 2 who will be active during period t. In that time period, only those agents will be active; all others will be inactive. When they are active, the agents will play the "game of perfect competition" in the static Edgeworth market depicted in Figure 4.7. What this means is that during the time period in which they are active, the agents existing will act as price takers in the static economy defined by their endowments and preferences and offer their demands and supplies parametrically to the auctioneer, who yells out prices for them to take. If we wanted to, we could think of this setup as depicting a society with an infinite number of generations, each of which lives for one period and then dies, only to be replaced by their identical successors, who partake for one period in the same economy as their predecessors. It is by analyzing the various rules of thumb and institutions that are created in such multigenerational economies that we can get an idea of exactly when institutions other than the auctioneer-led market institutions described above would evolve and what their exact function is.

To pursue this end, let us assume that time starts in period 1, when agents a_{11} and a_{21} are active and all other agents are not yet born. In period 1 we assume that the only institution existing is the auctioneer-led market institution, whose origin is left unexplained by the model. The economy at period 1 looks exactly as we have pictured it in Figure 4.7. It is now assumed that the length of time available in any time period is finite, in fact quite short. Consequently, as the auctioneer announces prices, it is assumed that he only has a

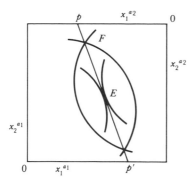

Figure 4.7. The strictly convex barter game.

finite and small amount of time to find the equilibrium price for the economy
and reach a Pareto-optimal allocation. Since the market institution is a *tâtonnement* mechanism, we will assume that if equilibrium trades are not achieved
by the time the period ends (within the lifetimes of the active generation), no
trades will be consummated and the agents in that generation will have to consume their initial endowments (α and β). The payoffs to the traders from playing this game of perfect competition can then be specified as follows:

$$\Pi_{it} = \begin{cases} \max \alpha_i^{t-1}[u^{it}(x_1, x_2)] \text{ such that} \\ \overset{\bullet}{p}_{x_1}x_1^{it} + \overset{\bullet}{p}_{x_2}x_2^{it} = \overset{\bullet}{p}_1 w_{x_1}^{it} + \overset{\bullet}{p}_2 w_{x_2}^{it} = I \quad \text{ } \\ \alpha_i^{t-1}[U^{it}(w_{x_1}^{it}, w_{x_2}^{it})] \end{cases} \begin{aligned} &\text{if equilibrium} \\ &\text{if no equilibrium} \end{aligned} \qquad (4.1)$$

where $i = 1, 2$

$\overset{\bullet}{p}_{x_j}, j = 1, 2$ = equilibrium price for good j

$x_j^{\overset{\bullet}{*}it}$ = equilibrium quantity of good j consumed by agent a_{it} at the equilibrium price $\overset{\bullet}{p}_{x_j}$

α_i^{t-1} = discount factor associated with agent a_{it}

The reason markets may not clear is that, given the length of each time
period, the *tâtonnement* process may be too slow to achieve equilibrium.

Finally, let us assume that after they make their play of the game of perfect
competition, each generation is free to pass on to the next generation of players
on their team a message specifying the type of behavior that can be expected
from the active agents of the next generation that he will face. More will be
said about the exact nature of this message, but for now it is sufficient to say
that it is upon this information that the agents decide to act in the next period.

If the auctioneer has instantaneous calculating speed, as we will assume,
then, as can be expected, because of the strictly convex preferences of the traders, the economy will evolve in a trivial manner. In each period equilibrium
will be achieved by a vector of competitive prices and each agent will maximize
their utility at those prices. The payoff to the teams will be

$$\Pi^1 = \sum_{t=1}^{\infty} \max \alpha_1^{t-1}[\,U^{1t}(x_1^{*2t}, x_2^{*1t})] + \lambda(I - p_{x_1}^* x_1^{1t} - p_{x_2}^* x_2^{1t}) \qquad (4.2)$$

$$\Pi^2 = \sum_{t=1}^{\infty} \max \alpha_2^{t-1}[\,U^{2t}(x_1^{*2t}, x_2^{*2t})] + \lambda(I - P_{x_1}^* x_1^{2t} - P_{x_2}^* x_2^{2t}) \qquad (4.3)$$

In addition, the informational content of all messages sent from any agent a_{it} to a_{it+1} ($i = 1, 2$) will be null, because at any time t, to reach an optimal equilibrium decision each existing agent needs no more information than is available in the price vector. Prices are the only informational mechanisms developed in the economy, and the information content of the economy can be totally represented by a price vector. Therefore, the informational content of the economy $I = \{p\}$ contains only prices, and the single institution of perfectly competitive markets carries with it all the information necessary to coordinate the activities of the agents in the economy.

Consider Figure 4.8. This figure has a simple explanation. In each period the active agents transmit bids and offers to the auctioneer, who runs the economy's markets. Because the preferences of the agents are strictly convex and the auctioneer has instantaneous calculating speed, in each period a competitive equilibrium will be reached in which each agent behaves parametrically and the information available in the set of equilibrium prices, together with the behavioral rule associated with competitive markets–"behave parametrically"– is sufficient to coordinate Pareto-optimal activity. Consequently, in each period we observe Pareto-optimal competitive equilibrium trades occurring, and no messages need be sent from one generation to the next because the information available in equilibrium prices totally decentralizes the economy and decouples all agents' behavior.[3] The important point to realize is that such an economy is institutionally degenerate because the institutional structure existing in any time period $t > 1$ is identical to the informational structure existing in period 1–competitive markets–and no extra institutions were created as the economy evolved. This fact, however, is counter to our everyday observation of a great many complex social and economic institutions whose function is to help markets allocate goods efficiently. The reason our model differs so drastically from reality is that the assumptions necessary to achieve the derived results are too stringent to be realistic. For instance, if preferences were convex but simply not strictly convex, such an institutionally degenerate result would not exist. Consequently, as we admit even the slightest relaxation of the neoclassical model, the informational content of competitive prices fails to be sufficient for their purpose, and some additional institutional detail must be added to the economy as it evolves if efficient coordination is to take place. Let us investigate the exact function of this additional institutional detail.

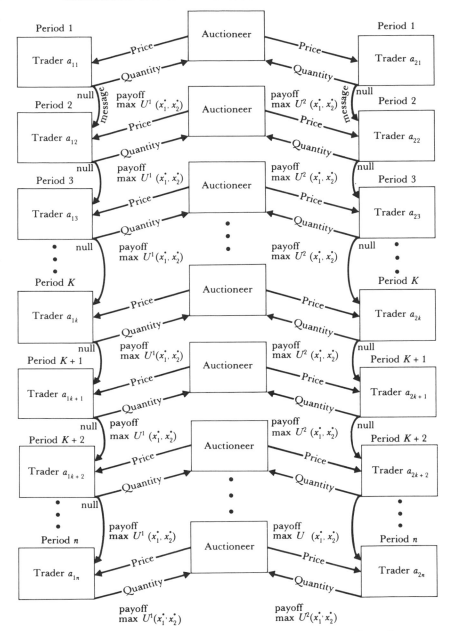

Figure 4.8. Information flows in the strictly convex barter game. In this chart x_1^* and x_2^* represent the amounts of goods x_1 and x_2 consumed at the equilibrium.

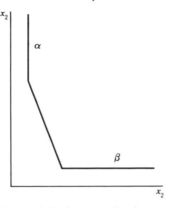

Figure 4.9. Preferences and endowments in the not-strictly-convex barter game.

Game 4.2: The not-strictly-convex barter game

As a result of our analysis of Game 4.1, we came to the usual conclusion that in "conventional" neoclassical economies (i.e., ones satisfying all of the most strict neoclassical assumptions), competitive markets are informationally sufficient to achieve Pareto-optimal allocations. In other words, as these economies evolve, they need not, nor will they, develop any other institutions, norms, or rules of thumb, because markets and prices are sufficient.

The situation will, of course, be different if we change even slightly the strict assumptions posited there. Therefore, let us investigate another economy identical to the first except for the fact that preferences, although convex, are not strictly convex.

Consider a barter economy with two types of traders, a_1 and a_2, who for convenience have identical utility functions depicted in Figure 4.9. Assume that the initial endowments of the traders are represented by the points α and β, where α represents the endowment of a trader of type 1 and β the endowment of a trader of type 2. There are an infinite number of traders of type 1 and an infinite number of traders of type 2, indexed $a_{1t} = a_{11}, \ldots$, and $a_{2t} = a_{21}$, ... The game is played as follows. Time is again divided into trading periods. At period 1, traders a_{11} and a_{21} are active and all other traders are inactive. The economy at period 1 looks like the Edgeworth box pictured in Figure 4.10, where F marks the initial endowments of the two traders.

The traders are required to act "competitively": to take the prices of a fictitious auctioneer (who has instantaneous calculating speed) as given and maximize accordingly. As prices are announced, the traders offer their supply and demand schedules, and if an equilibrium is achieved before the trading period is over, the payoffs to the two traders are utilities they achieve from their equi-

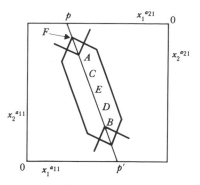

Figure 4.10. The not-strictly-convex barter game.

librium bundles. If not, they must keep their original endowments. Therefore, the payoffs may be specified as

$$\Pi_1 = \begin{cases} \max \alpha_i^{t-1}(U^{it}(x_1, x_2)) \quad \text{such that} \\ \dot{p}_{x_1}x_1^{it} + \dot{p}_{x_2}x_2^{it} = \dot{p}_{x_1}w_{x_1}^{it} + \dot{p}_{x_2}w_{x_2}^{it} = I \\ \alpha_i^{t-1}(U^{it}(w_{x_1}^{it}, w_{x_2}^{it})) \end{cases} \begin{array}{l} \text{if equilibrium} \\ \\ \text{if no equilibrium} \end{array} \tag{4.4}$$

where $i = 1, 2$ and $w_{x_1}^{it}$ and $w_{x_2}^{it}$ are the initial endowments of the itth trader of goods x_1 and x_2. The reason an equilibrium may not be achieved before the trading period ends should be obvious.

Consider Figure 4.10. At the equilibrium prices depicted by the line pp', each trader can maximize his utility by choosing any bundle on the line segment between A and B. For convenience we assume that only a finite number of bundles are available to be chosen along line $\overline{AB}$. However, if a_{11} chooses point C and a_{21} chooses point D, no trades can be executed because some excess demand will be positive. The problem, then, is one of coordination, in which the price system is sufficient to bring the traders to the segment AB but no further. A game of "hide and seek" or *coordination* is being played on line AB and a time limit is set for the seeker. Prices are then not sufficient to completely coordinate the action of agents, and some new mechanism is necessary. Finally, let us assume that traders cannot communicate directly with each other but must communicate through the price system by making quantity offers to the auctioneer. When the period ends, a new period is started (or a new *vintage* economy is created), say, period 2, and traders a_{12} and a_{22} appear. The process is then repeated for them. This is repeated infinitely. Finally, as before, we assume that traders can communicate with the immediate successors of their own type.

The situation described in this new model is isomorphic to a supergame of the coordination variety studied in Chapter 3, in which in each period an identical coordination game of hide and seek is played along line $\overline{AB}$ and the payoff to each team is the discounted present value of the payoffs of the agents on each team,

$$\Pi^1 = \sum_{t=1}^{\infty} \alpha_1^{t-1}[U^1(x_1^{1t}, x_2^{2t})] \tag{4.5}$$

$$\Pi^2 = \sum_{t=1}^{\infty} \alpha_2^{t-1}[U^2(x_1^{2t}, x_2^{2t})] \tag{4.6}$$

The only difference, of course, is that this supergame is not played by the same set of players but by a team of identical fiduciary agents each of which plays an identical static coordination game for one period. This difference, although not significant analytically, is significant intuitively, because although it may be possible to envision a game as having an infinite life, it is clearly impossible for the players who play it to be immortal. Social agents have finite lives and are replaced by other agents, who take their role in society. It is by creating social institutions that are passed on from generation to generation and prescribe equilibrium behavior for agents that life preserves its continuity.

Because the situation described is isomorphic to a supergame of the coordination variety, we can apply the analysis already developed in Chapter 3 to the problem at hand and investigate what is likely to evolve. To begin, in period 1 (the beginning of time) we assume that both agents have no information about the other and as a result must assign a subjective probability to the choice of bundles along $\overline{AB}$ expected to be chosen by their opponent. More specifically, because each agent knows that he is facing a team of agents that can communicate with each other (at least adjacent generations can), he will have to try to guess the various modes of behavior that can be expected from his opposing agent and assign a probability to the likelihood of each one. Both agents are expected to try to maximize the discounted payoff of their team, but this is not crucial because it will be in the long-term interest of each agent's team if he behaves myopically and simply maximizes his own utility. Agent a_{11} will then have to contemplate which plan of action the agents on the opposing team will follow, where a plan of action constitutes an intergenerational supergame strategy for the agents on the opposing team to use.

To illustrate what we mean, let us assume that the only pairs of bundles available to be chosen when the price line is pp' are the pairs of bundles (or allocations) labeled A and B in Figure 4.10 (i.e., only the end points of the segment $\overline{AB}$. Then assuming that the utility derived from consuming either bundle A or B at equilibrium is 6 for any agent a_{1t} and 4 for any agent a_{2t} and that the value of the disequilibrium endowment bundle F is 2 for each of them, the recurrent coordination problem shown by Matrix 4.1 is defined. In this

Agent a_{2t}

	a_{2t}^A	a_{2t}^B
a_{1t}^A	$\alpha_1^{t-1}(6),\ \alpha_2^{t-1}(4)$	$\alpha_1^{t-1}(2),\ \alpha_2^{t-1}(2)$
a_{1t}^B	$\alpha_1^{t-1}(2),\ \alpha_2^{t-1}(2)$	$\alpha_1^{t-1}(6),\ \alpha_2^{t-1}(4)$

Agent a_{1t}

Matrix 4.1. The allocation coordination game

game four plans of action can be defined for each player to follow in the infinite horizon supergame defined. They are

$$\Sigma^1 = (\sigma^1[a_{1t}^A/a_{2t}^A],\ \sigma^1[a_{1t}^A/a_{2t}^B],\ \sigma^1[a_{1t}^B/a_{2t}^A],\ \sigma^1[a_{1t}^B/a_{2t}^B]) \tag{4.7}$$
$$\Sigma^2 = (\sigma^2[a_{2t}^A/a_{1t}^A],\ \sigma^2[a_{2t}^B/a_{1t}^A],\ \sigma^2[a_{2t}^A/a_{1t}^B],\ \sigma^2[a_{2t}^B/a_{1t}^B]) \tag{4.8}$$

where, for instance, the plan $\sigma^1[a_{1t}^A/a_{2t}^A]$ can be written as

$$\sigma^1[a_{1t}^A/a_{2t}^A] = \begin{cases} a_{11}^k = A & \\ a_{1t}^k = A & \text{if } a_{2\tau} = A,\quad \tau = 1, 2, \ldots, t-1 \\ a_{1t}^k = A & \text{otherwise} \quad\quad t = 2, 3, \ldots \end{cases} \tag{4.9}$$

where $k = A, B$.

This strategy is basically an intergenerational plan of action for the players on team 1, specifying that they will choose bundle A at each iteration of the game. The norm $\mathbf{p}^t = (\mathbf{p}_1^t, \mathbf{p}_2^t)$ defines two four-dimensional probability vectors over each of these strategy sets, and this is the information that is transferred from generation to generation. In other words, the message space of the economy is the pair of simplices H^1 and H^2 since $\mathbf{p}^t \in H^1 \times H^2$.

Since agents a_{11} and a_{21} know nothing about each other (the game has no previous history upon which to draw inferences), we will assume that in period 1 they will assign an equal probability to each possible plan. Based on this pair of probability beliefs, we can apply the model we presented in Chapter 3 and assume that this probability pair $\mathbf{p}^1 = (\mathbf{p}_1^1, \mathbf{p}_2^1)$ represents an initial norm upon which they will employ a static Bayesian solution procedure, $\mathcal{M}$ (see Definition 3.2), to choose a plan of action in period 1 and take the first step called for by that plan.

At the end of period 1, they pass on to the agents active in period 2 an updated norm $\mathbf{p}^2 = (\mathbf{p}_1^2, \mathbf{p}_2^2)$ which they update based on the strategy choices made in period 1 using a norm-updating rule (see Definition 3.4). Furnished with this information, the period 2 agents again use the static Bayesian solution procedure $\mathcal{M}$ to choose a bundle in period 2. The process continues until in some period t an absorbing state is reached in which for each agent in period $t + 1$ onward, each expects with probability 1 that the agent on the opposing team will expect him to choose for example, the particular bundle $A \in \overline{AB}$, and he expects the agent on the other team to choose $A \in \overline{AB}$ with probability 1; such a common choice is a coordination equilibrium, so that is exactly what they do.

At this point all the prerequisites that David Lewis (1969) has laid down for the existence of a well-defined social convention or institution (in our terminology) are satisfied, and we call period t the *institution creation stage*. Diagrammatically, this can be represented as shown in Figure 4.11.

What we see here is a multistage evolutionary economy in which after each generation has played its part in the economy, it passes to the following generation a message in the form of an updated norm. Consequently, each agent in period t gets some pair $\mathbf{p}^t = (\mathbf{p}_1^t, \mathbf{p}_2^t)$ transmitted to it and each assumes that the other receives the same message. In Figure 4.11 period K is what we call the institution creation stage, in which the norm p^k (after updating the period $K - 1$ norm) is a degenerate pair of unit vectors each with weight 1 placed on the plan of behavior specifying the exact same bundle on AB. From period $K + 1$ onward, all payoffs will be equilibrium payoffs. At the end of period K, then, the economy has created a societal rule of thumb that can be summarized by the number λ, $0 \leq \lambda \leq 1$, in which λ defines the societally agreed upon bundle by defining the weights with which each agent weighs bundles A and B in his optimal choice of bundles. More precisely, from period $K + 1$ onward each agent will pass on the following equilibrium rule of thumb to his successor.

Rule of thumb 4.1. When at prices p, if your utility is maximized at a set of consumption bundles that is a segment $\overline{AB}$ of a linear hyperplane, $p_{x_1} w_{x_1}^{it} + p_{x_2} w_{x_2}^{it} = I$, always choose the bundle associated with the allocation $E = \lambda A + (1 - \lambda)B$, $0 \leq \lambda \leq 1$.

If traders follow this rule from period $K + 1$ on, equilibrium trades will take place in each of these periods. The final societal payoff from period $K + 1$ onward will be

$$\Pi^s = \sum_{t=k+1}^{\infty} \sum_{i=1}^{2} \alpha_i^{t-1} \{ U^{it}(\lambda A + (1 - \lambda))(B) \} \tag{4.10}$$

Consequently, we see that as this economy *evolves*, the price system is augmented by a rule of thumb which, together with the vector p, is sufficient to achieve a competitive equilibrium that is a Pareto optimum. Therefore, the sufficient information set, $I = \{p, \lambda\}$, does not merely contain the price vector p, but also λ or a rule of thumb.

With the addition of this rule, this economy is more complex than the one

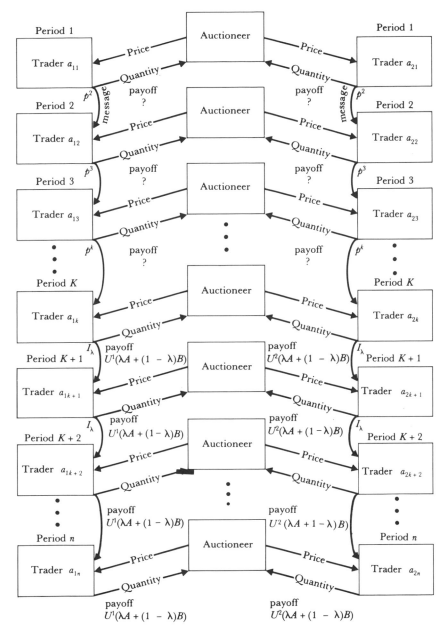

Figure 4.11. Information flows in the not-strictly-convex barter game.

studied before, because the institutional structure existing in period $K + 1$ is richer than the one existing in period 1. It is important to notice, however, that even though the economy has an informational structure that contains more than mere prices, the expanded information structure still coordinates the activities of the economy's agents in a totally decentralized manner. In other words, all any agent needs in order to behave optimally is the competitive vector of prices, knowledge of his own preferences, and the institutional rule of thumb λ. Knowing these, no thought need be given to the actions of other agents because this is taken care of by λ and the norm supporting it, which gives the agents the assurance that all agents will adhere to it. Consequently, the institutional rule furnishes all the information necessary to decentralize the economy given p and allows the agents to avoid the strategic second guessing involved in the coordination game of the economy. In addition, notice that λ is extremely efficient computationally because at any time $t \geq k$ no agent need remember any of the moves made by agents in generations before him. He has no need to store information. All relevant historical information about the game is distilled in the parameter λ, which is now a permanent feature of this economy. Even before period K, all relevant information necessary to make "intelligent" strategy choices was summarized by the norm $\mathbf{p}'$, which, in a convenient form, contains all the important information available in the economy's history. Consequently, the creation of economic norms and institutions is informationally efficient in the sense that they minimize the size of the informational storage and retrieval facilities that each agent must maintain for himself.

In conclusion, our economy is what we might call an *institution-assisted economy,* which we can define as an economy in which the information set necessary for the achievement of a decentralized equilibrium contains more than a vector of prices–a vector of prices plus at least one institutional or behavior rule. Neoclassical economies or economies that satisfy all the textbook neoclassical assumptions can be represented as degenerate special cases of institution-assisted economies because the set of institutional rules existing in the information set of the economy is null. Clearly, these economies are exceptional cases.

4.3 The extensive form representation: a game in agent normal form with imperfect recall

Our simple barter economy can easily be treated as a game in extensive form with an "infinity plus one" number of agents–an auctioneer and an infinite number of agents of each type. However, to capture the true flavor of the problem, it is best to treat the game as a three-player game in what is called *agent normal form,* composed of one auctioneer and two players, each player composed of an infinite set of agents. Each agent will be active at one information set of his player and endowed with a fixed and identical (with respect to agents of his own type) bundle of two goods, x_1 and x_2. Consequently,

$$w^{1t} = (w^{1t}_{x_1}, w^{1t}_{x_2}) = w^1 \qquad \text{for all } t = 1, \ldots$$
$$w^{2t} = (w^{2t}_{x_1}, w^{2t}_{x_2}) = w^2 \qquad \text{for all } t = 1, \ldots$$

and $w^1 \neq w^2$, where w^1 is the endowment of agents of type 1 and w^2 is the endowment of agents of type 2. The utility functions of the agents of the two players are identical, so that

$$U^{1t}(x_1, x_2) = U^1(x_1, x_2) \qquad \text{for all } t = 1, \ldots$$
$$U^{2t}(x_1, x_2) = U^2(x_1, x_2) \qquad \text{for all } t = 1, \ldots$$

The payoff functions of the players are the discounted utility payoffs of the agents on them:

$$\Pi^1 = \sum_{t=1}^{\infty} \alpha_1^{t-1}\{U^1(x_1^{1t}, x_2^{1t})\} \tag{4.11}$$

$$\Pi^2 = \sum_{t=1}^{\infty} \alpha_2^{t-1}\{U^2(x_1^{2t}, x_2^{2t})\} \tag{4.12}$$

The payoff of the auctioneer is the total number of periods in which equilibrium is reached in the economy. This ensures that the auctioneer will always choose the equilibrium price vector (which he knows, given perfect information about the utility functions and initial endowments of all agents). A similar type of assumption for the auctioneer was used by Arrow and Debreu (1954). Finally, in each period, each agent knows his utility function, the utility function of the agent of the other type active at that time, the initial endowment vector, and the price vector announced by the auctioneer. The agents are not allowed to communicate directly with each other and can only communicate through the auctioneer via quantity offers. However, they may transmit a message to their successors.

The game proceeds as it did in Section 4.2. Time is divided into periods of equal length. At each period, two agents are active (one of each type) and all others are inactive. For purposes of simplicity, we assume that the auctioneer instantly knows the equilibrium price vector and announces it at the start of each period. Also, for simplicity, assume that at the equilibrium price vector, p^*, each trader has only two vectors that maximize his utility at these prices. (This makes the resulting game tree easier to draw while preserving the essence of the problem.) These are the bundles associated with the points A and B in Figure 4.10, where at A player 1 is allocated (x_{1A}, x_{2A}) and player 2 is allocated $(X_1 - x_{1A}, X_2 - x_{2A})$, where X_1 and X_2 are the total stock of goods 1 and 2 existing. At point B the allocation is (x_{1B}, x_{2B}) for player 1 and $(X_1 - x_{1B}, X_2 - x_{2B})$ for player 2.

We will assume that each time period is so short that only one choice is allowed by each agent at any time period. If they both choose A or both choose B, equilibrium is achieved and the payoff vector is

$$(U^{1t}(x_{1A}, x_{2A}),\ U^{2t}(X_1 - x_{1A}, X_2 - x_{2A}))$$

if both choose A, and

$$(U^{1t}(x_{1B}, x_{2B}),\ U^{2t}(X_1 - x_{1B}, X_2 - x_{2B}))$$

if both choose B.

Notice that if both players choose bundle A, player 1 will be allocated (x_{1A}, x_{2A}) and player 2 will be allocated $(X_1 - x_{1A}, X_2 - x_{2A})$, so that $x_{1A} + X_1 - x_{1A} = X_1$ and $x_{2A} + X_2 - x_{2A} = X_2$, and $(x_{1A}, x_{2A}, X_1 - x_{1A}, X_2 - x_{2A})$ is the allocation in the economy depicted by point A. The allocation defined by point B can be similarly defined. If one chooses A and the other B, no trades can take place, and the payoffs are

$$(U^{1t}(w^1_{x_1}, w^1_{x_2}),\ U^{2t}(w^2_{x_1}, w^2_{x_2}))$$

As a result of our simplifying assumptions at each period, the active agents play the simple coordination game in normal form shown by Matrix 4.2, which we shall call the *ordinary coordination game,* with

$$U^{1t}(x_{1A}, x_{2A}) = U^{1t}(x_{1B}, x_{2B}) > U^{1t}(w^1_{x_1}, w^1_{x_2})$$
$$U^{2t}(X_1 - x_{1A}, X_2 - x_{2A}) = U^{2t}(X_1 - x_{1B}, X_2 - x_{2B}) > U^{2t}(w^2_{x_1}, w^2_{x_2})$$

where the top entry in each cell of the matrix is the payoff to player a_{1t} and the bottom entry is the payoff to player a_{2t}. Notice that these equalities hold because points A and B are points on the same indifference curves for both players.

Agent a_{2t}

		A	B
Agent a_{1t}	A	$\alpha_1^{t-1}(U^{1t}(x_{1A}, x_{2A}))$ $\alpha_2^{t-1}(U^{2t}(X_1 - x_{1A}, X_2 - x_{2A}))$	$\alpha_1^{t-1}(U^{1t}(w^1_{x_1}, w^1_{x_2}))$ $\alpha_2^{t-1}(U^{2t}(w^2_x, w^2_y))$
	B	$\alpha_1^{t-1}(U^{1t}(w^1_{x_1}, w^1_{x_2}))$ $\alpha_2^{t-1}(U^{1t}(w^1_{x_1}, w^1_{x_2}))$	$\alpha_1^{t-1}(U^{1t}(x_{1B}, x_{2B}))$ $\alpha_2^{t-1}(U^{2t}(X_1 - x_{1B}, X_2 - x_{2B}))$

Matrix 4.2. The ordinary coordination game

The game that is played between our two players is clearly a game of coordination. However, as we will see, unless the agents of a given player can communicate, the game will be one of imperfect recall because each player will

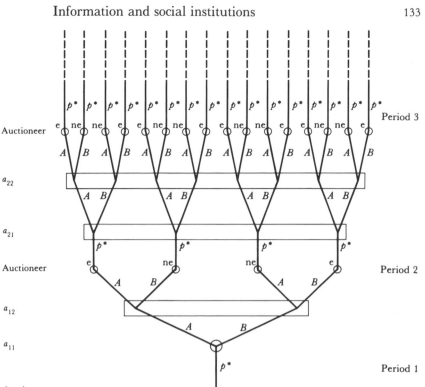

Figure 4.12. Institution creation in the strictly convex barter game.

forget the strategy choice made by his agent after the information set at which they are made is passed. Consequently, if succeeding generations could not communicate or if their communication were too costly, each and every pair of agents, when they were active, would have to solve the same coordination game for themselves, and the extent to which they fail to coordinate in any period is the extent to which society will fail to achieve Pareto-optimal results. Consequently, it would be desirable if the agents of both players could create some cheap communication device that would codify memory for themselves and inform them of how agents acted in the past and, consequently, of how they could be expected to behave in the future. Such a cheap communication device will be shown to be a social institution and represents a type of socialization process for the agents in the economy.

To investigate the problem more closely, study the game-tree representation of our economy shown in Figure 4.12, which represents our economy as a game in extensive form in which generations do not communicate with each other. We immediately see that the game has imperfect recall. In fact, for each player

1 and 2, all information sets all signaling information sets. Put differently, the players constantly forget the moves made by their agents each period as soon as it is over. Consequently, if equilibrium is reached in period 1, then in Figure 4.12 we see that in period 2 the players do not know that fact. This is forgotten because different agents are present in period 2 than in period 1. Consequently, some mechanism will have to be established that will allow the players to remember the moves made at previous information sets of the game. This mechanism, we will see, is an institution (rule of thumb, or convention), and this institution, once established, will be transmitted from agent to agent. Our point, then, is that institutions are established to help solve games that are iterated either a finite or an infinite number of times and become efficient by allowing agents to learn from the past and remember the societally agreed upon convention of behavior for these games. They avoid the suboptimal outcomes that might result if such institutions did not exist and agents were forced to repeatedly solve the same coordination problem.

4.4 Institution-assisted games

If you remember, when we described the rules of our barter economy, we stated that agents who are contemporaneous are not allowed to communicate directly, but are forced to communicate through the market by indicating their choices to the auctioneer. However, agents were allowed to transmit messages to the agents of their own type that follow them. These messages are of vital importance, for it is the system of such messages that create what we call social institutions. What happens in such games is that a new set of moves is added to the game tree pictured in Figure 4.12, called *message moves,* which allow each agent to inform his successor of the existing norm. If the norm is degenerate such that an institution is in existence, each active agent knows precisely how he is expected to behave and how the agents he faces will behave, and adhering to those expectations will be in all agents' self-interest.

Consider Figure 4.13, which represents a portion of the game tree that results when we include message moves in the game tree depicted in Figure 4.12. In other words, this diagram presents a partially drawn segment of a much larger game tree, which depicts the process of intergenerational message transmission. What we want to do here is follow the path of one fictitious play of our infinite agent Edgeworth barter game over the portion of the game tree represented here and demonstrate how social institutions come into being and are transmitted from generation to generation. To do this, consider the dark path in the tree, which will depict our hypothetical play of this game through three periods. The moves indicated as message moves are now added to the game and allow for the transmission of three types of messages: message I_A, which instructs the next generation of agents that an institution in which bundle A is always chosen has been established; message I_B, which instructs the next generation of agents that an institution in which bundle B is always chosen has been established; and message $p^{t+1} = (p_1^{t+1}, p_2^{t+1})$, called a noninstitutional *norm message*, which is a message indicating that no institutional rule has yet been established but that the norm in period $t + 1$ relevant for them is $p^{t+1} = (p_1^{t+1}, p_2^{t+1})$. I_A and I_B are actually pairs of degenerate unit vectors, indicating that with probability 1 each player is expected to choose bundle A, in the case of I_A, or B, in the case of I_B. Consequently, institutional messages I_A and I_B are drawn from the same message space as are norm messages (i.e., they are drawn from the products of simplices H^1 and H^2; see page 70 for a definition of H^1 and H^2). They do have a different qualitative meaning, however, because they affirm the existence of a social institution and inform agents exactly how they should behave. As a result, when an institutional message (I_A or I_B) is transmitted, each player knows uniquely what move was made by the agents immediately before him and how he should behave.

If no institution has been created by the time a given agent is active, he cannot be certain how his opposing agent will behave and will be forced to assign some subjective probability belief to his potential actions. This lack of knowledge can be depicted by assuming that when it is agent a_{it}'s turn to move, he somehow forgets what has transpired before him and in trying to reconstruct his memory can only arrive at probabilistic beliefs as to whether an equilibrium institutional rule involving A or B has been established.

The tree diagram demonstrates clearly how institutions or societally agreed upon modes of behavior (conventions) come into being and are transmitted from generation to generation. Let us say that we are looking at the game starting in period t, at which time we will assume that no institutions have been created. Assume that at that time the norm $p^t = (p_1^t, p_2^t)$ exists, instructing each player how likely it is that his opposing agent will be following any one of his four plans of action specified by (4.7) and (4.8). p^t is then a pair of four-dimensional vectors. Now assume that in period t the auctioneer announces the optimal price vector p^*. Because no institution exists yet, we depict the information sets for agents a_{1t} and a_{2t} as containing all nodes at their move (see information sets IN_I and IN_{II} in Figure 4.13). Consequently, the lack of an institution will be taken by us to mean that agents a_{1t} and a_{2t} will not remember what has transpired in the game up until that point and will consequently have to solve their coordination problem based only on the information contained in the tth period norm $p^t = (p_1^t, p_2^t)$. Now assume that in this period, based on the existing norm, the static Bayesian solution procedure being used by the players tells each of them to employ a strategy in which they are always supposed to choose bundle A. If this is so, then in period t we observe (see the dark path in Figure 4.13) both players choosing bundle A. This observation causes them to revise their tth period norm p^t into $p^{t+1} = (p_1^{t+1}, p_2^{t+1})$, which will be

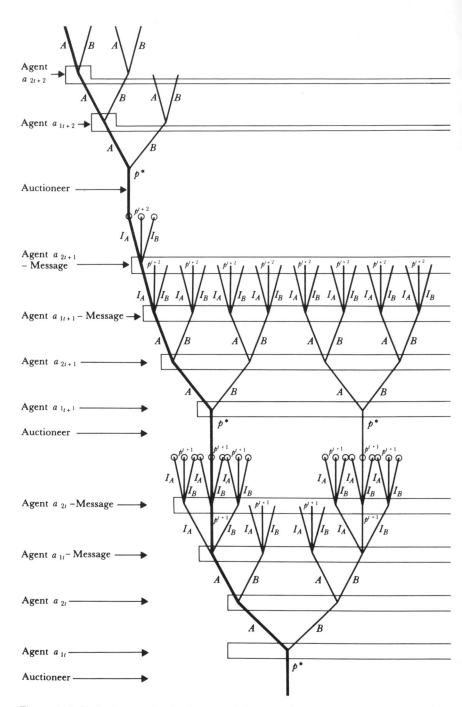

Figure 4.13. Institution creation in the not-strictly-convex barter game: institution-assisted games.

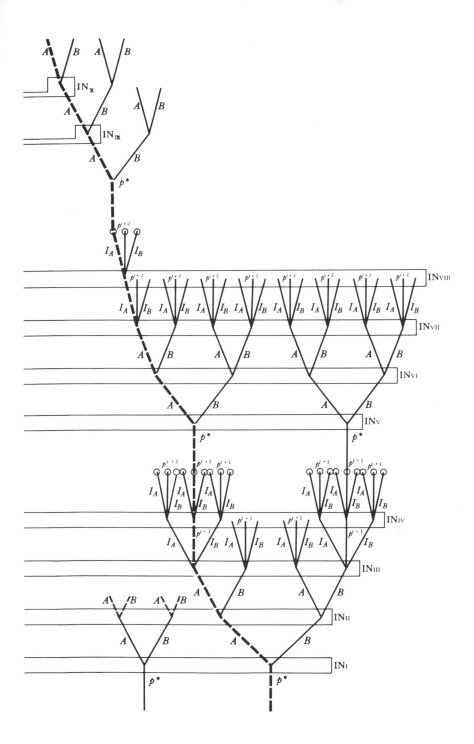

a norm in which it is more likely that the $t + 1$st period agents will follow a plan of action instructing them to choose bundle A. Now, because no institution has yet been created (the norms are not degenerate unit vectors), the agents in period $t + 1$ are again not totally certain how their opponent will behave, although they are more certain that he will choose a plan of action specifying the choice of bundle A than their predecessors were. Consequently, when the next generation of player goes to move, we consider the norm message they receive to be a garbled institutional message and represent this fact by the information sets depicted in the diagram by IN_{III} and IN_{IV}, which again contain all nodes at that move.

In period $t + 1$ we again depict the players as choosing a plan of action that instructs them to choose bundle A (see the dark path), but now we depict the $t + 2$nd period norm as a degenerate unit vector or institutional message I_A and assume that this institutional message is transmitted to the next generation. Consequently, from period $t + 2$ onward, all agents will have full certainty that the other will choose bundle A, and as a result bundle A will be chosen. This is depicted by the transmission of message I_A. Period $t + 1$ is what we call the *institution creation stage*. From period $t + 2$ onward, each player knows that both players before him chose A and expects with probability 1 that his opponent will also choose A. Consequently, he knows that he is on a branch of the game tree containing two consecutive institutional messages (I_A), yet he does not know the exact branch he is on, owing to his previous lack of recall prior to the institution's creation. This is depicted in the diagram by information sets IN_{IX} and IN_X, which contain only nodes that follow the transmission of two consecutive I_A message moves. As a result, when it is his turn to choose a bundle, he knows what his choice was in the previous period and, as a matter of fact, knows what all agents' moves were in every period since the creation of the institution. He does not, however, know when the institution was created–this information is not transmitted to him. Put differently, he does not know whether he is on the dark path in Figure 4.13 or on the dashed path in that diagram, but he does know that he is on a path of that variety. This is of no real consequence, however, because after an institution is created, all any agent needs to know to behave optimally at any time period is that an institutional rule governing his behavior exists. Therefore, in terms of the game tree, once an institution is created, we can assume that each player acts as if he knew exactly what the path of play was in the game since the creation of the social institution and hence has perfect recall about his moves. The game is transformed into a game of *institution-assisted perfect recall* because the institutional message is completely informative and distills all the relevant information about the path of the game's play up until that point.

Technically, the game still has imperfect recall because the creation of an institution offers no historical knowledge about the course of the game up to the creation of the institution. The point to be made is that this information is inessential because a myopic stationary behavioral strategy can be constructed without it. With this institution established, each player can proceed to employ a stationary behavioral strategy in the remainder of the game, which in our example is to always choose bundle A at each information set. Consequently, since stationary behavioral strategies are the most informationally efficient type of strategy for games in extensive (or agent normal) form, by allowing the players to employ them the institutional rule is an efficiency-increasing mechanism.

The point to be made, then, is that after the institution has been created, the economy moves myopically from one generation to another. The information existing at any point [i.e., the pair (p^*, λ)] consists of a price vector and an institutional rule (i.e., always choose bundle A), and these informational mechanisms help determine an economy that is informationally decentralized yet institutionally assisted. The analysis, then, demonstrates that individuals in pursuit of their own selfish interests will evolve institutions that help to allocate scarce resources to satisfy societal needs. These institutions are both market and nonmarket institutions. Yet, both are created as if by an invisible hand. Their purpose is identical, to help transmit information of a global variety (either about the scarcity of resources in the case of prices or about other agents' actions in the case of nonmarket institutions) to economic agents who have specialized decentralized information. They emerge "by human action but not human design" (Hayek 1955).

Finally, in terms of information storage, retrieval, and computation, the establishment of a social institution is extremely efficient because the only information relevant to decision making at any time period is contained in the norm, and if an institution is in existence, these norm vectors take on an especially simple form; they are unit vectors. No detailed history of the game need be kept by the players, nor does any other information need be stored. The institution tells all.

4.5 Entropy and the information content of norms and institutions

From our discussion so far one thing should be clear: social norms and institutions are devices that give structure or order to social situations. They do this by giving all of the agents in a particular situation an idea of what type of behavior they can expect from each other; and they act upon this information. At some time, however, a point is reached at which the actions that the agents observe completely fulfill all of their a priori expectations. At this point a social institution exists and the situation becomes totally structured, with each agent knowing exactly the type of behavior expected of him and everyone else and adhering to it. Our task in the remainder of the chapter is to try to quantify the exact extent to which social norms and institutions introduce order into previously chaotic social situations, and we propose to measure this using an entropy measure first developed by C. E. Shannon (1948) to measure the informational content of messages in a communication network. Before we proceed to our main discussion, let us pause and consider some simple concepts in information theory.

Information theory

In a pathbreaking work, C. E. Shannon (1948) developed a method to measure the informational content of messages sent in a communication network. This method was first formally applied to economics by Henri Theil (1967). To begin our discussion of Shannon's work, let us try to define the information content of a message stating that a certain state i has occurred, where $i \in N$, the set of all possible states. According to Shannon (1948), informational content of such a message can be measured as $h(X_i) = \log 1/X_i$, where X_i is the prior probability that state i will occur. This specific functional form is rationalized by the following argument [see Theil (1967)]. First, we would expect that the informational content of a message stating that state i has occurred should be inversely related to the prior probability of that state occurring. In other words, the more certain we are that a state i will occur, the less information we get when we find out it actually did.

In fact, if $X_i = 1$, we would expect that the informational content of a message stating that i occurred would be zero because that outcome was expected to occur, and if $X_i = 0$, the informational content of the message should be infinite. In addition, we would want our information measure to be continuously defined over the domain of X and monotonically decreasing. Finally, if states 1 and 2 are statistically independent, the informational content of a message stating that they both occurred, $h(X_1, X_2)$, should be simply $h(X_1) + h(X_2)$. The logarithmic function satisfies all these properties.

Given this function, we can derive an expression for the expected information existing in a situation with n states $i = 1, \ldots, n$ and probabilities $X_1, \ldots, X_n$ with $X_i \geq 0$, $\sum_{i=1}^{n} X_i = 1$. This is expressed as

$$\text{EI} = \sum_{i=1}^{n} X_i \log \frac{1}{X_i} \tag{4.13}$$

and measures the entropy or disorder in the situation. Note that this is maximized when $X_i = 1/n$ for all $i \in N$ and minimized when

$$X_i = \begin{cases} 0 & \text{for all } i \neq j \\ 1 & \text{for all } i = j \end{cases} \tag{4.14}$$

This expected information or entropy measure has a simple explanation. If a situation is very chaotic, so that all of the outcomes that could possibly occur are expected to occur with equal probability, then we have a great deal to learn from a message that actually tells us which outcome occurred. Consequently, when all outcomes are equally likely, the expected information of the message we receive is maximally informative. On the other hand, however, if we expect an outcome to occur with certainty, little can be expected to be learned from a message instructing us of the outcome. As a result, if the amount of chaos in a situation is equated to the amount of uncertainty existing about the situation's outcome, the amount of chaos can be meaningfully measured by the expected information existing in the situation.

Finally, we can measure the informational content of an indirect message or a message that does not indicate that a state i has definitely occurred but rather leads us change our original probability distribution for $X = (X_1, \ldots, X_n)$ to $y = (y_i, \ldots, y_n)$. It can be expressed as

$$H(X, y) = \sum_{i=1}^{n} y_i \log \frac{y_i}{X_i} \tag{4.15}$$

The expected information of an indirect message is actually the extent to which the entropy or disorder existing before the message is changed by the message.

Institutions and chaos

The applicability of these concepts to our analysis should be obvious. Assume that you are a third party observing the play of our infinite-agent Edgeworth institution-assisted economy. In addition, for simplicity, assume that in each period when the price vector pp' is announced, each agent has a choice between two bundles A and B with the resulting payoffs given by

Agent a_{2t}

		a_{2t}^A	a_{2t}^B
	a_{1t}^A	$\alpha_1^{t^{-1}}(6), \alpha_2^{t^{-1}}(4)$	$\alpha_1^{t^{-1}}(2), \alpha_2^{t^{-1}}(2)$
Agent a_{1t}			
	a_{1t}^B	$\alpha_1^{t^{-1}}(2), \alpha_2^{t^{-1}}(2)$	$\alpha_1^{t^{-1}}(6), \alpha_2^{t^{-1}}(4)$

Matrix 4.3. The allocation coordination game

Matrix 4.3 (same as Matrix 4.1). Now as stated before, each player can define four plans of action for himself to follow in this game [same as (4.7) and (4.8)]:

$$\Sigma^1 = (\sigma^1[a_{1t}^A/a_{2t}^A], \sigma^1[a_{1t}^A/a_{2t}^B], \sigma^1[a_{1t}^B/a_{2t}^A], \sigma^1[a_{1t}^B/a_{2t}^B])$$
$$\Sigma^2 = (\sigma^2[a_{2t}^A/a_{1t}^A], \sigma^2[a_{2t}^B/a_{1t}^A], \sigma^2[a_{2t}^A/a_{1t}^B], \sigma^2[a_{2t}^B/a_{1t}^B])$$

and at any time period t, a norm $\mathbf{p}^t = (\mathbf{p}_1^t, \mathbf{p}_2^t)$ exists which instructs each player as to the probability he should place on the other agent acting according to any one of these four plans of action. Now at time period t, when each agent chooses a bundle, according to the dictates of the static Bayesian solution procedure we can define the probability that one observes any particular pair of choices

$$b^{AA} = (a_{1t}^A, a_{2t}^A), \qquad b^{AB} = (a_{1t}^A, a_{2t}^B), \qquad b^{BA} = (a_{1t}^B, a_{2t}^A), \qquad b^{BB} = (a_{1t}^B, a_{2t}^B)$$

from our knowledge of the mixed strategies used by the players as dictated by the static Bayesian solution procedure. Let us denote these probabilities as follows:

$$\mathbf{1}_t = (l_t^{AA}, l_t^{AB}, l_t^{BA}, l_t^{BB}) \tag{4.16}$$

where, for instance, l_t^{AA} defines the probability that we observe the pair of choices $b^{AA} = (a_{1t}^A, a_{2t}^A)$ being made in period t when the norm is $\mathbf{p}^t = (\mathbf{p}_1^t, \mathbf{p}_2^t)$ and the players are behaving according to the mixed strategies dictated by the static Bayesian solution procedure $\mathcal{M}$. At each time period t, we can construct the vector $\mathbf{1}_t$ by multiplying the mixed-strategy vectors $\mathbf{s}_{1t}$ and $\mathbf{s}_{2t}$ appropriately. Consequently, if you were our fictional third party observing the evolution of this economy at each period t, there are four possible outcomes that could occur–observation of either the pair $b^1 = (a_{1t}^A, a_{2t}^A)$ or $b^2 = (a_{1t}^A, a_{2t}^B)$ or $b^3 = (a_{1t}^B, a_{2t}^A)$ or $b^4 = (a_{1t}^B, a_{2t}^B)$–and there is a probability distribution $\mathbf{1}_t = (l_t^{AA}, l_t^{AB}, l_t^{BA}, l_t^{BB})$ defined over these outcomes. Consequently, if at any time t we wanted to measure how orderly or chaotic the economy was, we could ask: What is the expected amount of information existing in a message that informs us of the bundles actually chosen by our agents in time t. This can then be answered by measuring the expected information existing in the vector $l^t = (l_t^{AA}, l_t^{AB}, l_t^{BA}, l_t^{BB})$ or

$$EI = \sum_{i=1}^{4} l_t^i \log \frac{1}{l_t^i} \tag{4.17}$$

where $l_t^1 = l_t^{AA}$

$\qquad l_t^2 = l_t^{AB}$

$\qquad l_t^3 = l_t^{BA}$

$\qquad l_t^4 = l_t^{BB}$

Notice what this means. If the norms existing in the economy are such that it leads to a situation in period t where we are equally likely to observe any pair of bundles being chosen (i.e., where $\mathbf{1}_t$ is a distribution giving equal weights to all four outcomes), then we are least likely to be able to predict what will happen. The situation will be most chaotic and our expected informational measure will be maximized. However, what happens when an institution exists? If this is the case, the vector $\mathbf{1}_t$ will be a unit vector, because once the institution exists, we know with certainty what outcome will be observed in period t, and the expected information of a message in this context is minimized: in fact, it is zero. Consequently, the creation of a social institution is an entropy-minimizing device that totally structures a given situation of strategic interdependence. Their purpose is to create order out of chaos, to make our lives more predictable, and thereby allow us to devote less of our resources to solving recurrent social problems repeatedly.

In addition to measuring the total amount of entropy existing at any time in a given social situation, our entropy measures allow us to measure how informative a particular observation is of the game being played. For instance, let us assume that it is time period t and the vector existing in our simple game is $l_t = (l_t^1, l_t^2, l_t^3, l_t^4)$, defining the probability of observing the occurrence of any one of our four bundles being chosen. If our institution has not yet been established, then on the basis of the tth-period observations, a new $(t + 1)$st-period vector, $l_{t+1} = (l_{t+1}^1, l_{t+1}^2, l_{t+1}^3, l_{t+1}^4)$, will be defined and we can measure the informational content of this observation, which leads us to change l_t into l_{t+1} as the informational content of an indirect message leading the players to change their estimate of l from l_t to l_{t+1} as follows:

$$H(l_t, l_{t+1}) = \sum_{i=1}^{4} l_{t+1}^i \log \left[\frac{l_t^i}{l_{t+1}^i} \right] \tag{4.18}$$

Again, notice that if the players in the game have not yet established an institution, each observation for each period t is informative, or the information value of each observation is positive. However, if an institution is established in period k, then $l_k = l_{k+1}$ for all $t \geq k$ and $H(l_t, l_{t+1}) = 0$ for all $t \geq k$. Consequently, the expected information value of an observation of a particular social situation for which a social institution has already been established is zero, because once the institution is established, we are certain what we will observe, so that actually observing it is not informative. In short, social institutions, once established, are fully informative, and nothing can be learned from observing adherence to them.

4.6 Conclusions

In this chapter I have tried to demonstrate that economic and social institutions are primarily informational mechanisms that complement the information contained in competitive prices when these prices fail to totally coordinate economic activities. In so doing they help to add structure and order to what would otherwise be a more chaotic situation of strategic interdependence. In short, we behave the way we do because in many of our social and economic encounters we know what type of behavior is expected of us and others, and behaving that way is the "equilibrium thing to do." The purpose of economic and social institutions is to transfer such information.

5 Toward a neo-institutional approach to economics

One of the demands that confronts social scientists is the demand for relevance. For many, this demand is a curse because it robs social scientists of their ability to justify total abstraction. The inevitable question in social science is always: "So what? What difference does this make to the real world?"

It is my belief that there are two methodological responses to this demand. One is a response in which the social scientist makes his work directly applicable to meaningful empirical questions. This is what the layman usually sanctions as "relevant" social scientific research. The other approach, however, and one that I feel is equally relevant, is an approach that aims not to change the real world directly but rather to alter the way we view the real world by changing the prevailing theoretical paradigm existing among scholars. In other words, one approach is to theorize directly about the real world, whereas the other is to theorize about the theory existing to describe the real world (i.e., to be metatheoretical). My aim in this book was closer to the latter approach than to the former. What I have written may not be as directly applicable to the real world as it is to the way we view that world. I have tried to broaden the institutional frame of reference that we use to analyze empirically relevant social phenomena and to open up a new set of questions that could be asked about such phenomena. Consequently, the theory presented here is one step removed from direct application, yet still potentially applicable.

In this chapter I outline what the consequences are for economics and other social sciences if one chooses to view the world through the institutional lenses constructed in this book. I do this by investigating the consequences that this type of analysis would have for a variety of specific topics both within and outside of economics, and by relating what we have done in this book to similar work done elsewhere.

5.1 Institutions, teams, hierarchies, satisficing, and bounded rationality

No idea is created in a vacuum. The works of other scholars and the intellectual climate existing at a given time are bound to influence, however consciously or unconsciously, any work that is done. This book is no exception. The ideas

144

contained here have a close relationship to the efforts of many other scholars who have been dealing with questions of organizational control and information over the past 10 years, and before we conclude our discussion I would like to point out these interrelationships and influences.

Teams

From our discussion in the first four chapters it should be clear that economic and social institutions, in our context, are behavioral rules of thumb that are created endogenously by the agents we are investigating. These rules of thumb or decision rules can then be investigated to discover whether they are efficient or not when compared to the decision rule that a social planner would choose under identical circumstances. If we consider the set of agents under investigation to be members of an organization whose goal is to reach Pareto-optimal outcomes, the investigation of the optimal decision rule for such an organization is a topic that is closely related to the study of the economic theory of teams originated by Jacob Marschak and Roy Radner (1972). To investigate the relationship of the team problem to the institutional problem being discussed in this book, let us briefly review what the team-theoretical problem is and contrast it to the game-theoretical types of problems we have been discussing up to this point

The static team problem concerns a set of n agents called team members whose preferences are identified in terms of the outcome of the team. In other words, their problem is to coordinate their decisions or actions in such a way as to maximize the objective function of the team. If their preferences differed, the problem would cease to be a team problem and would revert to an n-person game of the cooperative or noncooperative type, depending on the costs of communication and commitment. The problem is complicated by the fact that the world in which the team members live is uncertain, so that the team members do not know which state of nature x exists where $x \in X$, the set of all states of nature. The administrator of the team, on whom the analysis is centered, can, at a cost, decide upon an information structure that will associate for each team member a signal y with each $x \in X$. Such a function η_i from X to Y for all i $[y = \eta_i(x)]$ is an information structure, and each such η_i partitions the states of nature into disjoint sets of x that all have the same signal. After the team organizer has decided upon such a function for each member of the team, $\eta(x) = (\eta_i(x); \ldots, \eta_n(x))$, he must decide upon a decision rule for each member that will tell him what action to take if signal y is given, $y \in Y$. If we call such a function for the ith team player $\alpha_i = \alpha_i(y)$, then $\alpha(y) = (\alpha_1(y), \ldots, \alpha_n(y))$ and the team organizer must decide upon two n-tuples $(\eta_1(x), \ldots, \eta_n(x); \alpha_1(y), \ldots, \alpha_n(y))$, which maximizes the expected utility of the team. If information were free, the gross expected payoff of the team would be

$$Eu = \Omega(\eta, \alpha) = Ew(x, \alpha[\eta(x)])$$

where the expectation is taken over $x \in X$. However, information may be costly, and if we represent such costs by a cost function

$$\gamma(x, \alpha, \eta)$$

where $\gamma(x, \alpha, \eta)$ is the cost of the teams organization (α, η) when the state of nature is x, then the maximum expected net payoff to the team is

$$\max_{\substack{\eta_1(x), \ldots, \eta_n(x) \\ \alpha_1(y), \ldots, \alpha_n(y)}} Ew(x, \alpha[\eta(x)]) - E\gamma(x, \alpha, \eta))$$

Our institutional problem differs from the typical team problem in that there is no team organizer in the social situations we explore and the information structure is given and cannot be changed. Consequently, the institutions problem is a problem of optimal decision making in decentralized as opposed to centrally organized teams, and we claim that over time one specific team organizational structure will evolve as the same team problem is faced recurrently by succeeding generations of team members. Consequently, we claim that at any given period of time the team or societal information structure is given and that team members search for decision rules that are optimal, given that information structure and the fact that the other decision makers' decisions will affect their payoff. At any time, an equilibrium will exist if the decision made by the team players are what Marschak and Radner call person-by-person satisfactory. More formally, a decision vector $\tilde{\alpha} = (\tilde{\alpha}_1, \ldots, \tilde{\alpha}_n)$ is satisfactory for player i if given the decision vector $\overline{\tilde{\alpha}}_i$ of the other $n - 1$ team players, $\overline{\tilde{\alpha}} = (\tilde{\alpha}_1, \ldots, \tilde{\alpha}_{i-1}, \tilde{\alpha}_{i+1}, \ldots, \tilde{\alpha}_n)$, the payoff to player i, $\Omega^i(\overline{\tilde{\alpha}}_i, \alpha_i) = \Omega^i(\tilde{\alpha}_1, \ldots, \tilde{\alpha}_{i-1}, \alpha_i, \tilde{\alpha}_{i+1}, \ldots, \tilde{\alpha}_n)$ is maximized by the vector

$$\tilde{\alpha} = (\tilde{\alpha}_1, \ldots, \tilde{\alpha}_i, \ldots, \tilde{\alpha}_n)$$

If this is true for all $i \in N$, then $\tilde{\alpha} = (\tilde{\alpha}_1, \ldots, \tilde{\alpha}_n)$ is person-by-person satisfactory. It is exactly such regularity in behavior that, if established in an organization or team, becomes what we have called a social convention or institution, and the study of social institutions can be described as the study that investigates the evolution and function of person-by-person satisfactory decision rules, their optimality, and their transmittal from generation to generation. Such decision rules are, we feel, exactly what Menger had in mind when he discussed the organic creation of social institutions.

The description of the team problem above, although similar to the problem under investigation in this book, is different in three distinct ways:

1. The team problem is a static problem describing what decision n-tuple is person-by-person satisfactory. Our problem, however, as we have seen, is evo-

lutionary, so that we are not interested only in the emergence of a given social institution, but also in its transmittal to future generations as a fixed regularity in behavior. In other words, we are interested in the process of institutionalization of person-by-person satisfactory decision rules and the efficiency of such institutionalization.

2. The problems we investigate need not involve statistical uncertainty but may involve purely strategic uncertainty. In other words, we treat situations in which there is only one state of nature and payoffs depend only on the strategy choices of social agents. These may be called strategic coordination problems.

3. The situations we investigate need not involve problems in which all decision makers have preferences that are in accordance. In other words, we are interested in situations that are not only team problems but also noncooperative game problems, and because we take an evolutionary view in which the time horizon is infinite, we are therefore interested in a supergame-type problem posed by any given social situation.

Hierarchies

Looking back at what we have attempted so far in this book, it is clear that we are interested in the origin, evolution, and function of nonmarket institutions. In short, we have stated that there are circumstances where the information contained in market prices is not sufficient to efficiently decentralize the actions of agents. To compensate for this missing information, it becomes necessary for agents to create nonmarket institutions. Consequently, we have raised the question of when it may be more efficient to supplement or replace markets with other, nonmarket, institutions (see the traffic game of Chapter 1 for an illustration of this point). This exact point, however, is dealt with at length by Oliver Williamson (1975) in *Markets and Hierarchies*. Williamson basically investigates the question of vertical integration and asks when a given firm will find it advantageous to rely on markets to supply itself with inputs and when it would be advantageous to vertically integrate by buying up its suppliers. By doing that, the firm replaces the market by absorbing it into itself and transforms what was previously a market transaction with an intrafirm exchange. Consequently, for Williamson the market disappears and is absorbed into the firm through vertical integration. Other investigators have also dealt with this question and concentrated on when it is informationally efficient to vertically integrate [see Arrow (1975)]. Consequently, this literature implies that the set of institutions (i.e., markets or firms) through which firms interact is not given exogenously but is in some sense a choice variable, because by vertically integrating, firms can change what was previously a market transaction into a nonmarket transaction. In this context the set of institutions that emerges is determined primarily by efficiency considerations. To convince one-self that Williamson is primarily interested in institutional questions, one must only look at the first chapter of his book, where statements such as the following are common:

A broadly based interest among economists in what might be referred to as the "new institutional economics" has developed in recent years. . . . The spirit in which this present book is written very much follows the thinking of these new institutionalists. I hope, by exploring microeconomic issues of markets and hierarchies in greater detail than conventional analysis commonly employs, to achieve a better understanding of the origins and functions of various firm and market structures—stretching from elementary work groups to complex modern corporations. I focus on transactions and the costs that attend completing transactions by one institutional mode rather than another. [Williamson 1975, p. 1]

I think that it should be clear that a fair number of modern economists have continued to work on institutional questions long after the "old institutional-ists" have ceased having the center of the economic academic stage, and I think it is safe to say that this book may be considered yet another addition to this tradition.

Satisficing and bounded rationality

Mostly through the work of Herbert Simon the tools of modern decision theory have been introduced into the study of economics. As Simon (1979) has recently pointed out, this introduction has been slow and has at times met with resistance from the neoclassical school. The major thrust of Simon's work and other work on the behavioral theory of the firm [see Cyert and March (1963)] is that economic agents do not necessarily always maximize, because maximizing usually requires an exorbitant amount of information and calcu-lation and if such commodities are not free, agents may find it to their interest to establish some rule of thumb for themselves and adhere to it despite the fact that some other maximizing rule might lead to globally higher profits. When we leave the realm of the individual and look at sets of individuals who repeat-edly face the same recurrent problem, we can ask if these agents collectively will search for what may be the optimal rule or whether they will rather tacitly establish a rule for themselves which, although not leading to globally optimal results, will at least lead to results that are better than the ones that would exist if no rule was established.

For example, consider the game illustrated by Matrix 5.1. This is a coor-dination game with two equilibria, both circled. Now assume that this game were repeated each period and that each period each player had to decide to choose either a_i^1 or a_i^2 $i = 1, 2$. If it takes time and effort to establish a con-vention to govern this situation, it may be in the interests of the players to

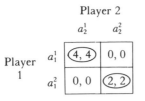

Matrix 5.1. A coordination game

establish some equilibrium rule and follow it even if the payoffs forthcoming
are not Pareto-optimal. This is especially true if the absolute size of the payoffs
is small, because the time and effort that might have to be devoted to improving
the rule may entail costs that greatly outweigh the benefits. To understand this
point better, let us assume that these same agents are simultaneously engaged
in another recurrent problem, whose payoffs are much greater than the payoffs
in Matrix 5.1. If this were true, it is very likely that the agents in the original
game would not devote a great amount of time and effort to establish the optimal convention for that game (in which they both choose their first strategy),
because their time might be allocated more effectively elsewhere (i.e., to the
more important problem). Hence, if an equilibrium institution or convention
were established in the first game in which both players repeatedly chose their
second strategy [with the resulting payoff of (2, 2)], no effort might be exerted
to changing this. The institution would determine "satisfactory" results but not
necessarily "optimal" results for the problem when viewed in isolation. Hence
the societal rules of thumb that we have called social institutions are really
satisfactory rules that solve recurrent problems once and for all but might not
always lead to optimal results. Their major benefit is that by solving unimpor-
tant problems quickly, they allow the agents in the economy to allocate their
effort elsewhere to solve more important problems.

5.2 The neo-institutional approach to economics and social phenomena

Institutions and neoclassical theory

Economics today, as seen in the works of Debreu (1959) and Arrow
and Hahn (1971), is an institutionally limited science. The only social or economic institutions that exist are markets of the competitive type in which all
agents act parametrically and in isolation. This lack of institutional detail must
be considered a weakness of the theory. To get a better idea of this point, let
us look at a typical neoclassical model of the phenomenon of general competitive equilibrium. The model proceeds first by announcing the fact that in the
theoretical world under investigation, only two types of economic agents exist–

the consumer and the producer. The consumers' job is to consume goods and offer their labor so as to maximize their utility given their budget and time constraints. The results of their maximization are summarized by a demand correspondence or function. The producers are assumed to maximize profits by transforming inputs into outputs. The results of their maximization is summarized by a supply correspondence or function.

To this point, the model is innocuous enough and simply describes the physical world in which the agents exist together with some simple behavioral assumptions of rationality. A problem arises in closing the model, however, because at this point a mechanism is required to coordinate the decision of the two types of agents. Rather than facing the problem head on, theorists have resorted to a deus ex machina. A fictitious auctioneer is envisioned whose job it is to call out prices to the consumers and producers and process the quantity demands and offers forthcoming at those prices. The problem with this assumption is not its lack of realism, because, although these fictitious auctioneers clearly do not exist, it can be said that markets do function *as if* they really did. Rather, the assumption has the following two weaknesses:

1. It robs the model of any behavioral or strategic complexity or interest. The neoclassical agents are bores who merely calculate optimal activities at fixed parametric prices. They are limited to one and only one type of behavior- that of acting as automata in response to the auctioneer. No syndicates or coalitions are formed, no cheating or lying is done, no threats are made–merely truthful parametric behavior. This strategic assumption has been called the Walras–Pareto fixation by Morgenstern (1972) and has been criticized strongly by game theorists, especially Martin Shubik (1973, 1974), whose recent work has been an attempt to close these models strategically in a non-cooperative framework of trade as opposed to the neoclassical method of the "magic wand."

2. More important for our purpose, however, the manner in which the neoclassical model is closed robs the model of any institutional sophistication. By this I mean that by positing the existence of a fictitious auctioneer, the theory is making an extreme institutional assumption: that the only institutions that exist in the economy are markets of the competitive type and that all information in the economy must be transmitted through the prices formed in these markets. This is clearly extreme. The economy has no money, no government, no legal system, no property rights, no banks–in short, none of the many social institutions that are created by societies to help coordinate their economic and social activities by offering information not available in competitive prices.

When we realize the impact that the seemingly innocuous existence of the fictitious auctioneer has on the results of the neoclassical model, we are able to retrace our steps and investigate the assumptions necessary for the model to work. When we do this, we immediately realize that these assumptions are the minimal assumptions necessary for the institutional structure forced on the model to be sufficient for its purposes–reaching a decentralized competitive equilibrium. The relaxation of any of these assumptions immediately makes the institutional structure of neoclassical economics inadequate for its purpose. The model really works backward. Given the assumed institutional arrangement–competitive markets–it investigates the types of economic environments for which decentralized economic equilibria exist. These environments then become the focus of study for the theory. Consequently, if one were to close the model in a less restrictive manner, economics would be freed to study a wider variety of economic environments [see Hurwicz (1973a)]–economies that include nonconvexities, discontinuities, and externalities, in a much more natural way. The job of the theory would then be to explain the type of institutional arrangement that would evolve from a particular environment or lead one to design institutions that, for any given environment, would reach "satisfactory" allocations. [For a further analysis of this point, see Hurwicz (1973a, b).]

If the neoclassical theory were just a theory in "positive" economics, the damage done by the misplaced institutional emphasis described above might be meaningfully contained. However, when the theory is made the basis of a normative theory, some attention must be paid. The two fundamental theorems of welfare economics, that each competitive equilibrium is a Pareto-optimum and that every Pareto-optimum can be achieved as a competitive equilibrium if the appropriate income redistribution is made, have extremely interesting consequences for what we have been discussing. Basically, they state that in terms of economic welfare, the only institutions that are necessary for welfare maximization are the very competitive markets assumed in the theory. The theorems are a vindication of the way in which the model is closed and justify the limited institutional character of the theory.

These theorems have grave consequences for the way in which economists approach social problems. When market institutions fail, as in the case of economies with uncertainty and externalities, the neoclassical economist does not, as he should, try to explain what alternative sets of institutions would be created to take their place. Rather, he attempts to redefine and expand the commodity space of the economy so that markets are again feasible institutions. For example, consider the analysis of Arrow and Hahn (1971) when their model comes upon the problem of uncertainty. When social groups in the real world face this problem, they devise a wide variety of schemes to help them spread the risks envisioned in the future. Farming cooperatives, insurance companies, and self-help groups all aim to deal with this problem. Economic theory, on the other hand, treats the problem as one that could be solved if the commodity space were sufficiently expanded to define goods as contingent quantities, conditional on the future states of nature. With this assumption, the fictitious auctioneer is once again called upon to call out prices, this time for an expanded "contingent economy," and market institutions are again proven sufficient for the allocation purpose.

The same trick is used by Arrow (1970) in treating the problem of externalities. Here, externalities are treated as market failures that can be corrected if an expanded set of commodities were created. This time the new commodities created are the externalities themselves, and markets in the externalities are invoked to allocate goods efficiently.

The important point to be made is not that this approach is ridiculous or even incorrect. What is being said is that economic theory, as it exists today, can be seen as an attempt to rationalize the extreme way in which the theory is closed and that the relaxation of this aspect of the theory is bound to expand its scope and make it more relevant to the world.

The game-theoretical revolution

The core and cooperative games: some disappointing results. Faced with the artificial nonstrategic manner in which all agents must behave in the neoclassical theory, cooperative game theory offered what appeared to be a way out, a way to free the science from the artificial auctioneer-led parametric *tâtonnement* process. It took exception to the fact that if the neoclassical model is closed in the manner it is, all behavioral and strategic complexity is robbed from the model and we are left with something of little intellectual interest.

Behaviorally, cooperative game theory is a great advance over neoclassical theory. It allows its actors unlimited strategic freedom within the rules of the economy and does not constrict them to a single type of parametric behavior. In this sense it must be considered a great success. The manner in which the theory developed, however, has proven to be a big disappointment, because its end result is to present an economy in equilibrium with an institutional structure no richer than the neoclassical model. This is particularly unfortunate because game theory holds real promise for the development of models that describe the evolution of institutional forms. This shortcoming in the theory is a consequence of a misplaced emphasis and misdirection that has characterized much of the game-theoretical research on the problem of general equilibrium. To understand this shortcoming, let us look at the way in which cooperative game-theoretical models are constructed.

To begin, the same agents exist in game-theoretical models as exist in the neoclassical model, as do the same commodity spaces, consumption sets, and technologies. However–and here is the first advance–cooperative game-theoretical models do not assume that competitive markets exist at the outset of the analysis. Consequently, no auctioneer is required and agents are free to act as they wish. This action takes the form of coalition formation among the agents in which each coalition strives to do as well for itself as it possibly can, given its productive capabilities and its resources. Institutionally, then, we are offered the opportunity of watching the evolution of an economy in which no institutions exist whatsoever at the outset–the economy exists in a state of economic nature–and the institutions that evolve can be explained endogenously.

In addition, the theory of games offers a wide variety of solution concepts, some of which, like the stable set solution, provide a rich description of stable institutional arrangements [see Hildebrand and Kirman (1976) for a good discussion of the relation between the Walrasian and Edgeworthian analyses]. At this point, game theorists made a mistake. They chose to use one particular solution concept, the core, which was particularly suited to their purpose because it could be shown that in market games the core was equivalent to Edgeworth's famous contract curve. The general equilibrium problem then became a search for allocations, without prices, which could not be improved upon by any coalition of traders. Such a set of undominated allocations constitutes the core of the economy.

The crowning achievement of the theory has been the proof of a conjecture made by Edgeworth (1881) that as the economy becomes larger in an appropriate way, in the limit the only core allocations that remain are also competitive equilibria. In other words, the theory did not assume that markets exist at the outset; rather, it made no assumptions about institutions whatsoever. What it did was formally prove that in the limit, competitive markets would be stable institutions. These limit theorems demonstrate that if the economies observed are conventional in the sense that all the typical neoclassical assumptions are satisfied, one particular institutional structure, competitive markets, will evolve. Consequently, the theory does what we expect it to do; it not only describes the equilibrium set of prices and allocations but also the equilibrium set of institutions that can be expected to evolve.

Unfortunately, in its present form the only institutions that evolve are competitive markets, so that in the limit the cooperative game-theoretical analysis offers us nothing more than the neoclassical analysis. Both are institutionally degenerate, although the game-theoretical analysis at least describes the evolution of markets instead of simply assuming their existence at the outset. Consequently, if the cooperative game-theoretical approach fails, it fails because although it at least explains the evolution of one type of social institution, competitive markets, it so restricts its analysis and concentrates so totally on the core as a solution concept that it is not able to explain the evolution of any other institutional form.

Actually, a word of modification should be added here. My point is not that cooperative game theory is an unprofitable area to investigate; far from it. Some of the most important applications in economics have come from the area of cooperative game analysis, as can be seen in the works of Lloyd Shapley and Martin Shubik as well as Lester Telser's recent treatment and application of the theory of the core in *Economic Theory and the Core* (1979). Rather, I am talking about the huge amount of effort that has gone into proving limit theorems whose results strip the entire game-theoretical analysis of their most interesting property, their ability to explain the evolution of nonmarket institutions [see Schotter and Schwödiauer (1980)].

Noncooperative games. In the past 10 years there have been some extremely promising game-theoretical advances in noncooperative theory, which hold out real promise for the systematical analysis of social and economic institutions. Basically, there are two streams of thought here. Martin Shubik, in association with Pradeep Dubey and Lloyd Shapley, has investigated a series of models in which the allocative properties of specific market institutions have been analyzed. All of the models deal with specific monetary institutions, and the games are all modeled in a noncooperative manner in which the Nash equilibrium is the solution concept employed as opposed to the core. In many of the models studied, the authors have proved that as the economies that employ these specific market institutions get large, the set of Nash equilibria of the games associated with them converges to the set of Walrasian equilibria of the economy. Consequently, the institutional detail of these models is very fine, and Shubik gives us a first look into an economy that is rich in institutional detail and theoretical interest.

The other approach to the study of social and economic institutions is most closely associated with the name of Leonid Hurwicz and a group of younger economists mostly centered at Northwestern University. The focus of these scientists is first to specify some desiderata that they feel any reasonably satisfactory allocating mechanisms should fulfill. However, since each allocating mechanism determines a different noncooperative game in normal form played by agents in the economy, the question resolves itself into which n-person game, if played by the agents in the economy, will yield results that are satisfactory. However, when we realize that an allocating mechanism is nothing more than a particular institutional setting, it becomes clear that these noncooperative models are really attempts at comparing the properties of alternative classes of economic institutions and, as such, are extremely promising.

Although these attempts are exciting, they emphasize a different aspect of the institutional problem from the one we are interested in here. First, our interests here are in the organic development and evolution of various social and economic institutions. Consequently, we are not interested in designing optimal institutions or in examining the properties of any particular class of them; rather, we focus on what types of institutional arrangements will be developed by the agents themselves. There are no planners in our analysis who have the ability to organize the economy. All there are are selfish maximizing agents who create institutions in pursuit of their own self-interest.

More important, however, the definition of what we call social and economic institutions differs from what are considered social institutions in the foregoing applications. More specifically, for Shubik and Hurwicz, social institutions are various rules of conduct that are defined by the planner and whose definition determines different n-person games. Consequently, for these authors the rules of the game and the institutional structure of it are synonymous terms. For us, however, what we call social institutions are not the rules of the game but rather the alternative equilibrium standards of behavior or conventions of behavior that evolve from a given game described by its rules. In other words, for us, institutions are properties of the equilibrium of games and not properties of the game's description. We care about what the agents do with the rules of the game, not what the rules are. This difference, however, merely reflects the difference of purpose between our two analyses. Our purpose here is positive and merely tries to describe the type of institutional arrangements that can be expected to evolve from a given situation, whereas theirs (at least Hurwicz's) is more normative and aims to prescribe which class of institutions ought to be designed if our aim is to achieve certain types of allocations at equilibrium. Consequently, as we will see in the next section, the two approaches are complementary.

The design of optimal institutions

As was stated before, the institutional question being asked in this book is not what institution, described as an abstract set of rules, yields results that are satisfactory according to some desiderata, but rather which regularity in behavior will emerge as the equilibrium regularity or convention prescribing behavior for the agents at each iteration of some *exogenously* given n-person recurrent game. In other words, we do not concentrate on the rules of the game but rather on the regularity of behavior that agents establish given the rules. Our emphasis may then be considered more positive than normative.

What I would like to demonstrate here is that these two types of analyses—the positive analysis described in this book and the comparative analysis referred to above—are not separate issues. In fact, I hope to demonstrate that the analysis I have been presenting is preliminary to the comparative analysis and that the two complement each other in an extremely convenient way.

To see this point, consider the problem faced by a community that has to construct a public good or a good that, once built, will be enjoyed by all members of society and is such that no member can be excluded from its use. In addition, assume that all agents will be asked to contribute to finance the construction of this good. As is well known, each member of such a society has an incentive to try to avoid revealing what his true preferences are for the public good, because he knows that once it is constructed he will be able to enjoy its benefits whether he has paid or not. An incentive or "free-rider" problem exists. Faced with this potential problem, there are two relevant questions:

1. Is the incentive problem, even though potentially real and theoretically possible, empirically significant–do people in fact lie about their preferences?
2. If it is an empirically relevant problem, what allocating institution can be designed that will lead people to act according to their true preferences?

The first question would be one attacked by the analysis presented here. Whether or not an incentive problem exists in a given society depends upon the norms and conventions of behavior established in that society, which regulate how people behave when confronted with such problems. Clearly, many societies exist in which it is possible to be a free rider in many situations, yet people do not because a "good-citizen" convention exists that people adhere to. Many examples, such as the tram system in Vienna, exist to prove this point. In other situations and in other societies, the incentive problem is a real one, because the society has established a free-rider convention in which all people expect the others to cheat and consequently decide to cheat themselves. Consequently, whether or not the state will be called upon to devise an allocating mechanism that will lead people to reveal their true preferences will depend upon the norms and conventions established to govern the situation. If the government has faith that people, even though they could, will not lie, it may not need to interfere in the allocation process in any way other than as a processor of information and as a coordinator. However, if it is clear that free riding is the expected behavior of its citizens, the government must explicitly enter into the allocating process. The question of devising optimal allocating mechanisms is then relevant only in those situations in which the equilibrium conventions or institutions existing in society lead to suboptimal allocations, and the extent to which this is true is an empirical question.[1] The point being made, however, is that the two types of institutional analyses, the positive and the comparative, merely attack different parts of the same problem and that logically one must be settled before we can decide whether the other is needed.

Market structure and the theory of industrial organization

In economic theory there is an extremely artificial manner in which different types of market structures are defined. In fact, three different types of structures are delineated and a separate theory posited for each one. Consequently, the move from the theory of perfectly competitive markets to the theory of oligopolistic or monopolistic markets is a highly discontinuous one. In addition, the market structures are defined in a rather artificial manner. For instance, perfectly competitive markets are defined as those markets in which there is a homogeneous good sold by a "large" number of firms selling to buyers who are informed perfectly about the prices charged by each firm and whose behavior is completely described by a demand curve. Oligopolistic industries have fewer firms–so few, as a matter of fact, that each firm must consider the impact of its actions on the behavior of the others. Monopolistic industries have only one seller.

This categorization is not satisfactory, however, because it is not clear when the number of firms is small and when it is large. Also, the criteria with which different structures are defined are not necessarily the critical criteria that actually differentiate them. As a result of our discussion in this book, however, there does exist one possible way to classify these market structures so that one unified classification is possible and we can avoid the discontinuous process of switching theories as soon as the market structure changes. Let me explain.

From what we have said in Chapter 4, social and economic institutions are informational devices that arise to help supplement the information contained in prices. The point there was that prices are mechanisms that provide information about the societal scarcity of resources, whereas institutions are mechanisms that supply information about the potential actions of other economic agents. Consequently, in markets where prices are not informationally sufficient to coordinate economic activity, some additional informational device will have to emerge to help in this coordination, because a problem of strategic interdependence among agents exists and the need to coordinate them has arisen. The informational devices that emerge to settle such problems are institutions or conventions. Now, to apply this to the classification of markets, all we need do is to classify markets with respect to the information necessary for the determination of an equilibrium in the market. For instance, if a market is perfectly competitive, the only information necessary to determine whether the market is in equilibrium is prices. All of the information that any firm needs to function in the market is contained in the price. Consequently, perfectly competitive markets are markets in which the equilibrium is completely characterized by prices.

In what are traditionally called oligopolistic markets, this is not true. One cannot determine whether the market is in equilibrium only by being informed of the price; one must also know the industry conventions of behavior or "code of conduct" before one can say that a particular price is consistent with that convention. Each firm must have information about the intended actions of others, and this information is transmitted through the existing convention of behavior. Consequently, in such markets, firms must be informed of both prices and institutions in order to behave in an equilibrium fashion and we, as outside observers, must be informed of both of these before we can decide whether the market is in equilibrium.

Market Structure

	Perfect Competition	*Oligopoly*	*Monopoly*
	Prices	*Prices and Conventions*	*Conventions*
Informational Mechanisms			

Figure 5.1. The classification of market structures.

In what are commonly called monopolistic markets, there is only one seller and he has the ability to set any price he so wishes. Consequently, any price he sets is an equilibrium as long as we know the convention he uses to choose prices. In such markets, the conventions of behavior developed are solely the conventions created by the monopolist himself, and knowledge of this convention is sufficient to define the equilibrium. More precisely, each market period the monopolist faces a recurrent one-person problem in which he is asked to choose a price. He is free to act in any way he wishes, because there are no other firms in the market; consequently, any convention of behavior (i.e., profit maximization, sales maximization, social welfare maximization) is a candidate for the equilibrium convention in the market. As a result, the only information it is necessary to know in such markets is the convention of behavior used by the monopolist.

From this discussion we can see that perfectly competitive markets are markets in which prices alone are sufficient information upon which to characterize equilibria, whereas in oligopolistic markets, both prices and institutions are required. In monopolistic markets, institutions or conventions alone are sufficient. A simple set of market structures are then defined informationally as shown in Figure 5.1. In this scheme market structures are classified only with respect to the type of information that is necessary and sufficient to reach equilibrium coordinated behavior. The number of firms in the market is irrelevant, so that the small–large problem does not exist and we can categorize markets consistently according to one information criterion.

International relations, conventions of war, and institutions

The world that has emerged from the Second World War is a world dominated by a few superpowers. These superpowers consistently confront each other in various parts of the world and test each other's will and fortitude. On the military side of this matter, these countries continually confront each other or decide to avoid such confrontations. For instance, although the United States lost 40,000 military personnel in Vietnam, it never launched an all-out invasion of the North. When the USSR invaded Czechoslovakia, the United

States, although protesting, never seriously entertained the thought of interfering. Such interventions are out of the question because they would serve to seriously disrupt the norms of behavior established in world politics and the conventions of behavior built upon them. The chaos that would result prevents the interference. The creation of "détente" during the Nixon years was first and foremost a norm of behavior that gave both the Soviets and the Americans certain expectations about each other. Upon these mutual expectations certain actions were taken and certain conventions evolved. In addition, certain actions were not taken because both sides knew that these actions would be counter to the spirit of détente. Both countries had a stake in maintaining the norm.

In addition to establishing conventions that define when an intervention or confrontation should be fought, there are also, as we have shown in Chapter 2, conventions that define how these confrontations are actually to be fought. In other words, there are "conventions of war." To illustrate, consider two countries that consistently are at war with each other. Assume that when they fight, they can fight with conventional weapons only or with both conventional and nuclear weapons. A typical recurrent prisoners' dilemma game is then defined as shown in Matrix 5.2.

Country II

		Conventional weapons	Conventional and nuclear weapons
	Conventional weapons	4, 4	2, 8
Country I	Conventional and nuclear weapons	8, 2	3, 3

Matrix 5.2. The rules of the war game

Clearly, as we already know, a convention of behavior will be established to govern the behavior of these countries. The important point about this example, then, is not that conventions are created to govern behavior in these situations, but rather the effect this knowledge should have on military strategists. The point is simple. Owing primarily to the influence of game theory in the 1950s, it has been commonly stated that military strategy should concern itself with an enemy's strategic capabilities and not with its intentions. In other words, the only relevant consideration for a military strategist should be the damage that the other side could do, and this damage should be minimized through appropriate actions. Consequently, classical thought is that even if the prisoners' dilemma game presented were a recurrent one, ruthless behavior is still militarily correct behavior. What is being stressed in this book, however, is that the knowledge of the other side's intentions is available through knowledge of the norms and conventions existing between the countries, and that truly rational behavior cannot ignore this information. There is more information available in a military situation than can be expressed in a game matrix. For instance, it may be rational in a war not to evacuate population centers if such evacuations are costly–not because the enemy does not have the capability of bombing them, but because it is known that they do not have the intention of doing so because the tacit conventions of war existing do not sanction this behavior and one has good reason to believe (knowledge of the norm) that the enemy adheres to those conventions. (In the Chinese–Vietnam War of 1979, each side refrained from entering into an air war even though both of them were capable of it.) Rational behavior involves the use of *all* relevant information–nothing should be ignored.

We are not unique in the world in establishing conventions that govern how we fight each other. Maynard Smith (1974) has presented a game-theoretical model to describe the fighting conventions that birds create to govern how they will fight each other. In these conflicts he demonstrates that a convention that involves the avoidance of fights to the death are often established by birds through the creation of a ritualistic fight in which neither bird gets killed. This type of behavior increases the fitness of the birds who possess it, and if the behavioral trait is genetically linked, the increased reproductive success of these birds will cause this gene to spread throughout the population. Other conventions governing which bird retreats from a fight between a bird with and one without property are also established. Obviously, then, the evolution of institutions is not a distinctly human characteristic. The unique aspect of human convention establishment is the way in which conventions are transmitted–to a large extent through a process of culturalization, learning, and socialization–not so directly through genetic transmission. Still, the purpose of all such conventions is the same–to solve recurrent societal problems once and for all so that each new generation does not have to solve them anew.

5.3 Sociobiology, behavior, and social institutions

Before I close this chapter and the book, I would like to raise the following question: To what extent are we the masters of our own institutional fate, or to what extent are the institutional structures we see evolving somehow the reflection of a deeper innate biogenetic predisposition? In short, do social agents, when they create social institutions, do so without innate biases, or is what we see emerging as a particular regularity in behavior somehow predestined or preprogrammed in us? I simply raise the question of whether the assumption of rationality in social science is both necessary and sufficient to yield an orderly social world, or must social scientists look toward the new field of sociobiology initiated by E. O. Wilson (1975) for the additional information required to analyze the evolution and emergence of social institutions? Because the application of sociobiology to economics is an emotional issue these days, I stress that I am merely raising the question, not advocating a particular answer.

It has been the main contention of this book that institutions or conventions emerge to help economic agents solve a set of recurrent coordination and prisoners' dilemma problems. The societally adhered to solution to these problems determines regularities in behavior that form the basis of our definition of a social institution. The question that arises, then, is whether there are preexisting innate biases in people that make certain solutions to these problems seem more natural than others and that therefore influence the probability that they will arise. A classic example that could be offered to support the belief that there are indeed such biases was given by Thomas Schelling in *The Strategy of Conflict* (1960). What Schelling did was to informally ask subjects to solve the following problems (among others), with the specification that their objective was to pick the solution they thought most likely to be named by other subjects. In short, they were asked to solve a series of coordination problems. The problems were as follows:

1. Name "heads" or "tails." If you and your partner name the same, you both win a prize.
2. Circle one of the numbers listed in the line below. You win if you all succeed in circling the same number.
   7   100   13   261   99   555
3. Put a check mark in one of the 16 squares below. You win if you all succeed in checking the same square.
   □   □   □   □

   □   □   □   □

   □   □   □   □

   □   □   □   □
4. Write a positive number. If you all write the same number, you win.
5. Name an amount of money. If you all name the same amount, you can have as much as you named.
6. You are to divide $100 into two piles, labeled *A* and *B*.

Schelling reported the following results of his informal survey. In problem 1, 36 people chose "heads" and only 6 chose "tails." In problem 2, the first three numbers got 37 of the total number of 41 votes. In problem 3, the upper left-hand corner received 24 of the total of 41 votes, and all but 3 of the remaining 17 were placed in boxes on the diagonal. Problem 4 showed a variety of answers, but two-fifths of all persons succeeded in choosing the number 1. In problem 5, 12 people chose $1,000,000 and only 3 chose numbers that were not a power of 10. In problem 6, 36 of the 41 subjects split the money $50–$50.

The point that Schelling makes is that in these types of coordination problems there are certain "salient" or natural solutions that seem to call attention to themselves and tend to be focused upon. The question arises however, as to exactly why these "salient" solutions are so salient. What is it that makes them seem so natural?

One obvious answer is simply that all of the people answering Schelling's questions shared a similar cultural background and that because of their cultural training, certain solutions (such as the number seven–"lucky seven"–in problem 2) seemed more natural than others. This answer may indeed be all that is needed to explain all the similarities. (It does not seem to explain why the upper left-hand corner box in problem 3 was salient, however, because that problem, at least, appears to be culture-free.) Another answer might possibly be that some of these solutions are more consistent with certain basic biogenetic structures which exist in our minds that predispose us to these solutions and make them seem natural.[2] These structures have evolved *possibly* because social coordination is essential for successful social existence and reproduction, and these patterns or structures facilitate such coordination and hence increase the fitness of human beings possessing them. Consequently, the view of *homo oeconomicus* as a rational agent acting with perfect information and free will may have to be modified, at least to some extent, to incorporate these biologically determined biases. Human beings may not be as purely calculating as we had once thought. They calculate, but some of the most important numbers punched into the calculator may be preprogrammed.

To illustrate our point, let us consider some biological examples of these types of preprogrammed biases in lower animals. We begin by noting that human beings are not the only species that create social institutions. In an extremely interesting article entitled "Wolves, Chimps and Demsetz,"[3] Fredlund (1976) demonstrates that animals are perfectly capable of creating territorial property rights and distributive systems that are remarkably similar to ours and function primarily in the way that ours function. Another social convention that animals, especially birds, create is a communication convention. More specifically, as Lewis (1969) points out, the use of one language in one place is a social convention created by human beings to coordinate their activities through communication.

Among birds it is noticed that each species employs a unique and different call to help it communicate danger and mating signals to those birds with whom it mates. The question is: How do birds as a species decide upon the same call? Are they taught it in the nest? Is it purely instinctual, or are there merely predispositions to these calls which, when mixed with the experience of hearing them, allow them to be established?

To answer this question, Barash (1977) reports upon the results of the following experiment. Male white-crown sparrows were taken, separated at birth from their parents, and kept in total acoustic isolation. At a later date some were exposed to a variety of sounds, including their own call; the remainder were exposed to no sounds at all. The results were that the birds who were kept in total isolation did not develop a call of *any* type, whereas the birds that were exposed to a variety of sounds, including their own species' call, were somehow able to pick their own call out of the sounds presented to them and developed a perfect version of the usual call of their species. The point, then, is that for birds, learning one's own call is not purely instinctual, because if it were, the birds that were kept in total isolation would have developed a perfect call without ever hearing it. Instead, there seems to be an internal structure in the bird's head that makes its own call seem natural and allows the bird to pick it out of a maze of sound presented to it. This preexisting structure influences the type of call that is established as the "conventional" call among the species.

To illustrate, if we view the bird-call problem as the recurrent coordination game of Matrix 5.3, in which a bird can either whistle its own call or whistle

		Bird II	
		Whistle own call	Whistle "Dixie"
Bird I	Whistle own call	4, 4	0, 0
	Whistle "Dixie"	0, 0	4, 4

Matrix 5.3. The bird-call game

"Dixie," and if we specify (through the specification of payoffs) that all that is important is that birds of the same feather whistle the same tune (as the payoffs imply), then the point being made is that the eventual solution to this game is not unbiased, a priori, because there are biogenetic structural biases determining which situation will evolve, and these structural biases greatly influence the type of institutional structures (bird calls) that evolve.[4] Man builds social institutions that in some sense mimic his biological reality. If our bodies are symmetric, we are likely to evolve symmetric institutions (e.g., split $100 50:50, as in Schelling's problem 6). That seems natural to us. We cannot escape our bodies, even in our social behavior.

The point that I am making is simply that the type of social behavior that we exhibit when we evolve certain regularities in our behavior–certain social institutions in this case–may not be independent of certain preprogrammed predispositions that we all share. Of course, human beings do differ from lower animals in their communicative skills and in their ability to learn, create, and preserve culture. Consequently, if we were to pick up the metaphor with which we started this book–an economy evolving and adapting through the creation of social institutions–the best hereditary model to use is not the Mendelian model but the Lamarckian. This is true because in Lamarck's theory it was possible for species to pass on to future generations traits that are presently acquired, and this is precisely what economies do when social institutions emerge in one period and then are passed on from generation to generation.

In summation, I have tried to raise the question of whether, when one attempts to analyze the creation and evolution of social institutions, one may have to incorporate some biological information heretofore considered irrelevant to the social sciences. It has not been implied, however, that these biological factors, if they are indeed important at all, would, by themselves, determine the shape and form of social institutions, but rather that they would bias the process in various directions.

5.4 Summary and conclusions

I could continue to spell out different categories of problems for which the analysis discussed in this book is relevant. However, the point of all these examples is the same. It is that to fully analyze any social situation, one must use all the information relevant to that situation. That information must include knowledge of the norms and conventions that have evolved to guide and govern agents' actions. This information is typically ignored in the analysis of most social problems. In addition, I have tried to stress, at least in this chapter, that institution or convention building is not a distinctly human characteristic and that we are not unique in the world in our ability to evolve regularities in behavior that are adhered to. Many birds, primates, and social insects are also institution builders, and one must speculate whether the factors that bias their institutional development also bias ours. We do not enter the social world as *tabula rasa*. We have predispositions and innate biases nudging us gently in certain directions. In the final analysis, the social world emerges from the chaos of a state of nature into the order of modern society through the evolution of institutions. The process is stochastic, so that what we observe as actually happening is merely one spin of an institutional roulette wheel. The only question is whether or not the wheel is biased.

Notes

Chapter 1. The nature and function of social institutions

1. This emphasis on disequilibrium analysis is seen in the works of the neo-Austrian economists, best represented by Kirzner (1973). Shubik (1973) also places emphasis on what he calls a "process"-oriented approach as opposed to an equilibrium approach.

2. See Marshall (1920, app. B, pp. 764–5).

3. In the eighteenth century, David Hume (1888) presented a description of the way a system of legal justice evolved in a society that was strikingly similar to Menger's "organic" view.

4. Nozick's entire analysis in the first part of his book can be reformulated game-theoretically, and the state's evolution can easily be seen to be the core solution to a game that is convex (i.e., Nozick's protective associations contain increasing returns to scale).

5. Duncan Foley (1975), writing on institutions from a radical perspective, rejects this view entirely. He argues that institutions cannot be explained from a functionalist point of view as socially efficient mechanisms that are capable of fine tuning and change, but rather emerge historically from a class struggle. Consequently, they serve no particular purpose and cannot be altered in the way we envision in order to increase social welfare. Foley (1975, p. 235), writes: "The organization of society is not a technical question because institutions are not designed to perform certain functions; they are rather molded historically out of a process of struggle and compromise, so there is simply no place for a technician to intervene from outside to adjust and improve them."

6. Rule utilitarianism is discussed probably for the first time as such by an economist in R. F. Harrod's "Utilitarianism Revisited," *Mind*, vol. 45, 1936, pp. 137–56. Others, such as David Lyons in *The Forms and Limits of Utilitarianism* (New York: Oxford University Press, 1965), argue that rule utilitarianism collapses into act utilitarianism. The argument is simple. Say that there is a rule R that specifies behavior and a circumstance under which any individual should break this rule. Then a new rule, saying conform to R except in this situation, results. But the new rule is such that it results whenever the old rule should be violated, so that any time an act utilitarian would break a rule R, a rule utilitarian would change the rule. Hence the two are the same. See also *Utilitarianism For and Against* (New York: Cambridge University Press, 1973), Essay I, "An Outline of a System of Utilitarian Ethics," by J. J. C. Smart and Bernard Williams. This issue is still open, however.

7. For a further discussion of coordination problems, see Schelling (1960).

8. Of course, if the situation were modeled as a supergame, it could be shown, using certain discount rates, that property rights are a noncooperative equilibrium institution in the supergame and need no external enforcement. This basic point is made in a different manner by Buchanan (1975).

9. This definition is consistent with the following definition offered by Blaine Roberts and Bob Holdren (1972, p. 110):

An institution will be defined as a system of rules applicable to established practices (or situations) and generally accepted by the members of a social system. These guidelines of interaction may be either explicitly delineated by laws, charters, constitutions and so forth or they may be implicit to a particular culture, such as customs, mores, generally accepted ethics, and so forth. The essential point is that an institution specifies consequences of individual or group action which can be expected. Given an existing institution, an individual or group knows to some extent the reaction its activities will evoke.

Chapter 2. State-of-nature theory and the rise of social institutions

1. As we will see in Chapter 3, what we mean when we talk about a norm is not the same as what we mean when we talk about a social institution, because a norm is merely a shared belief among agents that allows the agents to assess the probability of each other's behavior, whereas a social institution is something that is built upon a set of norms and is a rule prescribing behavior in various recurrent situations. In other words, the norm "honor among thieves" does not tell you how to behave in a prisoners' dilemma game if you are forced to play one recurrently; it merely gives you some information about how you might expect others to behave, and you will act upon this information.

2. A. Sen (1967) describes the following type of coordination game, which he calls an "assurance game."

Player II

		1	2	3
	1	6, 6	0, 0	2, 2
Player I	2	1, 1	4, 4	3, 3
	3	2, 2	3, 3	5, 5

What Sen discusses is the fact that in this game, as opposed to prisoners' dilemma games, each player, in order to choose strategy 1, needs only the assurance that the other will choose strategy 1; he need not have a binding contract to that effect. This assurance, as we see later, will be built up among the players as they iterate the game and begin to trust each other. They will build up a norm of cooperation, and it is upon this norm that the institution of always choosing strategy 1 in this game will evolve.

3. Another approach to the problem of preference revelation would be for the planner to change the rules of the game or its payoff function in such a way that telling the truth was either a dominant strategy for each player or at least determined a Nash equilibrium for the game. Such schemes have been devised by Theodore Groves (1973) and Groves and Ledyard (1977) and others, and have been experimentally tested by Vernon Smith (1978a). The problem with these mechanisms and the experimental evidence supporting them is that they are static theories with static experimental support. As a result, it has not been established that such schemes are actually required in order to elicit the truthful responses from agents in such situations if the players know that they will play the same game repeatedly. In such cases, the players might establish the convention of telling the truth by themselves and thereby obviate the need for an explicit or imposed preference revelation scheme (see Chapter 5).

4. This example was offered to me by Carlos Varsavsky both in conversation and in the first chapter of his most interesting manuscript, *Why Seven Days in a Week?* (1978, unpublished manuscript). A similar analysis can be found in a book entitled *The Week: An Essay on the Origin and Development of the Seven Day Week,* by Francis Colson (1926).

5. The 7-day week is by no means universal, however. Many different societies have had weeks of other than seven days. For instance, in Peru the Incas established a 10-day week, and in ancient Mexico the week had 5 days. The most common length has been 7 days, however. [These facts are from Varsavsky (1978).]

6. To understand this situation more formally, consider the following description of the extensive form of the game being played by the farmers. Time starts on day 1. At the end of the day each farmer must decide, in isolation, whether to go to the city, G, or stay at home, S. On day 1 his payoffs if he goes to the city are

$$P_i = \begin{cases} \xi^i(1) - c_i & \text{if } |s| = N \\ -c_i & \text{if } |s| < N \end{cases}$$

where $|s|$ is the number of farmers in the city at the end of day 1. Whether or not he has gone to the city on day 1, on day 2 he faces the same problem and must decide again, at which time his payoff is

$$P_i = \begin{cases} \xi^i(\tilde{t}) - c_i & \text{if } |s| = N \\ -c_i & \text{if } |s| < N \end{cases}$$

where $\tilde{t}$ in this case is a vector of either 1s or 2s. Consequently, on every day, each farmer must decide whether or not he will go to the city on that day. The game shown in Figure N.1 in extensive form is determined.

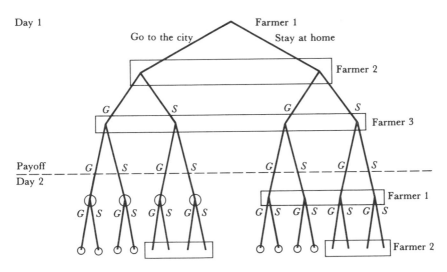

Figure N.1. Farmer coordination problem: the week game–three farmer extensive form representation. Notice that the information sets indicate that if a farmer decides to go to the city on a given day, he is able to observe who else decided to go on that day. Consequently, when he makes his next move he has this information at his disposal.

The game described by this tree is very simple. On day 1 all farmers must decide in isolation whether they will go to the city. Because this is the first time period, all decisions are made in ignorance of past choices. But on day 2 we can assume that their decision is eased by the knowledge of who was present on day 1. This additional information is indicated by the circle at the information sets of the players on day 2. If a farmer does not go to the city on day 1, he must make his decision whether to go on day 2 in total ignorance of what occurred on day 1. Such is the case for all days $t \geq 1$, in that all farmers are assumed to be able to see when they go to the market who else decided to go on that day, but when they are there they are not allowed to communicate with each other about when they want to return. The game is strictly noncooperative.

7. Varsavsky (1978), in *Why Seven Days in a Week?*, argues that the 7-day week, which is virtually universal today, is not an efficient size for the week and that a 9-day "continuous work-week" is preferable because it fits the technological facts of today's life better than does the conventional week.

8. The total demand for chips by a farmer must not exceed his income, so that we need not specify what happens if $r_m^i < \Sigma_{i=1}^n f_{mj}^i$ for any chip.

9. For additional references, see Harsanyi (1978) and Hare (1974); with reference to rules of war, see Brandt (1974).

10. The existence of détente between the United States and the USSR is equivalent to a social convention in which both sides are supposed to adhere to certain constraints on their behavior in various parts of the world. It is a convention that, if not adhered to by both sides, could determine a state of affairs that neither side would want.

11. In Nozick's analysis, of course, a protective association does not form to rob other people but rather to protect each member and to adjudicate disputes among its members. The offensive nature of my associations is included for convenience. The possibility that such associations could be offensively minded is certainly a real one, however.

12. *Proof:* This is true if for any coalition $P, Q \subset S$ such that $P, Q, P \cap Q$, and $P \cup Q$ are all different, we have

$$v(P) + v(Q) < v(P \cup Q) + v(P \cap Q)$$

which can easily be demonstrated as follows. Let coalition P have $|P|$ members and let coalition Q have $|Q|$ members, and let the number of members in their intersection ($P \cap Q$) be $|L|$ with $|L| < |P|, |Q|$ obviously. Then the following relations hold:

$$\begin{aligned}
v(P) &= |P|(M - c) - g(|P|) \\
v(Q) &= |Q|(M - c) - g(|Q|) \\
v(P \cap Q) &= |L|(M - c) - g(|L|) \\
v(P \cup Q) &= |P \cup Q|(M - c) - g(|P \cup Q|)
\end{aligned}$$

and

$$\begin{aligned}
&|P|(M - c) - g(|P|) + |Q|(M - c) - g(|Q|) \\
&\overset{?}{\underset{>}{\lessgtr}} |P \cup Q|(M - c) - g(|P \cup Q|) + |L|(M - c) - g(|L|)
\end{aligned}$$

or

$$\begin{aligned}
&|P + Q|(M - c) - g(|P|) + g(|Q|) \\
&\overset{?}{\underset{>}{\lessgtr}} [|P \cup Q| + |L|](M - c) - g(|P \cup Q|) - g(|L|)
\end{aligned}$$

But since $P + Q = P \cup Q + P \cap Q$, we know that

$$|P + Q|(M - c) = [|P \cup Q| + |L|](M - c)$$

so that

$$|P|(M - c) - g(|P|) + |Q|(M - c) - g(|Q|)$$
$$< |P \cup Q|(M - c) - g(|P \cup Q|) + |L|(M - c) - g(|L|)$$

if

$$g(|P|) + g(|Q|) > g(|P \cup Q|) + g(|L|)$$

which follows from the strict concavity of $g(\cdot)$. Hence $v(\cdot)$ is convex over the region S. Q.E.D.

Chapter 4. Information and social institutions

1. See G. Thompson (1953a, b) for a full presentation of the concept of signaling information sets and games of perfect recall. Thompson gives the following definition of a signaling information set.

"*Definition 4.3: A signaling information set.* Let U be an information set for player i and let $U_v = \{Z \mid Z$ follows some move in U by the vth alternative$\}$. Then U is a signaling information set for player i if for some v and some information set V of player i, $U_v \cap V \neq \emptyset$ and $V \not\subset U_{v'}$."

2. These terms and the statement of this theorem in this manner can be found in Selten (1975).

3. We are, of course, implicitly assuming that all agents are reporting truthful preferences to the auctioneer and not dissembling strategically. If they were lying, we would have to analyze whether an institution would evolve in which all agents told the truth to the auctioneer about their preferences or lied in such a manner that the outcome was still Pareto-optimal. If such institutions would not evolve organically, or if the probability of their evolving were sufficiently low, it might be necessary to force an institutional mechanism on the traders to make them behave truthfully. Such incentive compatible mechanisms have been investigated by Groves and Ledyard (1977), Clarke (1971), Green and Laffont (1979), and Tideman and Tullock (1976).

Chapter 5. Toward a neo-institutional approach to economics

1. Michael Taylor, in *Anarchy and Cooperation*, expressed the belief that in the proper super-game setting, what I am calling the good-citizen convention will be the rule and not the exception. For a formal treatment of the problem, however, see Berman and Schotter (1980).

2. For a further discussion of the concept of a biogenetic structure, see *Biogenetic Structuralism* by Laughlin and d'Aquili (1974).

3. For those readers who are not economists, it should be explained that a Demsetz is not a wild beast but rather a breed of economist inhabiting the Department of Economics at UCLA and interested in the function of property rights.

4. Clearly, this is the same point that Noam Chomsky makes in his analysis of the innate language abilities of human beings.

Bibliography

Arrow, Kenneth. "Political and Economic Evaluation of Social Effects and Externalities." In *The Analysis of Public Output,* (Julius Margolis, ed.). New York: National Bureau of Economic Research–Columbia University Press, 1970.

"Vertical Integration and Communication," *The Bell Journal of Economics,* vol. 6, no. 1, Spring 1975, pp. 173–84.

Arrow, Kenneth, and Debreu, G. "Existence of Equilibrium for a Competitive Economy," *Econometrica,* vol. 22, 1954, pp. 265–90.

Arrow, Kenneth, and Hahn, Frank. *General Competitive Analysis.* San Francisco: Holden-Day, 1971.

Aumann, R. "Acceptable Points in General Cooperative n-Person Games." In *Contributions to the Theory of Games,* vol. 4, Annals of Mathematics Study no. 40 (R. D. Luce and A. W. Tucker, eds.). Princeton, N.J.: Princeton University Press, 1959.

Barash, David P. *Sociobiology and Behavior.* Amsterdam: North-Holland, 1977.

Berman, S., and Schotter, A. "Supergames and Diffusion Processes." Discussion paper 79-01, C. V. Starr Center for Applied Economics, New York University, January 1979.

Berman, S., and Schotter, A. "When Is the Incentive Problem Real?" Paper presented at the Oskar Morgenstern Symposium on Mathematical Economics, May 28–30, 1980, Vienna.

Billingsley, P. *Convergence of Probability Measures.* New York: Wiley, 1968.

Brandt, R. B. "Utilitarianism and the Rules of War." In *War and Moral Responsibility* (M. Cohen, T. Nagel, and T. Scanlon, eds.). Princeton, N.J.: Princeton University Press, 1974.

Buchanan, James. *The Limits of Liberty: Between Anarchy and Leviathan.* Chicago: University of Chicago Press, 1975.

Buchanan, James, and Tullock, Gordon. *The Calculus of Consent: Logical Foundations of Constitutional Democracy.* Ann Arbor, Mich.: University of Michigan Press, 1962.

Clarke, E. "Multipart Pricing of Public Goods," *Public Choice,* vol. 11, Fall 1971, pp. 17–33.

Colson, Francis. *The Week: An Essay on the Origin and Development of the Seven Day Week.* Cambridge: Cambridge University Press, 1926.

Commons, John. *Institutional Economics.* Madison, Wis.: University of Wisconsin Press, 1961 (first published in 1934).

Cyert, R., and March, J. *A Behavioral Theory of the Firm,* Englewood Cliffs, N.J.: Prentice-Hall, 1963.

Debreu, Gerhard. *The Theory of Value.* New York: Wiley, 1959.

Debreu, G., and Scarf, H. "A Limit Theorem on the Core of an Economy," *International Economic Review,* vol. 4, 1963, pp. 234–46.

Demsetz, H. "Exchange and Enforcement of Property Rights," *Journal of Law and Economics,* vol. 7, October 1964, pp. 11–26.

"Toward a Theory of Property Rights," *American Economic Review,* vol. 57, May 1967, pp. 347–73.

Dynkin, E. B., *Markov Processes,* vol. 1. New York: Academic Press, 1965.

Edgeworth, Francis Y. *Mathematical Psychics.* London: Kegan Paul, 1881.

Feller, W. "The Parabolic Differential Equations and the Associated Semigroups of Transformations," *Annals of Mathematics, 55,* 1952, pp. 468–519.

"Generalized Second Order Differential Operators and Their Lateral Conditions," *Illinois Journal of Mathematics,* vol. 1, 1957, pp. 495–504.

An Introduction to Probability Theory and Its Applications, vol. 1, 3rd ed. New York: Wiley, 1968.

Foley, Duncan, "Problems versus Conflicts: Economic Theory and Ideology," *American Economic Association Papers and Proceedings,* vol. 65, May 1975, pp. 231–7.

Fredlund, Melvin. "Wolves, Chimps and Demsetz," *Economic Inquiry,* vol. 45, no. 2, June 1976, pp. 279–291.

Friedman, J. W. *Oligopoly and the Theory of Games.* Amsterdam: North-Holland, 1977.

Green, J., and Laffont, J. J. *Incentives in Public Decision-Making.* Amsterdam: North-Holland, 1979.

Groves, Theodore. "Incentives in Teams," *Econometrica,* vol. 41, July 1973, pp. 617–31.

Groves, T., and Ledyard, J. "Optimal Allocation of Public Goods: A Solution to the 'Free Rider' Problem," *Econometrica,* vol. 45, 1977, pp. 783–809.

Hare, R. M. "Rules of War and Moral Reasoning." In *War and Moral Responsibility* (M. Cohen, T. Nagel, and T. Scanlon, eds.). Princeton, N.J.: Princeton University Press, 1974.

Harsanyi, John C. "The Tracing Procedure: A Bayesian Approach to Defining a Solution for *n*-Person Non-cooperative Games," *The International Journal of Game Theory,* vol. 4, issue 1, 1975, pp. 61–95.

Rational Behavior and Bargaining Equilibrium in Games and Social Situations, Cambridge: Cambridge University Press, 1976.

Hayek, Friedrich A. "The Use of Knowledge in Society," *American Economic Review,* vol. 35, September 1945, pp. 519–30.

The Counterrevolution of Science. New York: Free Press, 1955.

Hildebrand, W., and Kirman, A. P. *Introduction to Equilibrium Analysis.* Amsterdam: North-Holland, 1976.

Hume, David. *Treatise on Human Nature.* New York: 1911 (first published in 1888).

Hurwicz, Leonid. "The Design of Mechanisms for Resource Allocation," *American Economic Review,* Papers and Proceedings, vol. 63, no. 2, May 1973a.

"On the Concept and Possibility of Information Decentralization," *American Economic Review,* vol. 59, May 1973b, pp. 513–54.

Jones, Robert. "The Origin and Development of a Medium of Exchange," *Journal of Political Economy,* vol. 84, no. 4, pt. 1, August 1976, pp. 757–76.

Kirzner, Israel M. *Competition and Entrepreneurship.* Chicago: University of Chicago Press, 1973.

Kuhn, H. W. "Extensive Games and the Problem of Information." In *Contributions to the Theory of Games,* vol. 2, Annals of Mathematics Study, no. 28 (H. W. Kuhn and A. W. Tucker, eds.). Princeton, N.J.: Princeton University Press, 1953.

Kurz, M. "Altruistic Equilibrium." In *Economic Progress, Private Values and Public Policy* (B. Balassa and R. Helson, eds.). Amsterdam: North-Holland, 1977.

Laughlin, C. D., and d'Aquili, E. G. *Biogenetic Structuralism.* New York: Columbia University Press, 1974.

Levy, P. *Processus stochastiques et mouvement Brownien,* 2nd ed. Paris: Gauthier-Villars, 1965.

Lewis, D. *Convention: A Philosophical Study.* Cambridge, Mass.: Harvard University Press, 1969.

Marschak, J., and Radner, R. *The Economic Theory of Teams.* New Haven, Conn.: Yale University Press, 1972.

Marshall, Alfred. *Principles of Economics.* 8th ed. London: Macmillan, 1920.

Menger, Karl. *Untersuchungen über die Methode der Sozialwissenschaften und der politischen Ökonomie insbesondere* (1883). Translated by Francis J. Nock as *Problems in Economics and Sociology.* Urbana, Ill.: University of Illinois Press, 1963.

"On the Origins of Money," *Economic Journal,* vol. 2, June 1892, pp. 239–55.

Principles of Economics (J. Dingwall and B. F. Hoselitz, trans.). Glencoe, Ill.: Free Press, 1950 (first published 1923).

Morgenstern, Oskar. "Thirteen Critical Points in Contemporary Economic Theory: An Interpretation," *Journal of Economic Literature,* vol. 10, no. 4, December 1972, pp. 1163–89.

"Pareto Optimum and Economic Organization." In *Selected Writings of Oskar Morgenstern* (Andrew Schotter, ed.). New York: New York University Press, 1976.

Nozick, Robert. *Anarchy, State and Utopia.* New York: Basic Books, 1975.

Owen, G. *Game Theory,* Philadelphia: Saunders, 1968.

Parzen, E. *Stochastic Processes.* San Francisco: Holden-Day, 1962.

Radford, R. A. "The Economic Organization of a P.O.W. Camp," *Economica,* vol. 12, 1945, pp. 189–201.

Rawls, John. *A Theory of Justice.* Cambridge, Mass.: Harvard University Press (Belknap), 1971.

Robbins, Lionel. *On the Nature and Significance of Economic Science.* London: Macmillan, 1935.

Roberts, Blaine, and Bob Holdren. *Theory of Social Process.* Ames, Iowa: University of Iowa Press, 1972.

Schelling, Thomas C. *The Strategy of Conflict.* New York: Oxford University Press, 1960.

Schotter, A., and Schwödiauer, G. "Economics and the Theory of Games: A Survey," *Journal of Economic Literature,* vol. 18, June 1980, pp. 479–527.

Selten, R. "A Re-examination of the Perfectness Concept for Equilibrium Points," *International Journal of Game Theory,* vol. 4, issue 1/2, 1975, pp. 25–55.

Sen, Amartya. "Isolation Assurance and the Social Rate of Discount," *Quarterly Journal of Economics,* vol. 81, 1967.

Shannon, C. E. "A Mathematical Theory of Communication," *Bell Systems Technical Journal,* vol. 27, 1948, pp. 379–423, 623–56.

Shapley, L., and Shubik, M. "Trade Using One Commodity as a Means of Payment," *Journal of Political Economy,* vol. 85, no. 5, October 1977, pp. 937–69.

Shubik, Martin. "Edgeworth Market Games." In *Annals of Mathematics* Study no. 40 (A. W. Tucker and R. D. Luce, eds.). Princeton, N.J.: Princeton University Press, 1959, pp. 267–79.

"The General Equilibrium Model Is the Wrong Model and a Noncooperative Strategic Process Model Is a Satisfactory Model for the Reconciliation of Micro and Macroeconomic Theory," *Cowles Foundation Discussion Paper 365,* November 1973.

"A Trading Model to Avoid Tatonnement Metaphysics." In *Bidding and Auctioning for Procurement and Allocation* (Y. Amihud, ed.). New York: New York University Press, 1974.

Simon, Herbert. "Rational Decision Making in Business Organizations," *American Economic Review,* vol. 69, no. 4, September 1979, pp. 493–514.

Smith, Maynard. "The Theory of Games and the Evolution of Animal Conflicts," *Journal of Theoretical Biology,* vol. 47, 1974, pp. 209–21.

Smith, Vernon. "Experimental Mechanisms for Public Choice." *Game Theory and Political Science* (Peter Ordeshook, ed.). New York: New York University Press, 1978a.

"Incentive Compatible Experimental Processes for the Provision of Public Goods," NBER Conference on Decentralization, Northwestern University, April 23–25, 1976. To appear in *Research in Experimental Economics*. Greenwich, Conn.: J. A. I. Press, 1978b.

Taylor, Michael. *Anarchy and Cooperation*. New York: Wiley, 1976.

Telser, Lester. *Competition, Collusion and Game Theory*. Chicago: Aldine, 1972.

Economic Theory and the Core. Chicago: University of Chicago Press, 1979.

Theil, Henri. *Economics and Information Theory*. Chicago: Rand McNally, 1967.

Thompson, G. "Bridge and Signalling." In *Contributions to the Theory of Games*, vol. 2, Annals of Mathematics Study no. 28 (H. W. Kuhn and A. W. Tucker, eds.). Princeton, N.J.: Princeton University Press, 1953a.

"Signalling Strategies in n-Person Games." In *Contributions to the Theory of Games*, vol. 2, Annals of Mathematics Study no. 28 (H. W. Kuhn and A. W. Tucker, eds.). Princeton, N.J.: Princeton University Press, 1953b.

Tideman, T. N., and Tullock, G. "A New and Superior Process for Making Social Choices," *Journal of Political Economy*, vol. 84, December 1976, pp. 1145–59.

Ullman-Margalit, Edna. *The Emergence of Norms*. New York: Oxford University Press, 1978.

Varsavsky, Carlos. *Why Seven Days in a Week?* 1978 (unpublished manuscript).

Veblen, Thorstein. "Why Is Economics Not an Evolutionary Science?" *Quarterly Journal of Economics*, vol. 12, 1898.

von Neumann, J., and O. Morgenstern. *The Theory of Games and Economic Behavior*, 2nd ed. Princeton, N.J.: Princeton University Press, 1947.

Weinberger, H. F. *A First Course in Partial Differential Equations with Complex Variables and Transform Methods*. Waltham, Mass.: Blaisdell, 1965.

Wentzell, A. D. "On Boundary Conditions for Multidimensional Diffusion Processes" (in Russian), *Teoriya Verojatnostei i Ee Primeneniya*, vol 4, 1959, pp. 172–85.

"General Boundary Problems Connected with Diffusion Processes" (in Russian), *Uspehki Matematicheskikh Nauk*, vol. 15, no. 2(92), 1960, pp. 202–4.

Williamson, O. *Markets and Hierarchies: A Study in the Economics of Internal Organization*. New York: Basic Books, 1975.

Wilson, Edward. *Sociobiology: The New Synthesis*. Cambridge, Mass.: Harvard University Press (Belknap), 1975.

Index